PRAISE FOR *SHOULD YOU MEDICATE YOUR CHILD'S MIND?*

"This is an outstanding resource for parents from one of America's most important child psychiatrists. If you are a parent with a child who is taking psychiatric medications, or you are thinking about starting your child on these medications, this is a *must read*."

—TOBIAS DESJARDINS, LCSW, family mediator,
creator of the Divorce Survivor workshop series

"A carefully thought out, down-to-earth analysis of a sensitive problem many parents face. It should be reassuring to lots of moms and dads."

—THOMAS W. PHELAN, PhD, author of
1-2-3 Magic: Effective Discipline for Children 2–12

"Any parent who is considering placing their child on psychiatric medications should first read this book. Dr. Roberts takes an extremely complicated issue and, using common sense and solid medical knowledge, distills it down to no-nonsense advice that is enjoyable and informative to read."

—BRYAN D. YATES, MD, psychiatrist

ELIZABETH J. ROBERTS, MD, is a board-certified medical doctor specializing in child and adolescent psychiatry who has been guiding and caring for children over the past thirty years, half of those years as a physician. Dr. Roberts has worked as a child and adolescent psychiatrist in private psychiatric hospitals, public state hospitals, psychiatric emergency rooms, public county clinics, and private group practices, and she has served as a consultant to pediatricians and psychologists. The former medical director for young adults of Hazelden, the world-renowned drug and alcohol rehabilitation clinic, she is currently the medical director of a psychiatric emergency room for children and in private practice. Dr. Roberts has lectured to parents and professionals on the subject of children's mental health at hospitals, schools, professional symposia, and at ChADD (Children and Adults with Attention Deficit Disorder) meetings. Dr. Roberts has appeared on *The Oprah Winfrey Show*, ABC News, and been featured in numerous publications, including the *Chicago Tribune*. She lives in Canyon Lake, California.

SHOULD YOU MEDICATE YOUR CHILD'S MIND?

A Child Psychiatrist Makes Sense
of Whether to Give Kids
Psychiatric Medication

ELIZABETH J. ROBERTS, MD

FOREWORD BY DREW ROSS, MD

MARLOWE & COMPANY
NEW YORK

Should You Medicate Your Child's Mind?:
A Child Psychiatrist Makes Sense of
Whether to Give Kids Psychiatric Medication
Copyright © 2006 by Elizabeth J. Roberts
Foreword copyright © 2006 by Drew Ross

Published by
Marlowe & Company
An Imprint of Avalon Publishing Group Incorporated
245 West 17th Street • 11th Floor
New York, NY 10011-5300

The information in this book is intended to help readers make informed decisions about their
health and the health of their loved ones. It is not intended to be a substitute for treatment by
or the advice and care of a professional health care provider. While the author and publisher
have endeavored to ensure that the information presented is accurate and up to date, they are
not responsible for adverse effects or consequences sustained by any person using this book.

Library of Congress Cataloging-in-Publication Data is available.

ISBN: 1-56924-333-6
ISBN-13: 978-1-56924-333-6

9 8 7 6 5 4 3 2 1

Designed by Pauline Neuwirth, Neuwirth & Associates, Inc.

Printed in the United States of America

This book is dedicated to my husband, and best friend,
Thomas Jozaitis.

CONTENTS

FOREWORD
by Drew Ross, MD

SHOULD YOU MEDICATE your child who has some problem with her behavior? I've been asked that question hundreds of times, and since I don't see children in my clinical practice, I don't get to really answer it. Instead, I usually respond with a longer winded version of "it depends."

I don't envy you if you have that question. The answer isn't confusing just because of the overwhelming mass of information out there about psychiatric diagnoses and treatments. I think it is especially hard because of what is mostly missing. What's almost not there is the middle ground.

Many if not most Americans think that psychiatrists are the way that we're depicted in the cartoons in *The New Yorker* or on television; that we dispense both medications and psychotherapy—that we're agile with and keen on both, and balance them well. In fact, there's a quiet war going on. The winner in terms of money and popularity in the profession at this time is the side that favors medications over psychotherapy, often to the point of disparaging the value of therapy. The partisans from this side of the conflict have rather successfully convinced the profession as well as the populace that almost all emotional difficulties arise from chemical imbalances.

The underdogs in the conflict are not well organized, and are not cohesive in terms of agenda or even belief systems. Some are old-timers who practice psychiatry the way it was done in the past, with psychotherapy front and center, and medications on the side or ignored. Others have more identification with alternative medicine, and believe that psychiatric medications are harmful or at least vastly overused.

While this quiet war goes on (it would seem that it smolders more than rages), there is an information gap for parents of children with behavioral issues. While there are tons of books and other information promoting or trashing any given medication or medications in general, there is nearly nothing in the middle. Few researchers, observers, and authors have the wisdom, grace, or sensibility to rise above the smoldering war to tell you what to do with your child in a way that honors your child above this conflict.

What you need is not propaganda from either side in the war. What you need is the truth, which is almost certainly in the middle. The truth is that psychiatric medications are helpful, and can be harmful. They're overused in many settings and underused in others. They treat symptoms, not disorders, and they work better when combined with psychotherapy.

Thankfully, Dr. Elizabeth Roberts has written this remarkable book—a practical, hands-on, no-nonsense guide to making one of the most difficult decisions in modern parenting. She's laid out the issues, the confusions, the problems, and the solutions without getting into partisanship in the war. Her allegiance is to you and your child, to helping you to neither give your child medications he may not need nor to avoid them when they might help. In this book, your child gets to be your child rather than a poster kid for either side of the war going on in psychiatry.

It isn't that we've been holding out on you. It hasn't been easy to be in the middle as psychiatrists. There are tremendous pressures to pick a side in this conflict, and the lack of information in the middle goes all the way through to the data available to us as professionals. Thankfully, Dr. Roberts has the training, experience, and wisdom to not only have crafted a path down the middle, but to have come up with the words to describe it so that you can join her, right where you belong when trying to decide if and when it makes sense for medications to be used for your child.

The next time that someone asks me whether their child should be on psychiatric medications, I won't start down the path of my "it depends" speech. I'll send them straight to this book. When you read it, you will be far better able to access the help that you need to make a difficult decision about a very important issue. The one thing that Dr. Roberts hasn't told you in this book is how remarkable it is that it exists, and how necessary it is for parents to have a guide who doesn't have an agenda besides the children.

DREW ROSS, MD, is the author of *Looking into the Eyes of a Killer*, a book about the roots and meaning of violence. He is working on a forthcoming book that paints a surprisingly optimistic picture of the future by predicting an unexpected increase in conscious behavior, essentially a spiritual revolution. He has a spiritual psychiatry practice in Kona, Hawaii.

PREFACE

I HAVE BEEN guiding and caring for children over the past thirty years, half of those years as a physician. It started when I was fifteen years old: I began my work with mentally ill children by volunteering my time caring for an institutionalized autistic girl. In the fourteen years that followed, I sheltered and counseled runaways, coached sports in poor neighborhoods, ran the local soup kitchen for the homeless, provided direct care for profoundly mentally retarded teenagers, and completed my teaching degree from the University of Michigan. My experience as a teacher ran the gamut from some of the most prestigious private schools to public schools in the more impoverished neighborhoods of Chicago.

In 1988, I went to medical school as a single mother when my children were eight, seven, and four years old. I completed my medical education with a Fellowship in Child and Adolescent Psychiatry from the Medical School at Northwestern University in Chicago. Since then, I have worked as a child and adolescent psychiatrist in private psychiatric hospitals, public state hospitals, psychiatric emergency rooms, public county clinics, private group practices; served as a consultant to pediatricians and psychologists; and had my own private practice. I have held positions as the medical director of Hazelden, a drug and alcohol rehab clinic for teens, and as the medical director of a psychiatric emergency room for children. I have lectured to parents and professionals on the subject of children's mental health at hospitals, schools, professional symposia, and at ChADD (Children and Adults with Attention Deficit Disorder) meetings. I have been quoted in newspapers and television news, and once appeared on *The Oprah Winfrey Show* as an expert on addictions in teens.

Throughout my above career, I have treated children with frighteningly severe psychiatric disorders, such as schizophrenia or methamphetamine-induced psychotic disorder. At the other end of the spectrum, I have treated children from intact, loving homes where the child was simply overindulged or was experiencing a difficult adjustment to a common life change, such as starting at a new school.

In every instance where I treat children, I am asked two questions:

What is wrong with my child?
What will help?

I believe that, if you desire to help children succeed and be happy, whether they are struggling with mental health problems or not, the proof of your methods lies in your outcomes. So, when the famous pediatrician and author, Dr. Spock, gave advice on raising children, it was difficult for me to take him seriously after learning how unhappy and dysfunctional his own children turned out to be. I have many successful outcomes in treating children professionally as well as in rearing my own children, who are now all adults. Their happiness and ability to lead fulfilling lives are the finest evidence of my understanding and treatment of children and adolescents. My methodology works.

However, the parents of the children I am called in to treat often complain that they have received conflicting advice from teachers, family, friends, media, and doctors—and they don't know who to believe. The other, even more common complaint is how little time and attention they and their child receive from their child's psychiatrist. Parents are appalled that they are shooed out the door with a prescription in twenty minutes, after a minimum of discussion about—or with—the child. Even more shocking, it has been reported to me that, pediatricians can, and do, assess and medicate in even less time. A five-minute appointment with a pediatrician culminating in a prescription for powerful **psychotropic** medications is fairly standard, according to my patients. (Terms in **boldface** are defined in the glossary in the back of this book.) Not surprisingly, parents tell me they often leave a doctor's office feeling completely clueless about a medication's potential side effects, and frustrated by never having had a chance to fully discuss the aspects of their child's condition that meds may not even treat! Ultimately, this poor line of communication between parent and doctor leads to problems for the child. The most serious and dangerous consequence of this lack of in-depth diagnosis and parent education is that children are being inappropriately medicated or overmedicated, without nonmedical therapy options being adequately discussed or utilized.

My broad knowledge and experience as a child psychiatrist, a teacher, a counselor, a coach, a child-care worker, and a parent has given me a unique perspective on behavior problems that encompasses every aspect of mental health in children. I have cared for the most disadvantaged and abused children of our society, and the most privileged and gifted, who yet had problems requiring my care. Regardless of their socioeconomic group or the nature of their psychiatric condition, the heavy-handed approach taken by some physicians who attempt to solve all behavioral problems with a pill can cause more problems for children instead of less.

Recently, I evaluated a seven-year-old who had been given five different psychiatric medications by the child's prior doctors: two **antipsychotic** drugs, a **mood stabilizer**, an **amphetamine**, and an **antidepressant**. He had been previously diagnosed with both **Bipolar Disorder** and **AD/HD**. It might help to understand that this child had experienced extreme chaos, neglect, and unspeakable physical and sexual abuse at the hands of his drug-addicted parents. His home life alone would have been enough to explain why this child was angry and agitated! He was living in foster care at the time I met him. Unfortunately, I was only able to see the boy once in the psychiatric emergency room where I work part of each week. I eliminated one of his many prescriptions and encouraged his new caregivers to seek competent outpatient treatment for the correct diagnosis of **Post Traumatic Stress Disorder**. I explained the diagnosis and the different treatments that could help him recover, and assured the foster parents that, with time, in a stable environment, and lots of reassurance from them plus psychotherapy and close monitoring of the proper medications, their new foster child had hope of recovery. In doing so, I dealt a commonsense blow to two troubling roots of the boy's prior, ineffective treatment: a too-hasty and downright wrong diagnosis by his previous physicians, and their overloading his system with unnecessary chemicals that did not properly address his real psychiatric needs.

In another case, I evaluated a *three-year-old* girl who had been previously diagnosed with both Bipolar Disorder and AD/HD as well. She had been raised by a drug-addicted mother who had provided little if any supervision. Instead of receiving guidance, nurturing, and discipline, this child had been pacified and indulged whenever she became belligerent or demanding, by a mother who wanted not to be bothered. There was no routine or structure in this three-year-old's life. Every day was another day of unpredictable chaos at the hands of her drug-using mother. The girl had developed a behavior pattern of being defiant and even physically aggressive whenever she didn't get her way. This was another situation that involved the child's eventual removal to a more caring and attentive foster home. By educating the girl's new parents about the legitimate and proper diagnosis of **Oppositional Defiant Disorder**, and its effective treatment by introduction of consistency and discipline to the child's daily life, I was able to convince them that medications were entirely unnecessary. In this instance, no medication was prescribed; the girl's "cure" required only good parenting.

How had this seven-year-old boy been diagnosed incorrectly and given so many strong medications with serious potential for permanent physical side effects? Why is a child as young as three, who is simply defiant, being brought to a psychiatrist? A multitude of societal influences and modern medical practices has converged to create problems in the treatment of childhood mental illness. Foremost among these problems is a rush to medicate children with psychiatric drugs, a tendency by parents and doctors alike that is growing at an alarming rate.

This growing epidemic of misdiagnosing and overmedicating children needs to be urgently addressed. As a lifelong advocate for children—who themselves have no power to shape public policy, and little voice in their parents' medical decisions—I feel compelled to appeal to parents on their children's behalf. *Should You Medicate Your Child's Mind?* is my attempt to address this unrestrained frenzy to place children on medications that may not improve their children's well-being and might just make matters worse. Before you join the rest of the parents flocking to their doctor's office demanding psychiatric medications for their children, read this book and decide for yourself whether a drug will truly resolve or merely mask your child's behavioral problems.

I wrote this book not to *replace* appropriate psychiatric care but to help you prepare for, and then proceed from, what may be a very brief encounter with your child's psychiatrist. With the accurate information on diagnoses and appropriate treatments in hand, the time you *do* get to spend with your child's doctor will be more efficient and productive. You will be able to determine quickly if the doctor's advice seems poorly suited to your child's condition, as well as whether the doctor is answering your questions adequately.

When I see a patient for the first time, I start with a thorough evaluation that takes at least one and a half hours, sometimes longer. I spend a lot of time in the first few sessions answering questions about the diagnosis, explaining how I arrived at my conclusion, what the child's prognosis is, and what treatment options exist. Unfortunately, due to the time constraints of managed care, doctors cannot usually take the time required to provide this kind of care and instruction to their patients. If you are unable to find a doctor who can spend the time necessary to bring you up to speed on your child's condition and his treatment options, you will simply have to push for this information from the doctor that you do have. Knowing what questions to ask is half the battle. That is how *Should You Medicate Your Child's Mind?* will prove invaluable to you as you seek help for your troubled youngster.

Your child may, in the end, require some form of medication, but it is my fervent hope that my advice within these pages will guide you toward making an informed choice, one that may affect your child for many years to come.

Introduction

Does Your Child Need Help?

YOUR CHILD HAS a behavioral problem, one you have finally admitted to yourself may need outside help. Perhaps you have been aware of his or her difficulties for some time, or maybe they have been brought to your attention by a teacher, a similar situation affecting a child you know, or a story in the media. One thing is certain: you want the problem resolved. So the question becomes "How?" That simple word unlocks the door to many other questions:

- How can you distinguish good advice from bad?
- What environmental/social triggers may produce symptoms that mimic those of psychiatric problems?
- Does your child have a condition that may respond positively to medication?
- Should you medicate your child?
- Which medication is the right one for your child's problem?
- What are the side effects associated with such a drug?
- Do you even *want* your kid to be on a medication?
- When is it more appropriate to use behavioral techniques instead of psychiatric drugs?
- How can you tell which behaviors are simply the result of willfulness or bad habits?

Complicating this already controversial subject are reports in the media about the harmful effects psychiatric medications may have upon children. In 2004, Congress held hearings to investigate the connection between anti-depressants and child/adolescent suicide. In the spring of 2005, the Canadian government outlawed the sale of the very popular AD/HD drug, Adderall XR, due to the sudden cardiac deaths of twelve boys in the United States. Adderall was reinstated in Canada in the fall of 2005. Psychiatric medications are powerful tools, not to be taken casually even by adults, and yet they are increasingly prescribed for children by physicians and psychiatrists. Why is this happening, and how may this trend affect your child?

MEDICATION-BASED SOLUTIONS ARE ON THE RISE

Are more children becoming disturbed, are diagnostic techniques improving, or is it simply a quick-fix convenience for educators, doctors, therapists, and parents alike to turn to the pharmacy to treat behaviors now deemed a "chemical imbalance" in our nation's youth? Does this last suggestion seem exaggerated? Just consider the following:

- The Surgeon General's 1999 report estimated that *21 percent* of children ages nine through seventeen experience the signs and symptoms of a psychiatric disorder in the course of any given year.
- The Center for Disease Control reported in 2002 that almost *20 percent* of the office visits (to pediatricians surveyed) were for psychosocial problems, eclipsing both asthma and heart disease.
- According to the DEA, the number of prescriptions for medications like Ritalin (an amphetamine-class drug) has risen by *500 percent* since 1991.
- In 2002, an *estimated 10.8 million* prescriptions were dispensed for patients younger than eighteen—minors are beginning to outpace the elderly in the consumption of pharmaceuticals, according to FDA, as reported by the *Wall Street Journal*.

These startling figures demonstrate how many children's problems are diagnosed as chemically based and treated with psychiatric medication. Can it be possible that so many misbehaving children are really physically ill? To the author of *Running on Ritalin*, Lawrence Diller, the increased use of doctor-prescribed drugs for children says volumes about our society's tendency to think there is a pill that could solve anything: "How we deal with our kid's problems reflects our thinking and a much larger problem in our culture."[1]

Many doctors who prescribe such medications are all too aware that our society is increasingly turning to the use of medication to "fix" a child's behavior . . . and yet they also understand that, thanks to the media, Internet, and other sources of advice, parents who believe that the only answer is medication, will simply go to another physician for a prescription if none is forthcoming from a doctor who refuses to write one. This is not to say that a pill may not be an appropriate treatment—a particular drug, administered responsibly, may indeed bring a situation under better control with minimal side effects. As a parent without a degree in child psychiatry or pharmacology, how might you go about identifying the cause(s) of your child's problem and determine the best solution for him or her?

WHO ARE THE "EXPERTS"?

COMPLICATING YOUR DESIRE for the best care for your child, the medical community is split on the use of drugs to "cure" behavioral problems in children. On the one hand, numerous psychiatrists and pediatricians explain away *all* behavioral problems in children as psychiatric disease; in consequence, they recommend psychiatric medications for most behavior problems. On the other, many experts condemn the use of psychiatric medications in children and adolescents, instead recommending an exclusively behavioral solution. These two approaches are in complete contradiction to each other. Is there a gray area—are there doctors who take a more balanced approach, where a drug may indeed be a safe and effective partial solution, while behavior-altering methods are also applied? Complicating the issue still further, self-proclaimed nonmedical child-care authorities in the media are endlessly touting their own wonder cure for various behavioral or learning difficulties. Where can you turn, to sort through so many sources of conflicting information?

You hold the key toward finding a solution in your hand. *Should You Medicate Your Child's Mind?* will answer your questions on how to decide whether or when psychiatric medications are right for your child, providing facts currently available to the medical community concerning the diagnosis and treatment of behavioral conditions in children and adolescents, to enable you to make an *informed decision* about the health and happiness of your child.

As a child psychiatrist (a medical doctor), a therapist, a schoolteacher, and a parent, I have approached children and their problems from every possible angle. I am not a staunch advocate of either side in the above argument; rather, I find solutions specific to each child's circumstances—as should you. In this book, I will help you distinguish between those problems that *are* caused by a chemical imbalance and *can* be treated with psychiatric medications, from those behaviors that *are not* caused by chemical imbalances and *cannot* be treated with medications. The first step in the process is to locate a responsible professional with whom to evaluate and treat the situation; next, to determine *what* problem is affecting your child; third, whether your child might need medications and what these medications can actually do or not do for your child; and, finally, what nondrug solutions may support a medication therapy or even take the place of it.

Should You Medicate Your Child's Mind? will guide you through the sea of confusing medical advice with hard facts and tough love, not an automatic reach for the prescription pad. Remember at all times that, as a parent, your goal is to have a healthy, happy child functioning to the best of his or her abilities . . . the goal of *every* parent of *every* child. And that this *may* be achievable with minimal use of medications or no drugs at all.

What You Will *Not* Find in this Book

Should You Medicate Your Child's Mind? is not intended to be used as a diagnostic tool. I am not attempting to deputize you as pseudopsychiatrists. Nothing can replace the trained eye of a competent, *licensed* child psychiatrist, if you want your child evaluated for treatment for a behavioral problem. If your child needs the help of a psychiatric professional, you want the best doctor you can find, not a self-proclaimed expert lacking a medical degree. Remember, too, that it is impossible for you to be objective about your own child. The best assessment and treatment plan will be obtained, with the help of your input, from an unbiased and highly trained clinician. Such professionals spend many years studying their area of expertise and have worked with many clients presenting myriad facets of similar circumstances to the one your child is in. Please resist diagnosing your child with a specific ailment and then seeking out an "expert" in only that ailment—by starting with too narrow a focus, you may both miss signs supporting another diagnosis altogether. It is all too possible, as well, to slip into "medical student's syndrome," via which hearing too much about a behavioral problem falsely convinces you that your child has it! Let me state it once again: to achieve the best results for your child, *do not attempt to diagnose and treat your child's problem on your own.* That said, *do* use the information you gather here to steer you toward asking the right questions and to present your child's problems and your willingness to listen in such a way that stimulates a thorough evaluation and discussion of your child by a qualified doctor.

What You *Will* Find in This Book

BECAUSE OF THE current trend in psychiatry to overdiagnose and overmedicate children, to use the strongest and most dangerous medications available even in the youngest children, parents need a guide that explains the risks associated with seeking mental health treatment for their children. This book is intended to provide guidance through the difficult process of finding help for your child's behavioral problems. Specifically, I will clarify exactly which behaviors constitute the basis of a psychiatric diagnosis, which behaviors and conditions in children do not need medication and which do. For the diagnoses that would benefit from treatment with psychiatric medications, *Should You Medicate Your Child's Mind?* will clarify which meds do what and what risks associated with each. While it is not intended to be an exhaustive resource on everything related to making a mental health diagnosis and choosing appropriate treatment, I *will* cover the most common childhood psychiatric diagnoses. More important, I will provide very specific recommendations on how to find the right type of mental health clinician and tell you how to communicate effectively with these professionals to achieve the best outcome for your child.

I have divided the subject into four sections. The first presents a brief overview of dealing with doctors and psychiatrists, and their possible biases as regards the to-drug-or-not-to-drug issue. This section is also intended to teach you how to most effectively present your child's symptoms to the doctor— clearly, accurately, using the kind of language psychiatric professionals may in turn use in their own observations.

Part 2 is a sampling of the most common childhood psychiatric disorders. It is not by any means a complete list, but presents a good starting point toward the resolution of the most typical behavioral problems affecting children. Each chapter in this part is dedicated to one of the mental illnesses covered in this book, to enable you to zero in on the diagnosis you think your child might have, learn which alternative diagnoses might be worth looking into, and eliminate diagnoses that are unlikely, based upon your child's particular symptoms and circumstances. Finally, part two addresses which drugs are typically associated with the treatment of each of the discussed diagnoses, as a preliminary for part three.

Part 3 walks you through the most commonly prescribed psychiatric medications for children, with disclosure of the risks and benefits of each type of medication. In this section you will learn about the most common and dangerous side effects of specific medications that might be prescribed for your child. I have lost count of the number of times I have heard from a parent, "The doctor never told me that my child could experience that side effect." Being prepared with questions about medications will ensure that these important issues are covered during the doctor visit, before the physician or psychiatrist even writes the prescription. This section will also help you bring to the doctor's attention other health issues regarding the medications he is prescribing your child, such as potential interactions with prescriptions already being administered for common conditions like asthma or allergies.

Part 4 deals with solutions other than, or in addition to, medication, outlining a variety of nonmedication treatments that should also always augment your child's medication treatment. Particularly if you are completely opposed to the use of any medications, this section provides practical information about the alternative means by which your child's condition may be effectively approached. This section contains time-tested advice on how to manage your child's behavioral issues through a variety of disciplinary techniques. These chapters are not meant to completely cover the very broad subject of parenting. What you will find is the heart and soul of a solid and effective parenting approach for any child, but especially for one with psychiatric problems.

I hope that what readers learn here will translate to a nation of healthier, happier children. Let's proceed!

PRELIMINARY STEPS TOWARD A PROFESSIONAL DIAGNOSIS

1

IDENTIFYING YOUR CHILD'S PROBLEM

PARENTHOOD

Raising children may be the greatest challenge you will ever face in life. It is a daunting, often thankless job. At the same time, there is no more important mission in the world, and no greater joy when done well. Parenting is already hard enough, but it becomes even more difficult when your child starts developing "problems."

Maybe it is something that your relatives or the parents of your child's classmates have brought to your attention, or you were alerted to your child's misbehavior by a teacher. Or, perhaps you were the first to identify that your child's behavior has changed from what you recognize as his or her norm, or that what you first deemed a "phase" has become regularly disruptive or pronounced to an unusual degree. No matter how your child's problems come to light, you will probably respond to the revelation with a sinking feeling. You may feel overwhelmed; you may feel angry and frustrated; you may feel embarrassed and ashamed. The prospect of your child having a mental health problem may be frightening to you . . . and, in our age of soaring health-care costs, wondering how to pay for diagnosis and treatment may be a very real worry. Perhaps you have already experimented with rewards, punishments, or other solutions that did not work. And so now you ask yourself: "Is it something I did?"

"Something I *didn't* do?" "Was my child born with this condition?" "*What* is wrong with my child, and what can I do about it?" Perhaps the situation has reached a point where you are willing to try just about anything, to help your child feel better. But it is hard to know where to start.

FINDING THE RIGHT ANSWERS TO YOUR QUESTIONS

WHEN YOUR CHILD needs help, you look everywhere for answers. You want to be thorough. By now you have probably collected information from every available source: from the Internet, magazine articles, doctors, and well-meaning teachers, relatives, and friends—and, almost certainly, you have gathered such conflicting information that now you have still *more* questions! Perhaps most disturbing of explanations you may have encountered is the trend of the "experts" to portray any child's misbehavior as the result of a chemical imbalance, and that such imbalances must be treated with psychiatric medications. Before pursuing that line of treatment, it is vital that you *do* seek answers to the new questions you may have:

- How can you know if your child's behaviors are the result of a chemical imbalance?
- What medical condition may be responsible for the observed signs and symptoms?
- If your child's behaviors *are* the result of such a condition, should they be treated with psychiatric medications?
- Which medication is the right one for your child?
- Do you even *want* your kid on medication?
- As a parent, do you have the right to demand psychiatric drugs be administered to your child?
- Should you decide you do want your child placed on medication, do you seek out a child psychiatrist's help or will a general practitioner be enough?
- How can you separate the good doctors from the bad?
- What exactly are the medications supposed to be doing for your child and what are the risks?
- What behavioral techniques or alternative therapies are recommended as supplementary approaches to medications?
- What if your child is just willful? How do you turn that around without the use of drugs?

HOW SHOULD YOU HANDLE PSYCHIATRIC ADVICE FROM TEACHERS?

I LOVE AND respect teachers. I think the service they provide our children is invaluable and often underappreciated. In fact, I worked as a public and private school teacher for several years before attending medical school. Even today, as a child psychiatrist, my work includes an aspect of teaching. That said, teachers are not doctors.

Although teachers may be very useful in identifying behavioral issues, they are not medically qualified to diagnose psychiatric disorders, and should certainly not advocate the use of specific medications. A little bit of knowledge can be a dangerous thing. Too often parents report to me that their child's teacher has said, "I think Johnnie has AD/HD. You should think about taking him to see the pediatrician for some Ritalin." When your child's teacher tells you that your son or daughter has AD/HD, bear in mind that she has only observed your child at school. Also, a teacher's experience with childhood mental illness is usually limited to the one diagnosis, AD/HD, which receives the most press. What your child's teacher may fail to grasp is that there are a dozen different disorders that include the symptoms of poor concentration and hyperactivity. There is no way she could possibly know if your child has anxiety, depression, food allergies, poor sleep habits, or any number of other diagnoses behind the behaviors she observes in the classroom and schoolyard. Even if she is knowledgeable about child psychology, she has not been educated about the criteria for each and every psychiatric illness. Furthermore, viewing your child as but one among several dozen students at any given time, she has not conducted a formal, one-on-one psychiatric interview to collect all the necessary information to make a diagnosis. Therefore, without the complete information from you about your child or any of the necessary medical training, how accurate can a teacher's diagnosis be?

AN EXAMPLE OF HOW GOOD INTENTIONS GO BAD

I HAVE TREATED countless cases that elucidate the point that even the most concerned teacher is not qualified to diagnose your child. This was best illustrated in the case of a six-year-old child I will call Andy, who was brought to me for a second opinion by his adoptive mother. She had adopted Andy when he was six months old from a woman who was addicted to cocaine and alcohol. The baby, while in the care of the addicted mother, had been severely neglected.

Needless to say, Andy sustained long-term effects of this early abuse—although he would have no conscious memories of that time, the first months of life are critical to the development of a healthy psyche through the bonding process with the mother or primary caregiver. Five-plus years of parenting by another person did not enable Andy to form normal emotional connections, reversing the effects of those abusive formative months. As a result, Andy was socially awkward, and his poor social skills led to a lot of conflict with peers. He was withdrawn and unaffectionate with his adoptive mother, resisting her attempts to hug him. At school, he was obsessed with being first in line, and he rushed through his schoolwork to be the first to turn in his work.

Andy's teacher diagnosed him with AD/HD and directed the adoptive mother to get Ritalin from her pediatrician. The woman went as directed to the doctor and reported what the teacher had said. The pediatrician dutifully wrote out a prescription for Ritalin, a process which took no more than ten minutes, according to my client. She never saw much improvement with the Ritalin, and that was when she sought another opinion—mine.

After a thorough interview with the child, I diagnosed Andy with Reactive Attachment Disorder and changed his prescription to an antidepressant. Shortly thereafter, his adoptive parent mother reported back to me: With tears in her eyes, she told me that her son had actually offered her a hug for the first time since she had adopted him! She said that he was a new boy since treatment began with the antidepressant.

However, months later, she presented me with some disturbing news. After she had casually mentioned the change of medication to Andy's teacher, the teacher irritably "demanded" that the child be taken off the antidepressant and placed back on Ritalin. The woman felt trapped. Not wanting to anger the teacher, and yet not wanting to see her son lose the gains he had made on the new medication, she became creative. She told the teacher that on one particular day, she would be restarting the Ritalin—and that she would appreciate feedback from the teacher on how her son performed in class. When the day arrived, the teacher, believing that the Ritalin had been substituted for the antidepressant, reported to the mother that she had seen a huge improvement in the boy's behavior at school. But the meds had not been changed—the boy had taken the same antidepressant that day as he had for the previous two months!—Andy's mom had lied to the teacher, to avoid further reprimand and possible retribution from the teacher toward Andy. It was unfortunate that pressure from the teacher had forced her hand, but she felt it necessary to protect her son's mental health for the remainder of the school year. Because the teacher tried to be a doctor, parent-teacher trust between these individuals was shattered for the rest of that school year.

WHAT YOUR CHILD'S TEACHER DOES BEST

THIS TEACHER'S BEHAVIOR is not representative of the conduct of most teachers. Teachers can offer you important and valuable guidance in the area of education, and may find it necessary to point out that your child is falling behind or has been withdrawn or disruptive in the classroom. Noticing symptoms is one thing; but, when it comes to diagnosing your child with a psychiatric illness, stick to the advice of a qualified mental health professional!

My experience has shown me that when truly professional teachers think that your child has AD/HD or any other psychiatric condition, they are professional enough not to say so. Responsible teachers realize that, were they to say such a thing, they would be operating outside their licensing and education. However, such diagnostic advice from teachers is so widespread that some U.S. states have actually enacted laws forbidding teachers from giving parents psychiatric advice.

A responsible teacher will alert you to the problems your child is having that are worth addressing. Generally, teachers err on the side of caution by reporting everything and anything outside of the norm. My advice to you is not to try to sort out on your own what is worth pursuing and what can be ignored. If your child's teacher thought something was worth bringing up to you, then it is clearly something deserving of a trip to the doctor's office to evaluate. Remember, sometimes a teacher observes at school what you are not seeing at home.

Good communication between parents and teachers can only benefit the child. Go to all your child's teacher-parent conferences. Ask lots of questions and be prepared to develop a plan to address problems that are brought to your attention. Be sure to ask about your child's social functioning as well as his or her academic performance. Ask the teacher how well your child relates to her personally inside and outside the classroom. Finally, always ask if there is anything that concerns her about your kid's emotional well-being.

I advised a mother of a child named Betsy. Betsy was eight years old and had just moved to Hawaii. She was attending third grade at her new Christian grade school and appeared to be doing well academically. Betsy had started to gain a little excess weight but otherwise seemed to be adjusting well, at least judging from what the mother was hearing from Betsy. So, it came as a bit of a shock when the mother learned at teacher conference night that the other students had shunned Betsy because of her race (Caucasian) in a class in which all the other students were Hawaiian or Asian. When the mother questioned Betsy, she admitted that the other girls had told her they could not play with her until she developed a deep tan and dyed her blond hair black. Betsy had been feeling that the shunning was something she deserved because she was the "new kid," an outsider—so she did not tell her mother. But an alert teacher had made it possible for a socially tormented child to get the help she needed. My advice to the mother was to transfer Betsy to a school with a more racially diverse student body. Eventually, Betsy found a school where she felt accepted. She enjoyed a healthy social life and lost all her excess weight without much effort.

DIAGNOSING YOUR CHILD YOURSELF

WHEN YOU TRY to research your child's problem yourself, several obstacles will keep you from arriving at the correct diagnosis. Your first obstacle is bias. The second is what may be only your partial understanding of what criteria make up a psychiatric diagnosis. The third is psychiatric jargon. Let's start from the top.

OBSTACLE 1: BIAS

You cannot be unbiased about your own children. You do not see their faults and misbehaviors objectively. There have been many instances when a mother has described her child's symptoms to me one by one, making a perfect case for a particular diagnosis . . . and yet, when I tell the mother what the proper diagnosis is, given the symptoms she has reported, she denies it is possible. She simply will not believe that her child has that particular disorder. So, I walk her through the diagnostic criteria in the *Diagnostic Manual* that defines her child's diagnosis. Frequently, even then, although on one level she agrees that her child meets all the criteria, on another—call it a mother's instinct to defend her young—she cannot accept the truth. This is a natural reaction . . . as is its converse, a desire beyond any support by actual symptoms, to believe that an incorrect diagnosis, a more socially acceptable diagnosis, must be true.

That latter bias can also affect adults who try to diagnose themselves. I once had an adult crying in my office, begging me to diagnose her with AD/HD. Her actual diagnosis of depression was too devastating for her to accept about herself. She viewed AD/HD as a more socially acceptable and trendy diagnosis for adults. Given how emotionally charged one diagnosis can be versus another, it is understandable that you may be incapable of being objective about your own child's problems, whether this be based on your fear of and lack of knowledge of mental illness in general, your denial that family issues may be having a negative impact upon your child, or your inability to concede that your child is not fulfilling the dreams you had envisioned for him or her.

Although your perspective is absolutely essential for helping a clinician to understand your child's problem, ultimately, it is always best to find an impartial third party to evaluate your child's mental health. Such a professional will be able to take an overview of your child's entire situation: physical health, emotional state, home life, and social life, including perhaps uncovering background information about your child's past—such as being the victim of bullying, or sexual abuse—that she may have balked at disclosing to you.

OBSTACLE 2: PARTIAL UNDERSTANDING

When you look up a diagnosis on the Web, read a description in a book, or complete a survey in a magazine, you are only seeing part of the picture. Remember the anecdote about the three blind men who each tried to describe an elephant? Each one held a different part of the elephant: a leg, trunk, and tail. Consequently, each man came up with a different description of an elephant. One man insisted an elephant is like the base of a tree, another said an elephant is like a snake, and the third man reported that an elephant is like a rope. The body of information that covers all the psychiatric disorders is quite large. Like the blind man who believes an elephant is like a snake while holding on to its trunk, when you are exposed to only a small portion of the available psychiatric literature, it is easy to be misled. You may, for example, be completely unaware of the fact that the symptoms of poor concentration, hyperactivity, and agitation are common to a dozen different psychiatric diagnoses aside from the one condition you may feel familiar with. Furthermore, you may not realize that children do not have the same symptoms as adults with the same diagnosis. For example, adults with depression feel sad, whereas depressed children may feel irritated, angry, and cranky. Depression also includes the symptoms of poor concentration and "psychomotor agitation" (medical jargon for hyperactivity). Obviously, a magazine survey or Web page that confirms that your child attends poorly in school and sits restlessly in his seat because he has AD/HD, is not enough information upon which to base a diagnosis. Take advantage of the years of training and clinical experience that a mental health professional can offer you. Utilize the expert's greater access to and understanding of the entire elephant—the complete bank of psychiatric knowledge. That you wish to learn more about your child's problems is not unreasonable; the difficulty lies in how much accurate data you can be exposed to as a layman on the subject. You could collect a mountain of information—and misinformation!—from the Internet, and still be no closer to correctly diagnosing your child. Put all that energy into finding a qualified professional to perform your research for you.

OBSTACLE 3: JARGON

Every profession has its own language and jargon. When it comes to describing psychiatric symptoms, psychiatrists have their own language; common words and phrases have very specific meanings to a doctor. Therefore, when a survey in a magazine or on a Web page asks if your child has mood swings, understand that the term may mean to a psychiatrist something that you may not have intended. Thus, when trying to describe your child's symptoms to your doctor, be very careful what terms you use. If you don't know exactly how your doctor interprets certain words, you may give him the wrong impression about your child. To communicate effectively with your child's doctor, you need to be aware of psychiatric jargon, and to be careful how you use it. Otherwise, without realizing what you have done, you may assign a symptom to your child that is not even the case. When you put together a string of misconceptions about symptoms, especially if you begin with a predisposition to diagnose your child's problem as a particular condition, you may end up with an out-landishly incorrect diagnosis, one that a professional listening to you may believe as the truth, and that may ultimately lead to improper treatment. I will cover more on the specific misunderstandings of jargon in the next chapter. For now, let me simply stress once again that a competent mental health profes-sional is far better qualified than you are alone, to analyze the signs and symp-toms of your child. Get help.

2

Choosing a Doctor
for Your Child

What Professional Resources Are
Available for Your Child?

WHEN YOU SET out to find a mental-health professional to evaluate your child, it is important to know which performs which services, and what their qualifications are—including whether they are licensed to practice medicine. Understanding who does what will help you choose a professional best able to diagnose and treat your child.

The following is a brief description of the clinicians most often involved in treating children with behavioral problems. Each type of clinician provides a different kind of service, depending on such factors as training, specialty, and licensing.

- **Marriage and Family Therapist (MFT)** These clinicians have a masters-level education and postgraduate clinical experience, with supervision from a fully trained MFT, prior to licensing. MFTs provide talk therapy to individuals, couples, families, and groups. They are not medically trained and cannot prescribe medications.
- **Licensed Clinical Social Worker (LCSW)** These, too, have a masters-level education, plus postgraduate clinical experience, with supervision from a fully trained LCSW, prior to receiving their license. LCSWs

provide therapy to individuals, couples, families, and groups. They also work in the courtroom, rendering opinions to judges on custody and child welfare cases. In hospitals and a variety of other settings, LCSWs may provide case management, arranging placement and other support services for patients who are being discharged from an institution or care facility. They are not medically trained and cannot prescribe medications.

- **Therapist or Counselor** For any number of reasons, therapists may opt not to complete a conventional licensing program after completing their degree in social work, psychology, or child development. They may be excellent therapists for children and families, nonetheless. The worth of individual therapists directly relates to their ability to empathize, understand, and guide. Thus, although a license may prove that the therapist has completed the requirements of a licensing program, it does not guarantee the quality of the therapy you might receive. Unlicensed therapists are not medically trained and cannot prescribe medications. If you do have health insurance, the cost of services provided by any *licensed* clinician might be covered by your insurance company, depending on your policy. However, you should not expect the services you get from any *unlicensed* therapist or counselor to be covered by your insurance benefits.

- **School Psychologist** The name "psychologist" in a faculty member's title can be misleading. Sometimes a "school psychologist" is actually a licensed psychologist (see below) but not necessarily. Some may have a masters degree. School psychologists provide a very specific service to the schools. Their job is to evaluate the educational needs of the students sent to them for assessment by teachers and school counselors. They are trained to determine what learning disorders, and what social or emotional barriers may exist, that prohibit a child from acquiring an education or may be causing a child to act out negatively within the school setting. Though psychologists may be called "doctor," they are not medically trained and cannot prescribe medications.

- **Psychiatric Nurse (RN)** Psychiatric nurses are registered nurses with a masters degree in psychiatric nursing, and received postgraduate clinical experience with supervision as a prerequisite to being granted their license. They provide therapy to individuals, couples, families, and groups in an outpatient clinic setting. They are also an integral part of every psychiatric hospital unit or psychiatric emergency room. Psychiatric nurse practitioners have received more extensive training than registered nurses. Thus, psychiatric nurse practitioners can *recommend* medications, but only under the direct supervision of a medical doctor who writes the actual prescriptions. Although they are medically trained, they have not completed a medical doctor's training and cannot write a prescription for medication alone: all of the prescriptions provided by a psychiatric nurse practitioner are actually written by the medical doctor supervising her.

- **Clinical Psychologist (PhD or PsyD)** Both a PhD and a PsyD have a graduate degree in psychology, but only a PhD psychologist has completed a dissertation. Both have to complete postgraduate clinical experience with supervision, from a fully trained psychologist, prior to receiving their license to practice. Psychologists provide therapy to individuals, couples, families, and groups. They also perform a very special service that no other specialist can provide: psychological testing. When patients need personality testing, intelligence testing, mental condition testing, or learning disability testing, they are evaluated by a clinical psychologist. Though these psychologists are called "doctor," they are *not* medically trained and cannot prescribe medications.

- **Pediatrician or Family Practice Physician (MD)** These MDs (medical doctors) are specialists trained to diagnose and, if necessary, medicate children. Pediatricians assess, diagnose, and treat children exclusively, whereas family practitioners provide the same services to people of all ages. MDs have a medical doctor's degree and complete a medical internship and residency training in hospitals and outpatient clinics, focusing upon their specialty. This internship and residency takes three years to finish after completion of four years of medical school following the earning of a bachelor's degree in science— typically, eleven years of training in their field altogether. When treating children with mental health problems, pediatricians and family practitioners can prescribe psychiatric medications. However, they are not trained psychiatrists and do not provide psychotherapy. The pediatrician and family practitioner both refer the child to MFTs, LCSWs, psychiatric nurses, or psychologists for individual or family psychotherapy services.

- **Psychiatrist (MD)** A psychiatrist is a medical doctor. Psychiatrists have a medical doctor's degree obtained after completing a medical internship and a psychiatric residency in hospitals and outpatient clinics. Combined, their internship and residency take another four years after they have completed the four years of medical school and earned a bachelor's degree in science; in other words, they typically have twelve years of training altogether. Unlike pediatricians or family practitioners, psychiatrists can provide psychotherapy to individuals, couples, families, and groups although, in actual practice, very few psychiatrists offer conventional outpatient psychotherapy. Generally, psychiatrists assess, diagnose, and treat patients with mental health problems, including, if necessary, by administering psychiatric medications. Psychiatrists are trained to treat patients of all ages, though primarily they work with adults.

- **Child and Adolescent Psychiatrist (MD)** A child and adolescent psychiatrist is a medical doctor. Child psychiatrists have a medical doctor's degree, complete a medical internship and a psychiatric residency training in hospitals and outpatient clinics. Following three years of a general psychiatry residency and internship, child psychiatrists also complete a two-year fellowship in child and adolescent psychiatry. Their internship, residency, and fellowship take five years to complete. This is after they have attended four years of medical school and earned a bachelor's degree in science; thus, they typically have thirteen years of training. Child psychiatrists are legally permitted to treat patients of all ages, but their specialty is the treatment of children. Unlike pediatricians or family practitioners, child psychiatrists provide psychotherapy to individuals, couples, families, and groups, although in actual practice, very few child psychiatrists offer conventional outpatient psychotherapy. Generally, child psychiatrists assess, diagnose, and treat children with mental health problems, and are licensed to prescribe psychiatric medications.

How to Match the Right Clinician to the Problem

THE TYPE OF clinician you choose really depends on the type of services you are seeking. If you desire counseling services only, then you are looking for a therapist. If you want someone to prescribe medications, then you will need a medical doctor's help. If you think your child may need both therapy and drugs, or don't want to rule out the possibility of one or the other, then the starting point would be to visit a psychiatrist. Most psychiatrists do not provide therapy, although there still are a few of us that do; what they will do if necessary is provide a referral to a therapist trained to help children in situations comparable to your child's.

No matter what type of clinician you seek, getting a referral is a good way to begin your search. Whenever possible, try to find a competent clinician, ideally in your community. Don't settle for whoever is simply most convenient, inexpensive, or in your insurer's address book of providers. Start with the suggestions of doctors you already work with or from parents who already use particular clinicians. Don't just select a clinician blindly: some therapists and doctors outline their clinical approach and philosophies about treatment in a brochure, on an Internet site, or may even be willing to do so in a brief phone conversation. Doing a little research ahead of time will save your wasting time, money, and perhaps placing your child at risk for misdiagnosis or mistreatment, in the hands of a professional ill-suited to your particular needs. In the end, nothing can take the place of your own personal experience with the clinician. Sometimes, during or after even your first visit, you can tell if the doctor or therapist is going to be a good fit for your child. Usually, however, the best appraisal of a doctor or therapist is made only after you have visited with the clinician at least three times, so please don't be too quick to form a judgment. The first visit or two might be too new or stressful to you or your child, for the true dynamics of the developing relationship between you and the professional to emerge.

I have treated many children whose parents had taken them to the community's expert on AD/HD and, not surprisingly, their children were diagnosed with AD/HD. When one such local expert, Dr. Z, retired, I adopted her practice and the care of all her patients. Out of the roughly three hundred patients transferred to my care, only five people had not been diagnosed with AD/HD. Among the AD/HD patients referred to me by Dr. Z, was a nine-year-old boy, Charlie, who was having trouble in school. He had been failing to complete his schoolwork and disrupting his classmates. Naturally, his teacher and mother had come to the conclusion that Charlie had AD/HD and sought out treatment from the expert on AD/HD, Dr. Z. She placed Charlie on an amphetamine-class drug, which did seem to help him complete a little more of his work but not enough to ensure his academic success. On top of the weak response to his medication, Charlie also had suffered some side effects to the drug. He had even more trouble sleeping than he had been having prior to treatment, and his anxiety and agitation had increased as well. When I reviewed Charlie's case I found that his problems with attention and his disruption in the classroom were much more involved than were originally thought. Upon further investigation, I learned that Charlie's parents had been engaged in a bitter custody battle for the past five years after an ugly divorce. Furthermore, Charlie had been experiencing other symptoms aside from inattention during this same period of time, including anxiety, anger, agitation, sadness, insomnia, social isolation, and lowered self-esteem. Dr. Z had explained away these additional symptoms as Charlie's response to his AD/HD frustration. His mother was eager to accept this justification because the alternative explanation would have involved examining the role her hostile marriage had played in the development of Charlie's problems. Initially, Charlie's mom was resistant to the idea that AD/HD might *not* be the correct diagnosis but, eventually, she accepted my revised diagnosis of **Adjustment Disorder** with mixed disturbance of emotions and conduct. Charlie started feeling better and enjoyed greater success in the classroom, once his medication was changed to an antidepressant and his family started working on their issues in therapy.

One final comment: remember, a medical doctor's specialty does make a difference. If you have decided that you want your child to be evaluated for possible treatment with medications, don't settle for less than the most highly trained doctor, and one that specifically has the training to correctly prescribe psychiatric medications to children. As much as you may feel comfortable bringing your child to your usual family doctor or pediatrician, this situation may be outside his or her professional depth. A child psychiatrist has the most training and clinical experience in the area of mental health for children of any of the medical specialties.

3

PREPARING FOR
YOUR FIRST VISIT

A DOCTOR'S VISIT can be very brief. Child psychiatrists are under a great deal of financial pressure from insurance companies to make your visit as brief as possible—this is a sad reality of managed care medicine. Make the most of the little time you will have with your child's doctor by being as prepared as possible.

To prepare for your first visit, it helps to know what kinds of questions you will be asked. If you know the questions, then you can be ready with the answers. In fact, it is a good idea to write down answers to some of the standard questions and provide the doctor with a copy at the time of your first visit.

- **What are your child's current symptoms?** Jot down all of your son or daughter's problem behaviors. Please exercise caution here. It is extremely important that you choose your words very carefully as you describe your child's symptoms; don't employ psychiatric jargon that may misrepresent the situation in advance of professional diagnosis. (This will be covered in more detail in the next chapter.) You will be asked how well your child is sleeping, eating, concentrating, and interacting with peers, family, and teachers. You may want to make a note of these features, and begin now to observe your child and formulate answers. Wherever possible, use specific yet plain language and cite dates when any unusual behaviors became apparent or changed, and the frequency/setting of particular symptoms. For example, if your child has begun to have nightmares, try to note when they began, and their frequency. This is the one part of the interview that the doctor will want to discuss with you in the office. Writing down this information beforehand simply ensures that the most basic and important characteristics of your child's condition are covered carefully in that first interview.

- **Safety situation?** No psychiatric evaluation is complete without an investigation into your child's thoughts and attempts to harm him- or herself, or others. You may also be asked if your child has been abused or neglected. Do not be offended. This is a standard question that all child psychiatrists are trained to ask. Keep in mind that many people of either sex may be with your child when you are not there to supervise the interaction. These typically include classmates, babysitters, relatives, teachers, coaches, and clergy. Your psychiatrist will probably ask your child about possible abuse history when interviewing him or her separately.

- **Past psychiatric treatments?** You will be asked to describe any type of psychotherapy, drug rehabilitation treatment, or intensive outpatient programs your child has attended. It would be helpful to list all of the psychiatric medications he has ever taken in the past, and how long they were administered. Also, if you can remember or still have the containers, record the dosages that were prescribed and your child's responses or adverse reactions to each of these medications. If your child was ever hospitalized in a psychiatric facility, include this fact in your report, and the dates that your child was admitted and discharged.

- **Substance abuse history?** This is information that you may not be fully aware of, but write down what you do know or even suspect. If children or adults your child associates with have had substance abuse problems, it is important to the health of your child to admit this to the doctor. The standard procedure in a psychiatric interview of an adolescent is to ask these questions when she is alone with the doctor.

- **Medical history?** Write down all of your child's current and past medical conditions. Be sure to include all the prescription and over-the-counter or herbal medications he is currently taking for nonpsychiatric conditions. These may include vitamin supplements, pain or allergy medications, and cough syrups. List all the surgeries your child has had and the dates of those operations. Describe, for the doctor, any head trauma, loss of consciousness, unusually high fevers, or seizures your child may have endured. Give the date of your child's last physical examination and note whether his immunizations are up to date. Be sure to list any medications to which your child has an allergic reaction. Note any other allergies and intolerances relating to food, food additives and dyes, environmental substances (such as pollens, dust, and sensitivities to scents, soaps, or latex), insect bites, and animal hair or dander.

- **Developmental history?** Although this history is always of interest to a child psychiatrist, this information is particularly useful if your child is under twelve years old. Tell your child's doctor how long you were pregnant and how the pregnancy went. Be sure to mention any medications or substances you used while pregnant, and any substances the child's father may have been using during the period immediately preceding conception. Describe how the delivery went, including any adverse events or complications for your child. If you can recall, list the ages she first crawled, sat up, walked, and talked. Otherwise, just include a general impression of whether your child reached her developmental milestones on time, prematurely, or late. Have there been any periods of marked regression in any area? Include whatever information you have about any recent sight or hearing tests.

- **School history?** In your write-up, describe how your child is doing in school. You want to be sure to include his grade level and the type of school: public, private, or religious. State what type of classroom your child attends: special education, regular education, or gifted, and the size of the classes. Be specific about the type of any special education environment, noting whether it is for students with behavioral problems or learning disabilities, and whether your child is receiving any extracurricular tutoring. If your child is home-schooled, is the teacher a parent or a licensed professional; how large are the classes and in what kind of setting are they held; and are children of different ages and levels of learning in the same class together? List your child's grades on his last report card, or bring contrasting report cards if grades/behavioral comments have changed significantly from one term to another. Give an account of how he behaves in the classroom, including detentions and suspensions. Finally, tell the doctor, in your prewritten history, how well your child gets along with other children—peers, younger children, and older children. Does your child get into fights often? Does he have many friends at school? Do his classmates exclude him from their social activities, or does he avoid mixing with his peers?

- **Social history?** In your report, it is useful to describe your child's family life. State your marital status and, if separated, for how long. If you are living with your partner, describe how well the two of you are getting along. Are you the child's biological parent? Is your partner the child's other biological parent? If the child has other parents, what is the visitation situation, if any? If you are dating or in a new relationship, is your child exposed to your partner(s) and how do they get along? Parents often underestimate how fluctuations or discord in their relationship(s) can affect their child's mental health. Be sure to be as frank and honest as you can. Your child really does pick up on more than you may realize. Has your child ever been placed in temporary foster care or lived with another guardian for any extended period of time?

Include here how many brothers and sisters your child has, their ages, and whether they still live at home. If the family is a merged one of step- or half siblings or adopted, provide the details. If any of your other children are having mental health problems or social crises, this would be extremely useful information to include in your record.

Describe how big your living space is and where your child sleeps. Does your child have his own room? Does he share a room or bed with another child or adult? What is your child's usual bedtime? Has he been having nightmares or begun wetting the bed? Do family members listen to loud music or television, or talk loudly, while your child is trying to sleep or study? Is your child exposed to music, TV shows, or videos containing adult or negative themes? Is his bedroom full of electronics, such as a TV, a DVD, a VCR, a computer with Internet access, a Play Station, an X-Box, and so on, and does he have adult supervision while he uses the Internet? Does he prefer a secluded area rather to joining the rest of the household?

You should report who is working outside of the house and what jobs they hold. Is your child now or has he been in daycare? Who watches your child when you are not available to do so? Is he a "latchkey" child or is an adult waiting for him at home when he returns from school? Have any siblings moved out or left for any other extended period recently, such as to attend college or join a military unit, or has anyone recently been added to the household?

Have any important family members become very sick or injured? Has any close elderly relative exhibited personality changes that may be affecting your child's relationship with him or her? Has anyone close to the child—including any pets—recently died? Has the family seen any sudden change in its finances or physical safety? When did you last move house, and did it involve changing schools? How often has your child changed schools? These are all important influences that can affect your child's health.

Be sure to list your child's hobbies and after-school activities. Does your child begin and complete his homework without argument or your doing some of the work for him? How many hours each day does he typically watch television or videos, play with electronic games, or use the Internet for nonhomework purposes? Does your child have a particular interest, skill, or talent that absorbs his time and attention, and has that pursuit diminished, intensified, or stayed about the same since his problems began? For instance, if a child who has always practiced without anxiety on a musical instrument begins to spend an obsessive number of hours every day attempting to perfect his skills, that is a change to note for the doctor.

In what clubs or sports does your child participate? If a teenager, does your child have a curfew and does she observe it? Does your child have an after-school job? Does your child have any friends outside of those she sees in school? Does she prefer to be with children younger or older than her peers, or adults? Have you met the people with whom your child socializes in and out of school? Does your child have a pet, and does she care for it responsibly? Has a close friend of your child recently moved away or severed the friendship? Have any of your child's friends been diagnosed and treated for behaviors now exhibited by your child?

Finally, let the doctor know what responsibilities your child has around the house. Does your child keep his own room clean? Does he have any chores? If there are multiple siblings, how do you keep track of who is doing their chores? Do you reward cooperative behavior at your house? How do you respond to uncooperative behavior? Are you and your partner in agreement about such responses, or does each of you employ different techniques, with different thresholds as regards what constitutes noncooperation, to discipline your child?

- **Family history?** Under this heading, list all the other people in your family related to your child by blood, such as grandparents or aunts/uncles, who have any mental illness or addiction history. State what treatments or medications helped in each case, if you know. Of course, if your child is adopted and you know nothing about the biological relatives, then state that here instead.

Arrive at your first doctor's appointment fully prepared with complete answers to these standard kinds of questions asked in a psychiatric interview. This will make the most of your visit, allowing more time for arriving at and discussing your child's diagnosis and treatment. In fact, you would get more out of every session with your child's doctor if you always attended your visits prepared like this: Between appointments, keep a journal or a log of your child's condition from day to day, noting answers to questions you may not have been able to answer the first time around. Then you can arrive with a complete report about your child's progress, including his response to any medications.

A blank form that includes all the above questions can be copied from Appendix A or downloaded from my Web site, www.DrElizabethRoberts.com. You can complete the form and take it with you to your appointment for reference. Making a copy for the doctor to keep in your child's chart is a good idea, too.

4

COMMUNICATING WITH
YOUR CHILD'S DOCTOR

THE TROUBLE WITH JARGON

PROBABLY THE MOST frequent reason that children are improperly diagnosed and medicated, is the miscommunication between parent and doctor. When you sit down with your doctor to discuss your child's condition, you must be aware of how psychiatrists interpret certain words. Common words that you may use to describe your child's behavior or symptoms may have very specific meanings to the doctor. You may both be using the same word yet it is one to which you each assign a very different meaning. If the doctor does not carefully review with you every term you use to describe your child's condition, and just what you mean by it, then he could arrive at a false diagnosis based on misinterpretations. Let's review the most common examples of everyday words that doctors have adopted as jargon.

- **Hyperactivity** If you examine this word, you notice two parts: *hyper* and *activity*. To an average person, this word means a very active kid who loves to get into everything, run around, and have as much fun as he possibly can. If you have a young son, you are familiar with the typical behavior of boys under twelve years old. Doctors, however, regularly use the word prefix *hyper* to describe a number of disease states.

For example, hyperthyroidism is a condition where there is an excess of thyroid hormone in the body, an excess that is enough to cause the malfunctioning of other organ systems. When you tell your doctor that your child is "hyperactive," you are telling him that he is outside the range of normal "little boy behavior." (Yes, of course, there are little girls who are as active as little boys.) Therefore, if you are trying to tell your doctor your child is an active kid, use the word *active* and leave it at that. Eliminate the prefix *hyper* unless you want to communicate to your doctor that your child's level of activity is clearly in the abnormal range. Additional terms used by psychiatrists to mean *hyperactive* are: psychomotor agitation, agitation, restless, keyed up, and on edge. Hyperactivity is very often associated with impulsivity.

- **Inattention** This term is used to describe a person who cannot attend to a task *even when he wants to pay attention*. This term does *not* apply to a child who does not *want* to pay attention. That latter behavior is referred to as *defiance*. If your child can spend long periods of time focused on Legos, Yu-Gi-Oh cards, or computer games that require planning and strategy, but then appears to be deaf when you ask him to do his homework, he may be defiant but he is not inattentive. Your child may just be consciously ignoring the things that he does not like or want to do. Inattentiveness, as it is understood in psychiatry, is a condition that is outside of a person's control or choice. Try this test. Ask your child to do a chore while standing next to him. If he ignores you, tell him that you will give him twenty dollars if he does the chore. If he responds to the offer, ". . . to give him twenty dollars," then you know that he hears only what he wants to hear. Now you know that he can attend to you when a subject is important to *him*.

To a psychiatrist, inattention is synonymous with: poor concentration, easily distracted, forgetfulness, failure to finish projects, disorganized, poor attention to details, and losing things. Furthermore, when using this term clinically, doctors mean a degree of inattention that is *beyond* what is considered developmentally normal. Keep in mind what is developmentally appropriate for your child, given her age, and to what degree such behaviors need to be learned and reinforced. Being organized is not a skill that develops naturally on its own. This is something *taught* to children and reviewed repeatedly throughout the first thirteen years of life. Do not expect your child to develop organization skills by himself. Developing such proficiency requires guidance from teachers and parents who have already mastered these skills.

- **Mood Swings** This is a particularly treacherous term. To an average person, the phrase *mood swings* describes behavior of a person who displays an array of emotions that are not, individually, extreme. We've all known someone who may be laid back one day yet nit-picky or irritable the next. This term may also apply to a person who cries at the least little provocation and then recovers just as quickly. Psychiatrists have an entirely different meaning for the term *mood swings*. A person with mood swings has episodes of *mania* separated by episodes of *depression*. Each of these terms, mania and depression, have very specific meanings, whose definitions follow. When trying to describe a child's moodiness, in the sense of exhibiting a variety of moods, use a term other than *mood swings*: cranky, fussy, irritated, or grumpy might describe the more negative forms of such behavior. Only tell the doctor your child has mood swings if you intend to communicate that your child has genuinely manic episodes.

- **Mania** is a cluster of symptoms that occur together over a discrete period of time, usually four to seven days. To determine if a person is having a manic episode, consider whether the behaviors are fixed, everyday personality traits that are constant, or are the behaviors truly episodic. By definition, an *episode* has a beginning and an end. Generally, after recovering from a manic episode patients will be shocked and dismayed at their own behavior during the episode. Once they are no longer in that state they recognize the mania as being something abnormal for them. It must be clarified that a true manic episode occurs in the absence of intoxication. People bingeing on illicit drugs, especially amphetamines, do resemble those experiencing a manic episode, but they are not truly manic. During a manic episode, the person becomes delusional, acts bizarrely, and seems to be out of touch with reality. Even to the untrained eye, manic patients appear extremely mentally ill. There are a number of specific symptoms that clearly identify the person as manic:

  - They require almost no sleep for four to seven days straight. They are awake and hyperactive—in the medical sense—for the entire episode. This should not be confused with the loss of sleep that occurs in depression or anxiety. Depressed and anxious people are tired and want to sleep, but spend their nights in bed tossing and turning. Manic persons do not desire sleep—they appear not to need sleep, because they just keep moving tirelessly, night and day.

- They lose touch with reality. Typically, a person in a manic state believes he is famous or is the close friend of a famous person. These beliefs are termed *delusions of grandiosity*. They act on these delusions by doing strange, out-of-character things, such as waiting by the window for a famous celebrity's limo to arrive and take them on a date, or believing they are romantically involved with a rock star for whom they buy gifts.

- Manics are euphoric. They are excessively joyous and have grandiose thoughts, such as believing that they can save the world with their plans for world peace or that they have been selected as Homecoming Queen.

- Manic people become sexually focused. They are infamous for being out in public naked, and oblivious to the socially inappropriate nature of this behavior. Manic adults and teens typically have indiscriminate sexual encounters with multiple partners during the episode. In a manic preteen, excessive masturbation may be how this sexual focus is expressed.

- A person in a manic phase will spend money excessively on items he doesn't need and can't afford. I treated a manic man who tried to buy five cars on the same day. A teenager in a manic phase may purchase $5,000-worth of music online with his parent's credit card. Not every shopping spree becomes proof of a manic episode. Manic spending differs from normal overspending both in the magnitude of the spending and the lack of awareness. People in a manic episode spend with abandon, completely oblivious to the ramifications of the excessive expenditures.

- They have *pressured speech* and *racing thoughts*, also terms that require extensive definition (see below).

- **Pressured Speech** occurs during a manic episode. Afflicted persons will talk very rapidly while in the manic state. They speak so quickly and volubly that they are impossible to interrupt. Manics do not pause to allow others to respond. Pressured speech is different than the giddy ramblings of teenage girls on a Friday night. Normal teen girls talk about reality-based events, and enjoy exchanging ideas and stories. When a manic person has pressured speech, the content is usually delusional, bizarre, or grandiose. The abnormal quality of the content as well as the relentless drive with which it is delivered is evidence that the person is exhibiting the pressured speech seen in mania.

- **Racing Thoughts** is also a symptom of mania. When a person is experiencing *racing thoughts*, his mind jumps rapidly from one idea to the next in what is referred to as a *flight of ideas*. The content of his thoughts is unrealistic and disjointed. As his mind flies from one idea to the next completely unrelated idea, the patient feels unable to keep up with his own thoughts. Even if he tries to, he is unable to slow his thoughts down enough to focus on any one idea. Racing thoughts should not be confused with *ruminating*.

- **Ruminating** is the experience of reviewing and agonizing over past decisions or decisions that have yet to be made. Ruminating is going over and over again in one's mind guilty feelings, dissatisfying events of the past, or worries about the future. When you reexamine an event in your mind, repeatedly thinking about how you could have done things differently, or can't stop yourself from fretting about up-coming events, you are ruminating. To some degree, this is normal behavior; it tips into the realm of abnormal when it is interfering with one's ability to function within the present. Excessive, debilitating rumination is common in persons with depression or anxiety, but should not be confused with the racing thoughts experienced in mania.

- **Depressed** mood only becomes of clinical concern when it starts to consume a person and interferes with his or her day-to-day functioning. People tend to say someone is depressed when the person is just plain sad or subdued or doesn't want to join in; it is a term that should only be used to indicate profound despair or withdrawal that leads to the inability to cope with/move on within a reasonable time frame from an upsetting situation. A kid crying himself to sleep for a week over the loss of a friend who moved away is not depression, it's plain old grief. If the grief eventually resolves and he can otherwise function at school and in his extracurricular activities he may not even need therapy, much less drugs. More on the topic of clinical depression will be covered in chapter 9.

- **Obsessions** with hobbies or activities does not automatically constitute a mental illness. There is a tendency for people to claim an interest or an intensity of interest they do not share as an obsession. To consider a behavior an obsession in the medical sense it needs to be interfering with the person's everyday functioning. A kid who has three hundred dinosaur models is just a dinosaur enthusiast; a kid who has to arrange every one of them in alphabetical order before he can brush his teeth

may have an obsessive disorder. Chapter 13 covers the issues and symptoms of Obsessive Compulsive Disorder in greater detail.

- **Insomnia** is the inability to sleep soundly through the night. When you
  cannot fall asleep or sleep until the time you desire to be awakened,
  you have insomnia. Insomnia is a sleep problem that may occur in
  depression or anxiety: depressed and anxious people want to sleep, but
  cannot do so to any degree that will refresh them; the symptom feeds
  upon itself by making them feel increasingly tired with each wakeful
  night. This should not be confused with the loss of sleep that occurs
  during mania; as noted, manics do not desire sleep and do not appear
  tired from lack of sleep. There are three types of insomnia:

  - The first is the inability to initiate sleep; that is, for a long period
    of time you are unable to fall asleep when you first retire to your
    bed. How long is "too long" to fall asleep can be a subjective
    assessment. Generally, any longer than twenty minutes spent
    consciously trying to fall asleep would be considered an insom-
    nia of initiating sleep.
  - The second type of insomnia features frequent awakenings
    throughout the night, paired with difficulty returning to sleep.
  - The final type of insomnia is the early morning awakening. You
    find yourself awakening one or two hours earlier than you
    wanted. You then find you are tired, you want to return to sleep,
    but you are unable to do so.

- **Irritable** is another tricky term you must be very careful how you use with
  your child's doctor. Again, this is one of those expressions that an average person would use to describe the mood of a person who is quickly and
  easily angered or frequently cranky. If, indeed, your child is easily irritated,
  in this sense of the term, then tell the doctor, but specify that your child
  has a trigger temper or is often angry. Just be very careful with the word
  irritable, as some doctors have come to see this word as synonymous with
  the mood of manic patients. (See *mania*, page 25, for further explanation.)
  The average person may also use this term to describe a person who cries
  easily, someone who seems "touchy," around whom one must be careful what one says or does. This second description actually comes closer
  to the way doctors use this term, when such reactions are extreme
  compared with their circumstances. Whenever you report any symptom
  to a doctor, it is important to keep in mind that *doctors deal in extremes.*

Furthermore, doctors assume that a condition described by a psychiatric term of jargon impacts upon the person's functioning significantly. In other words, if your child indeed cries easily, you would only report this to your doctor as being an "irritable mood" if it is to an extreme degree and creates a significant loss of functioning for your child. Be aware as well that "irritable mood" is used by some doctors to describe the mood of Borderline Personality patients or the mood children experience when they have Major Depressive Disorder. More on these finer points in the chapters on Depression and Borderline Personality.

- **Hearing Voices** is a very specific psychiatric symptom that reflects grave mental illness. If your child has told you that he "hears voices," be sure to clarify exactly what he is experiencing. If your child is having disturbing thoughts that are unwanted but they are simply *thoughts* not actually perceived as *sound*, then he is not having auditory hallucinations (AH). These unwanted, distressing thoughts represent a symptom called *intrusive thoughts*. In young children, intrusive thoughts are very difficult to separate from their world of imagination, particularly when it involves an imaginary friend or a favorite fictional character. If your child reports actually hearing sounds and people's voices the same way he perceives other sounds, then he is experiencing auditory hallucinations. A doctor assumes that a patient who reports he is "hearing voices" is essentially saying he is having AH. Experiencing an auditory hallucination is a serious symptom that indicates your child may be psychotic. There are a number of diagnoses that include AH, such as schizophrenia, deep psychotic depression, or substance abuse–induced psychosis. What is important to establish with your child is whether the voices he hears are truly auditory or simply intrusive thoughts. This is one psychiatric symptom you don't want to over report and have your doctor jump to unwarranted conclusions.

The Importance of Effective Communication

THE KEY TO an accurate diagnosis of your child starts with a thorough history collected by a doctor who is communicating effectively with you. Therefore, it is essential that you and the doctor are both using language in the same way. When you meet with your child's doctor, choose your words very carefully and make sure you have not used one of the terms listed above in a way you did not intend. Give specific examples of behaviors to back up why you may employ one of these terms, to be clear that the doctor understands your usage.

Beware of self-administered surveys on the Internet and in popular magazines that use the terms listed above. These pseudopsychological tests can be
very misleading. Diagnosing genuine psychiatric conditions requires the doctor to integrate your child's symptoms into a cohesive package, always putting
them into the perspective of your child's and the greater family history. A self-
administered survey cannot place your child's behavior in the context of his life
experiences, traumas, and losses. Such tests may lead you to believe that your
child has a greater problem than she actually has, or may misinterpret the symptoms. Finding and communicating well with a responsible medical professional
is the first step toward getting the assistance you need to help your child feel
better and stay well.

Summary: Preparing for an Accurate Diagnosis

1. Find the right clinician to evaluate your child.
2. Make the most of your time by attending your visits fully prepared with
   a complete history of your child's health, school and social life, and living environment.
3. Have a thorough understanding of the jargon used by mental health
   professionals, and be very careful how you use it.

Now, you are ready to discuss your child with her doctor.

5

How Your Child Can Become Overmedicated or Incorrectly Medicated

STUDIES PUBLISHED IN the 2003 *Archives of Pediatrics & Adolescent Medicine*[1] concluded that three times as many children are receiving psychiatric medication than did fifteen years ago. How did this happen? Why are so many more children receiving psychiatric medications—and why are they being prescribed *more dangerous* medications than they were fifteen years ago? Are there really that many more children developing psychiatric illnesses?

While no one has done a study to answer these specific questions, as a child psychiatrist and parent I think I can explain how this problem may have developed. The following is a list of the major reasons why children may become overmedicated or incorrectly medicated.

- Misdiagnosis
- What's in fashion
- Overdiagnosis
- Partial response to medications
- Doctor's anxiety
- Doctor's faith in medications: lack of faith in psychological treatments
- Resembling another child the doctor treated in the past
- Pressure by the teacher on the parent

- Pressure by the parent on the doctor
- Parent's fear of confronting the doctor
- Doctor's fear of confronting the parent

Let's examine these reasons in greater detail.

Misdiagnosis

BEING MISDIAGNOSED IS probably the biggest contributor to the overmedication of children. Starting a treatment based on the wrong diagnosis usually leads to either the use of medications when they are completely unwarranted, or the wrong medications being prescribed. When your child's symptoms continue unchanged or perhaps even worsen while being treated with a mistakenly prescribed medication, it is often assumed that the medication regimen needs to be "adjusted." Rarely is the *diagnosis* reexamined. The "adjustment" usually consists of the doctor adding one or more other medications to those your child is already taking. Once your child is given the wrong medications, every readjustment simply leads to the addition of more medications. Chances are that a doctor will want to stand by his diagnosis as well as his preferred treatment regimen for that condition. This is how easily a misdiagnosis can lead to overmedicating or incorrectly medicating your child.

One common way your child can be misdiagnosed occurs when your doctor does not take the time to understand his or her problems thoroughly. Here is how a doctor might arrive at the wrong diagnosis, based on incomplete information about your child:

Let's take for our example a child who is easily angered, loses his temper when he doesn't get his way, and refuses to do his homework. He often argues with the teacher and other adult authority figures, and defies rules at school and at home. In class, he purposely antagonizes his teacher by clowning around and leaving his assigned seat to interfere with his classmates' studies. If your child had these symptoms, the likely diagnosis would be Oppositional Defiant Disorder (ODD). But imagine that your doctor only learned from you that your child was not doing his work and often left his classroom seat; then the doctor might reasonably conclude that your child had AD/HD. On the other hand, if you were only allowed time to explain that your child is easily angered, has tantrums, and clowns around in class, he might conclude that your child had Bipolar Disorder!

Both of these diagnoses, AD/HD and Bipolar Disorder, are usually treated with powerful psychotropic drugs that can cause significant side effects:

Amphetamines, the medications usually administered for AD/HD, would indeed help your child do his homework more efficiently, if he agreed to do his work at all. On the other hand, he might still refuse to do any of his work, while continuing to antagonize his teacher, argue with other adults, and behave defiantly. Now consider that the drugs used to treat Bipolar Disorder, mood-stabilizing medications, could help sedate and calm your child, causing him to be less angry and less agitated. These mood-stabilizers can achieve such calming results even when your child does *not* have a psychiatric diagnosis. Again, a sedated, less agitated child does not necessarily become more compliant and cooperative with adults.

The crime here is that, not only is your child subjected to powerful drugs for a condition he does not even have, but his real problem, Oppositional Defiant Disorder, *does not need to be treated with medications at all.* The solution to ODD consists of educating parents, to help them learn behavioral management techniques that stop their children's belligerent behaviors. But, because a diagnosis is rushed, and a psychotropic medication is hastily prescribed, you, the parent, never receive the proper advice on how to modify the behaviors of your ODD child. Without behavioral intervention, he will likely receive more and other drugs in an attempt to control each symptom not responding to the original medications. What a horrifying prospect!—but it happens every day in my profession, all for want of communication and thoughtful evaluation.

Making the correct diagnosis is essential to receiving the proper treatment. Otherwise, your doctor's false conclusions may lead to your child receiving medications he does not need.

What's in Fashion

Certain diagnoses come into fashion for a period of time. Unfortunately, your doctor can be influenced by a recent lecture he has heard or conference he has attended. Should your child be evaluated during a period of time when a particular diagnosis is popular, then he is more likely to be diagnosed with that disorder. Through the years, there have been several popular diagnoses:

- In the 1970s, **Multiple Personality Disorder** was very popular. The book and movie, *Sybil*, had just come out, and as a result many people were being diagnosed with this disorder. Today, the disorder is not even listed in the *DSM*.
- AD/HD has enjoyed a long, uninterrupted popularity as a diagnosis in children. After the year 2000, AD/HD also became a favorite diagnosis

in adults. Following AD/HD, Bipolar Disorder became a popular diagnosis.

- Prior to 1996, Bipolar Disorder was unheard of in children under the age of ten. Since 2000, however, Bipolar has become the newest explanation for tantrums in children. I regularly evaluate children who were diagnosed by the previous doctor as having this disorder. The youngest child I have seen wrongly diagnosed by a professional was a three-year-old girl! But it gets worse: I personally evaluated a toddler, eighteen months old, whose mother had diagnosed her own baby with Bipolar Disorder!
- Recently, Asperger's Disorder has become an increasingly common diagnosis. Researchers have found that, between 1987 and 2005, the diagnosis of autistic disorders, like Asperger's, has increased tenfold.[2] The Center for Disease Control has stated that the increased prevalence in the United States of autistic diagnoses cannot be verified as an actual increase in the number of real cases or whether they are "due to changes in how we identify and classify autistic disorders."[3]

One concept does emerge out of all of this. Diagnoses come and go in their popularity. What are the factors that influence these changes? Let us consider the following:

- Parents can play a part in promoting the popularity of a diagnosis. Stories about certain diagnoses and cures circulate among parents. They meet at schools or at community functions, or through the Internet and at such parent support meetings as ChADD (an AD/HD support group). They share anecdotes about behavioral problems in children and the diagnoses these children were given. For example, a story may start circulating about an angry, aggressive child who was finally diagnosed with whatever is the new, fashionable psychiatric disorder. The story may go on to say that, after this new diagnosis was made, the child was placed on medications that really helped him. These sorts of tales can generate a lot of excitement, and make a certain diagnosis very popular. As a result, parents will suggest to their child's doctor that this fashionable disorder or its wonder-drug cure might apply to their child.
- Information-sharing among parents can be misleading. For example, anger and aggression in children are common problems for which there are no easy answers. The assumption that a specific medication currently in vogue for treatment of a fashionable disorder will *only*

work to reduce anger in a child who has that particular diagnosis, is misleading. The truth is, medications that reduce anger in children will probably work at least to some degree no matter what her diagnosis or the reason for her anger. That the drug may appear to have a positive affect may blind parents to the fact that their child has a different, untreated problem altogether, fueling the popularity of one diagnosis over another receiving less press or acceptance.

- The print and television media can also fan the flames of what's popular in childhood psychiatric disease and medical cures. Sensational and alarming stories sell advertising time. Therefore, the media will scoop up these stories that circulate around the Web, and feature them as public interest stories. These "news" stories result in the promotion of whatever is trendy in psychology today. People are very impressionable. If they see it in print, or on TV, they assume it has to be true, but often what is presented may not be accurate, complete, or as broadly prevalent as the extensive news coverage would indicate. Therefore, media stories go a long way in promoting the popularity of a particular psychiatric diagnosis.

- Pharmaceutical companies also play a part in popularizing a diagnosis. Drug companies will seize upon any opportunity to find a new application for medications that are already approved and in use for some other diagnosis. For example, let us examine the relationship between the newly popular diagnosis of Bipolar Disorder and the upsurge in prescriptions for antipsychotic medications.

- Antipsychotics are sedatives that are effective in reducing anger and aggression. Children may have anger outbursts or tantrums for many reasons. Yet, tantrums in children are quickly becoming "proof" that your child has Bipolar Disorder. Because tantrums are common, this makes Bipolar Disorder an increasingly common diagnosis. Suppose you tell the doctor that your child is having tantrums and you think he may have Bipolar Disorder. The doctor may not look any further to make a diagnosis, and proceed to treat your child's tantrums with antipsychotic medications. When your child's tantrums are reduced by the antipsychotics, your doctor may conclude there is a connection between the medication's success and his diagnosis. In this simplistic manner, doctors can and indeed do reason that children whose anger is reduced by antipsychotics *must have* Bipolar Disorder. This popular line of reasoning is like saying that because dogs have four legs, all four-legged animals are dogs. Though reasoning such as this may not be logical, this is how trends in psychiatry can get started and snowball.

When this conclusion about tantrums, antipsychotics, and the diagnosis of Bipolar Disorder appears in a drug company–sponsored lecture— given by speakers they fund, not an impartial source—it only further popularizes the diagnosis of Bipolar Disorder. Accordingly, the doctors who have successfully treated tantrums with antipsychotics, come away from these lectures with their belief that tantrums are proof of childhood Bipolar Disorder confirmed by a reputable source.

- I do not mean to imply that, just because a diagnosis becomes popular, it is *never* the correct diagnosis. Children who have tantrums may *also* have Bipolar Disorder, of course. Nor do I mean to say that antipsychotics are not effective medications—when used correctly. They can be very useful medications for a number of conditions, including Bipolar Disorder. Furthermore, I am not implying that pharmaceutical companies are trying to mislead anyone. Doctors come to these conclusions on their own. Drug companies simply provide a venue for these ideas to be exchanged. Yet, when pharmaceutical companies finance lectures on the use of certain medications for fashionable diagnoses, your child could easily get swept up in whatever trend is popular at the time. Then your child could be medicated unnecessarily or overmedicated.

OVERDIAGNOSIS

OVERDIAGNOSIS STARTS WHEN your child's initial diagnosis is incorrect. Armed with the wrong diagnosis, your doctor may use medications that do not really address your child's condition. Then, to explain your child's symptoms that did not respond to the first medications, your doctor adds another diagnosis. This is how a misdiagnosis may evolve into an overdiagnosis.

Let us run through a common example of how a misdiagnosis can evolve into the overdiagnosing and ultimately the overmedicating of your child. Assume that your child is sad about the family's recent move, a move that required him to leave his old friends and start a new school. He is not paying attention in school. He is not sleeping well at night. He is withdrawing into his room to be alone. He is more restless, agitated, and more easily irritated than usual by his little sister. If your doctor is aware of only one or two of your child's symptoms and remains unaware of the rest of your boy's problems, the doctor might easily arrive at the wrong diagnosis. In this example, if your doctor zeros in on the inattention and restlessness, he could come to the conclusion that your child has AD/HD. As a result, your doctor may start your child on Ritalin or some other amphetamine that does not address the real problem.

Now, you may ask, "What about the symptoms that the doctor did not take into account?" Doctors defending their original misdiagnosis like to employ a new rationalization for dismissing one of the symptoms that your child is having in favor of focusing on another that better fits their theory. The explanation is the "this causes that" phenomenon. For instance, lecturers who promote AD/HD and the medications that treat AD/HD tell doctors at conferences that AD/HD causes "depressed mood." Using this line of reasoning, your doctor may claim that your child, who is depressed and therefore cannot concentrate, really has AD/HD and is only depressed because he is sad about his school failure! Yes, your child's ability to concentrate will be improved by his taking Ritalin, even when he does not have AD/HD, but his depression will continue untreated. It bears repeating that amphetamines, like Ritalin, will help just about *anyone* concentrate and pay attention better.

So, now your child is taking Ritalin and paying attention better in school, but he is still sad and withdrawn. At this point, your doctor may add the diagnosis of Major Depressive Disorder to his first diagnosis of AD/HD. A new diagnosis means new meds (as understood by many doctors). In short order, your child is taking an amphetamine *and* an antidepressant.

Let's roll with this one level further. While your child is taking his two medications, he is concentrating better and he is happier—good news. However, the amphetamine, Ritalin, is causing him to sleep even less and feel even more irritated, restless, and agitated. At this point, your doctor may want to add another diagnosis to explain the symptoms that remain or may have developed as a drug's side effect. A typical option when children are not sleeping well and are feeling agitated is the diagnosis of Bipolar Disorder. With Bipolar Disorder comes a whole new group of medications. Soon, you may find that your child has three diagnoses and is taking four or five different medications. This is not to say that more than one medication is always wrong. Sometimes it does take two or more drugs to treat a single diagnosis. But this example of overdiagnosis is actually a fairly common scenario in child psychiatry. It explains how children become overmedicated by the diagnosis of only a few symptoms at a time, instead of a single, comprehensive diagnosis that takes in the entire picture.

PARTIAL RESPONSE TO MEDICATIONS

A PARTIAL RESPONSE to medication is another way that children end up overmedicated. This overmedicating process starts when your doctor sees some improvement in your child on a medication he just prescribed. Generally, when your child's condition has improved, even mildly, with a medication the doctor prescribed with a particular diagnosis in mind, this validates his diagnosis of your child. The doctor may determine that because your child got a little better, his diagnosis must be correct. Hopefully, the doctor's diagnosis is correct. However, some doctors will not question their diagnosis when your child is getting better on the medications he prescribed. Instead, the doctor will forge ahead with the treatment by increasing the dosage of your child's medication. His thinking: if a little worked this much, a lot will work even better.

To illustrate this point, assume your child has all the symptoms of Oppositional Defiant Disorder (ODD). A child with ODD has symptoms of being touchy and easily annoyed, often angry and losing his temper, has tantrums when he doesn't get his way, argues with adults, provokes others, and is defiant. If your doctor has concluded that your child has the diagnosis of Bipolar Disorder, based on your child's anger and irritability, then he will likely prescribe powerful mood stabilizers or antipsychotic medications. On these powerful medications, your ODD child's anger and agitation may be somewhat reduced. When you tell your doctor that your child's agitation and anger are a little better, the doctor will be convinced that he is on the right track. He will likely perceive your child's slight improvement as proof that Bipolar Disorder is the right diagnosis. When you tell the doctor that the improvements are negligible and that your son is still defiant, oppositional, and belligerent, the doctor may conclude that what your child needs is to have his medications increased, or be treated with additional medications. The higher doses and additional drugs will likely sedate your child even more—while never addressing his belligerence. The cycle may continue until your child is sedated to the point of being lethargic. Is that the solution you want?

Even when your child is correctly diagnosed, his partial response to a psychiatric medication may lead to his being overmedicated. Same scenario as for a misdiagnosis: your doctor may decide that, to get better results, more medication is necessary. After all, it is not unreasonable to conclude that if your child got a little better on one dose of medication, then your child will get even better on a higher dose. Or you may request such an adjustment to the dosage, yourself. It is not often that you will find a cautious doctor who will tell you that you should just sit tight and wait for a fuller response to the medications, which can require many weeks with some psychiatric drugs.

On occasion, a medication may start to take effect early in treatment, but more often medications require weeks at any given dose before they achieve their full potential. Some drugs can take up to six weeks or longer to show a full response. This long response time is typical of antidepressants. Even such medications as mood stabilizers and antipsychotics—which have some effects that are immediate—can have further benefits six weeks later into treatment. If your child is taking an antidepressant, he may start to feel better after two to three weeks. Should you tell the doctor, prior to the obligatory six weeks, that your child is only a little better on the meds, your doctor is likely to increase the dosage, instead of allowing more time to see a fuller response. Such premature zeal can lead to overmedication.

The best results in mental health care are achieved when drug treatment is combined with other psychotherapeutic interventions. When medications are the only treatment used, your child can easily be overmedicated. Also, as your child starts to respond positively to the medication, other treatments are not likely to be added to the treatment regimen. Your child's mild improvement may be read by the doctor as proof that medication alone is all your child needs to make a full recovery. The doctor could decide that there is no justification to add psychotherapy or attempt any other intervention.

Take the case of a grieving child. Imagine your child is grieving the loss of a beloved grandmother. If her sadness is so consuming that she is seriously depressed, her doctor may prescribe antidepressant medications. In this case, medication would be a very appropriate step. When your daughter appears a little better on the antidepressants, her doctor may conclude that medications are all she needs. Psychotherapy may never be recommended. Your child may have unresolved issues related to her grandmother's death that can never be resolved by medication alone.

On the other hand, psychotherapy may help the child process or vent the issues related to her loss. Once the child has successfully come to accept her loss, her depression may lift all by itself and she may no longer need medications at all. If psychotherapy is never suggested or tried, the healing process could take much longer and medications be increased unnecessarily.

When any drug therapy is recommended, be sure to inquire into other therapies that may support, if not necessarily entirely replace, the use of medications. See chapter 25 for additional discussion of this important issue.

Doctor's Anxiety

Doctors are not comfortable with patients who are not getting better. Speaking as a member of the profession, I can tell you that we doctors see ourselves as helpers and healers. When the children we are treating are not getting better, we feel very uneasy.

Doctors have an equally hard time facing their patients' unhappy parents. When treating a child whose illness is not resolving, most doctors are driven to act in his capacity as a doctor. They feel that writing a prescription is one important action that they can take. Therefore, if you continue to return to the psychiatrist's office with reports that your child is still struggling with symptoms, then the doctor will most likely start new drug therapy, or continue to add medications to your child's medication cocktail.

Please do not stop voicing your concerns. You must continue sharing with the doctor your worries about your child's unresolved health problems. You are your child's best advocate. However, understand that some doctors feel that simply saying, "You need to wait a little bit longer for the medication's full effect," is like doing nothing. They fear that the parent will turn to someone else for a solution. Conversely, these doctors think that writing another prescription for your child is doing *something* at least. Some doctors may react by writing a prescription when they have run out of ideas. Although giving your child more medications may help relieve your doctor's anxiety with his proactive prescribing, he may actually be placing your child at greater risk.

DOCTOR'S FAITH IN MEDICATIONS: LACK OF FAITH IN PSYCHOLOGICAL TREATMENTS

MOST PSYCHIATRISTS AND pediatricians rely heavily on medications to treat emotional and behavioral problems in children. Many psychiatrists believe that the answer to almost all childhood behavioral problems can be found in a prescription medication. Some doctors do believe psychotherapy has an important role to play. Unfortunately, however, psychotherapeutic approaches may take a long time before one sees results. Many doctors find that the slow, tedious progress achieved with psychotherapy or behavioral modifications can be quite disappointing and frustrating for their patients. We live in an instant-gratification society, one that demands quick solutions. Therefore, even the doctors who do believe in psychotherapy are reluctant to recommend it to their patients, because patients don't want to work that hard and therapy simply takes too long.

Even though medications can get much faster results for some symptoms, recognize that not all of your child's problems can be solved with drugs. Some childhood problems will not respond to anything but psychotherapeutic approaches, such as one-on-one psychotherapy sessions for your child, learning new parenting techniques to modify your child's behavior, or family therapy focusing on improving communication. These approaches are not quick fixes for you or your child; they require dedication, discipline, patience, and time, all elements in short supply for any family in a crisis. For this reason, many doctors write a prescription when a referral for therapy would be more appropriate.

Returning to our previous example, if your child is belligerent, selfish, and easily angered, he requires discipline, limits-setting, and structure in his life. Behavioral modifications of this sort require a great deal of effort on the part of the child and parent alike. New parenting techniques can take a long time to implement and an even longer time to show results. After dealing with a belligerent child for a few years, most parents lack the energy or the drive to devote the needed time and effort into behavior modification. Parents, teachers, and doctors all recognize that medications are faster and easier. And although medication will not *correct* your child's belligerence and defiance, medication will *reduce* some of his anger and agitation. Pharmaceuticals may not be the best treatment, but they are clearly the easier option and certainly better than letting the problem slide without treatment at all.

Let's consider another kind of problem: how to help your child who is sad and grieving, as in our grandparent example. Clearly, the best and most appropriate treatment from the get-go would be to start with psychotherapy. Therapy could help your child identify the source of her hurt and help her learn how to cope with her loss. But psychotherapy may take months or even years to see results. While psychiatric medication may not completely eliminate your daughter's grief, meds will reduce her sadness. Though pharmaceuticals cannot help your child process her grief, as long as she takes her medication, her sad feelings will be partially addressed. Some parents prefer the rapid response of meds over the slow and thorough approach of therapy, even though the results are incomplete. No parents like to see their child suffer, and doctors are happy to accommodate parents who want medications for their children.

What I am trying to point out is that medications promise the magical eradication of symptoms, while not necessarily curing the underlying problem. Fast and easy results are far more appealing to parents and doctors alike, than are the alternatives: the slow and difficult process of personal growth and change. This is not to say that medications may not be a vital and essential *part* of treatment. They can be. My point is, if meds are administered without encouraging your child's personal growth and overall emotional health, drugs may end up being the *only* tool your doctor uses . . . and when they are not entirely effective, he will only treat with drugs rather than seek nonprescritive solutions.

Resembling Another Child the Doctor Treated in the Past

Your child's problems may remind your doctor of another child's condition that she has treated previously. Your doctor may conclude that your child might have the same success on the same medications that helped the child with the similar symptoms. This strategy might be a reasonable course of action, *unless* your child does not actually have the same condition as the first child and your doctor has not taken sufficient time to know your child thoroughly. Also, this "similar child" may have been prescribed four different psychotropic medications. Unfortunately, in her eagerness to help your child feel better quicker, your doctor may want to start all four medications at the same time. The safest approach is to treat each child as a new and unique individual. Hopefully, your doctor will take the time to know your child before she starts medication.

No two children respond to psychiatric drugs in exactly the same way. Prescribing more than one substance at a time, just because they worked well collectively in another individual, will leave the most astute doctor in the dark about which medication created the benefit and which caused a side effect in your child. Psychiatric medications should *always* be started one at a time. Treating your child just like the child with similar symptoms, with all the same medications, could lead to your child being overmedicated, and perhaps for a condition that your child doesn't even have.

PRESSURE BY THE TEACHER ON THE PARENT

SOME TEACHERS WANT their disruptive students to be treated with psychiatric medications. Other teachers are dead set against medications. Yet others remember their role is to educate, not diagnose, and defer to doctors to determine which children need medications and which do not. A teacher's feelings regarding medications are not always evident until there is an issue with a particular child who is not fitting in.

Unruly students can present quite a disruption in the classroom. Children on medication are usually much easier for some teachers to manage and instruct. If your child is oppositional and disruptive in the classroom, then you may come under pressure by his teacher to medicate him, thus making her job easier. When teachers pressure parents to place their children on medications, these parents, in turn, may pressure doctors to write prescriptions. Parents can be easily intimidated by the authoritative position of a faculty member. Patients have often told me that their child's teacher and principal had threatened to expel their child if psychiatric medications were not prescribed! Because this kind of interference from school staff had become so problematic, some states had to enact laws that expressly forbid teachers from giving parents advice on psychiatric medications.

Still, teachers can be very persuasive. When speaking with you about your child's problem behaviors, some teachers will hold themselves as experts. They are experts in educating children. But, teachers may be overstepping their licensure and, in some states, their legal bounds by pointing to their role as a professional to legitimize their psychiatric diagnosis of your child, and their recommendation that your child be medicated. Be aware that the bottom line here is often not your child's welfare, but to have a manageable classroom.

Some teachers may feel guilty when children in their classroom act out. They may feel responsible for the poor behavior of their students. Teachers may fear that their poor instructional skills are to blame because they have failed to hold the children's attention (which *may* be the case). Some teachers worry that when the students are out of control, others will view this as evidence of the teacher's ineffective classroom management skills (which, again, may indeed be the case). It only takes one or two children provoking the rest of the students to laughter, for the entire classroom to appear in chaos. If the troublemaking student can be pegged as having a mental illness, then the teacher cannot be held responsible for the disruption in her classroom. Subduing a disruptive child with psychiatric drugs who would otherwise bring shame to a teacher is one way the teacher can avoid appearing ineffectual but, of course, children can be unnecessarily medicated as a result.

This does not describe all or even most of the educators with whom I have worked. Unfortunately, this does describe some of them. Please be assured that most teachers have excellent classroom management skills and would only suggest a psychiatric evaluation when appropriate. However, there are times when even a well-meaning teacher may draw the wrong conclusions about your child's medical needs.

Pressure by the Parent on the Doctor

SOMETIMES IT IS the parents who push the doctors to write a prescription. If your child has a legitimate mood, anxiety, or thought disorder, then psychiatric medications are warranted—in such cases, *not* providing medication would deny her important relief. In a situation of legitimate need, I am the first to encourage the appropriate use of medications. However, there are times when medication is *not* the correct therapy, and yet parents insist that drugs be administered.

When your child has behavioral problems, you are likely to feel guilty. You may feel that you are responsible for his bad behavior. Some parents cannot bring themselves to be a tough disciplinarian, confusing discipline and the setting of limits with punishment or being too demanding of the child. However, some children need vigorous discipline to be successful in life. If you have a hard time saying no to your child, then you may have a parenting style that is too lax or overindulgent. Lenient parenting methods can result in very belligerent, demanding, and impatient children, who learn early that a good tantrum gets results. When friends and family start questioning your parenting practices, you may feel too defensive to recognize that, yes, you might be responsible for your child's behavior problems.

When your child spins out of control, a psychiatric diagnosis can be a great relief to the parent who has been feeling guilty. A diagnosis creates a legitimate reason for your child's misbehavior. No longer can friends and family blame your child's bad behavior on your poor parenting skills. It can all now be explained away as a "chemical imbalance." For a genuine chemical imbalance, psychiatric medications would be the right approach. However, if your son is simply undisciplined, treating him with medication would not be appropriate; the correct course of action would be to adjust your parenting approach to one that includes effective discipline.

Unfortunately, sedating a belligerent child lends credence to a parent's assertion that the child has a mental illness—because these drugs can diminish a child's negative behaviors albeit slightly. Subconsciously, a parent who is relieved by the results may become invested in keeping their child on psychiatric medications indefinitely. Doing so fails to address other problems that the child may still have.

Assuming your child does *not* have a psychiatric condition, his defiance may still cause academic failure and disruption in the classroom. Undisciplined children refuse to do what they do not want to do. This can include not wanting to do homework or follow classroom rules. When asked to comply against their will, they can become quite angry and agitated. You certainly can keep your child more subdued with mood-stabilizing medications and, with amphetamines, fairly focused on his schoolwork. However, these medications alone will not help your child build the skills he needs to become a responsible adult. He will not be learning the valuable lessons of life that every child needs in order to function in society, be happy, and respect himself. These concepts are: accepting that he cannot always get what he wants, learning to make do without, cooperating with others, respecting authority, coping with frustration, and waiting to receive a reward until after it has been earned. If your child is unable to grasp these important insights, he will continue to be demanding, defiant, belligerent, argumentative, uncooperative, and undisciplined.

Doctors trust the reports from parents about the symptoms and behaviors of their young patients. So, if you can convince your doctor that your child has a psychiatric illness and has benefited from psychiatric medications, then your child's drug regimen will certainly be continued or even increased should annoying "symptoms" continue to manifest themselves.

Parent's Fear of Confronting the Doctor

If you start questioning the doctor about the kind or the amount of medication that your child is being prescribed, you may be sharply criticized for meddling in affairs you lack the education to understand. He may dismiss your research into your child's diagnosis or treatment, as the meddlings of an amateur out of her league. This of course can be very insulting and also intimidating. The result is that you may be less likely to question the doctor the next time he wants to add another drug to your child's treatment regimen. This is unfortunate, because a parent who puts her foot down on behalf of her child is often the only brakes applied on the runaway train of medicating children with psychiatric drugs. Without an advocate trying to slow the all-too-common practice of automatically reaching for the prescription pad to address a child's behavior, overmedication is inevitable.

Doctor's Fear of Confronting the Parent

Sometimes it is easier for a psychiatrist to simply go along with the parent's assessment of the child rather than to challenge the parent. Doctors who try to assert their own clinical impressions will sometimes meet with great resistance from the parents who are fixated on *their own* diagnosis. If you have done some research into your child's condition, then you might be completely convinced that he has a particular psychiatric diagnosis. Furthermore, a parent can become adamant about the medications that she thinks will best help her child. If your doctor challenges your conclusions about your child's diagnosis and medication choices, you may become angry and defensive. In the face of this kind of hostility, many doctors will simply go along with a parent's assessment to avoid an ugly confrontation.

Parents can be very sensitive and guilt-ridden about their role in their children's dysfunction. In such an emotionally charged situation, a doctor can hardly feel comfortable suggesting that family therapy or parenting classes for you might solve your child's behavioral problems. To some parents, this would be tantamount to saying, "You are a failure as a parent and a person." In a situation such as this, two factors come into play. One factor is the parent's resistance to hearing or acknowledging the truth. The other factor is the doctor's fear and reluctance to face an angry, defensive parent. The result of this futile exchange is that the parent wins and the child loses.

Summary

MANY DIFFERENT PRESSURES come to bear on doctors to fix your child's problems. Unfortunately, most doctors usually reach for one tool: medication. Medicine is what they know best, and often what the parent or someone pressuring the parent comes to expect from a clinician. What I hope to impart to you is the importance of a careful, honest, and thorough evaluation prior to medicating your child. Don't be overly hasty for a solution or progress rooted in convenience for someone other than the child. And if your child is prescribed drugs, proceed with caution. *Correctly prescribed, a drug enables your child to function more capably, not just more calmly, than if he is not taking the drug.* Medications may save your child's life. Cavalierly prescribed, they might destroy it.

WHAT IS *REALLY* TROUBLING YOUR CHILD?

CRITERIA FOR DIAGNOSIS

WITH EACH DIAGNOSIS in the *Diagnostic and Statistical Manual of Mental Disorders (DSM)*, is a list of symptoms that determine whether the diagnosis applies. Almost as important as the symptoms that are included to confirm a diagnosis, are the exceptions and situations that would *exclude* a child from the diagnosis. Each diagnosis has a unique number of criteria that must be met to reach the threshold of symptoms required to qualify for that diagnosis. Thus there is no standard number of symptoms that always qualifies or disqualifies your child for any given disorder. On the other hand, some generalizations can be made about most psychiatric diagnoses, if not all.

- The *DSM* defines each diagnosis based upon the presence of a cluster of symptoms with no regard to what caused those symptoms. In other words, whether your child meets all the requisite criteria for Major Depressive Disorder because she is grieving or because she developed the symptoms for no other reason than a strong family predisposition, the diagnosis applies. There are notable exceptions, such as PTSD or Alcohol-Induced Mood Disorder, but overall the rule applies: If you meet the criteria for a diagnosis, no matter how you arrived at that point, you have the diagnosis.

- Most diagnoses have a specific minimum duration for which your child had to be experiencing the symptoms to meet the requirements for a given diagnosis. It is not enough to have met the criteria for enough symptoms, if they were not present for long enough to meet the time threshold for a given disorder. The requirement for the duration that your child has psychiatric symptoms varies with each diagnosis: anywhere from two weeks to six months may be required.

- As you contemplate whether a particular symptom applies to your child, keep in mind that the magnitude of the symptom must be outside of the normal range for a child that age. A two-year-old who sets a fire is simply poorly supervised, whereas a sixteen-year-old who purposely sets a fire may have a Conduct Disorder diagnosis. Likewise a four-year-old girl who cries often may be making normal adjustments to hearing "no" from her parents, but a twelve-year-old girl who cries as often may be clinically depressed.

- Taken altogether, the symptoms, to be considered severe enough to qualify as criteria for a diagnosis, have to have interfered with your child's normal functioning. This is a basic litmus test by which any psychiatric diagnosis is measured. Who hasn't known a time when their child had such a bad day that she misplaced everything, felt scattered and irritated, came home from school tired and defeated, and cried herself to sleep? If she got up the next day and went to school and passed her classes, then she did not fulfill the criteria for a psychiatric diagnosis. Anyone can expect to feel sad, lonely, anxious, worried, or angry from time to time, given the right set of circumstances. Sometimes after a great loss, change, or stress, your child's uncomfortable feelings can last well over two weeks, but if she continues to function adequately, consider the experience part of the pain of growing up, not a psychiatric diagnosis.

- Before any psychiatric diagnosis can be confirmed, it is imperative that other medical conditions that can mimic a mental illness first be eliminated as a possibility. When the symptoms that your child is having are really caused by other general medical conditions, such as allergies, thyroid conditions, diabetes, seizure disorders, or infections such as meningitis, the underlying medical conditions must be treated first. Only after all preexisting medical conditions have been properly treated and all other general medical conditions have been eliminated as a possibility can a psychiatric diagnosis be made with certainty.

- There is no one "right" treatment for a particular disorder. Some doctors believe that psychiatric conditions can only be treated with medication. Then there are other doctors who recommend that mental illness only be treated with psychotherapy alone. This second type of doctor never recommends the use medication for any psychiatric disorder. Then there are doctors like myself, who believe a combination of all modalities (biological, psychological, and social) produces the best outcomes for children with psychiatric diagnoses.

- For most psychiatric conditions it is possible to medicate your child for a year or so, and then slowly taper off the medication, eventually completely, *without losing the benefits achieved.* When I use psychiatric medications in children, I treat them for as brief a period of time as possible. Unfortunately, in some cases, even with supportive therapies, children *do* need to remain on medications for many years. Thankfully, these drugs will continue to bring your child some degree of relief and thus enable him to function better if not optimally.

- For further details on the risks and benefits of each of these medications, refer to part 3. The other biological, psychological, and social approaches that I mentioned are covered in more detail in part 4. After you have informed yourself sufficiently about the benefits and relative risks of each type of treatment, you need to work with your child's doctors and therapists to develop a treatment plan that suits your child best. Ultimately, the choice is yours as to which treatments your child receives. If you do not feel comfortable seeing your child treated with certain medications or you wish to pursue a completely drug-free regimen, make this clear to your doctor. Should you opt not to use meds, get help devising an alternative, professionally monitored behavioral modification plan based upon your son's or daughter's needs.

6

AD/HD:
ATTENTION DEFICIT/
HYPERACTIVITY DISORDER

WHAT IS AD/HD?

"ATTENTION DEFICIT," AS it is commonly known, is more properly called **Attention Deficit/Hyperactivity Disorder (AD/HD)**. AD/HD is the diagnosis whether you child is only inattentive, only hyperactive, or both. The way that doctors differentiate among the different types of AD/HD is to classify your child as either:

- AD/HD: Predominantly Inattentive Type
- AD/HD: Predominantly Hyperactive-Impulsive Type, or
- AD/HD: Combined Type (that is both hyperactive and inattentive)

INATTENTION

In the *DSM*, under AD/HD, is a description of inattention that lists nine different ways to define the symptom of inattention. First, your child's level of inattention must be causing him problems. Also, the degree of inattention must be outside of what is normal for a typical child his age. The term *inattention*, as used in the *DSM*, would only apply to your child if he were *not able* to attend to a task even when he *wanted* to pay attention. If your child does not *want* to pay attention, this behavior is referred to as *defiance*. If your child can spend long periods of time playing computer games that require planning and strategy, but then appears to be deaf when you ask him to do his homework, he may be defiant, *not* inattentive. If he *is able* to attend to tasks that are important to *him*, your child may just be ignoring the things that he does not like or want to do. To qualify for the inattentive type of AD/HD your child must demonstrate at least six of the following nine criteria:

1. Cannot pay attention to details even when he is trying to pay attention to the details
2. Cannot sustain attention even when he is trying to sustain attention
3. Cannot listen when spoken to directly even though he wants to listen
4. Cannot follow directions even when he wants to comply
5. Cannot organize his activities even though he wants to be organized
6. Avoids tasks that he knows he is *incapable* of completing even though he wishes he could
7. Cannot help losing items even though they are important to *him*
8. Cannot help being easily distracted even when he is trying to sustain attention
9. Forgetful about activities even when the activity is important to him

Furthermore, the degree of inattention has to be *beyond* what is considered developmentally normal for a child at that age. In other words, a five-year-old cannot be expected to remember to put away his bike when it is time to come inside for dinner. Five-year-olds hardly remember to pull up their pants after they use the bathroom. Whereas, if your sixteen-year-old child absentmindedly leaves his wallet in a public place three times a week, he has a problem.

HYPERACTIVITY-IMPULSIVITY

As for inattention, the *DSM* lists nine different ways to define the symptoms of hyperactivity and impulsivity. The level of hyperactivity and impulsivity must be causing your child problems. If your child is simply an active kid, then hyperactivity and impulsivity may not be an appropriate description. If your child can settle down when he *wants* to, but *chooses* to ignore your requests to do so, he is defiant, not hyperactive. To qualify for the hyperactive and impulsive type of AD/HD, your child must demonstrate at least six of the following nine criteria:

1. Cannot stop from fidgeting even though he wants to stop

2. Cannot remain in his seat even though he wants to comply
3. Cannot stop from running around and climbing excessively even though he wants to stop
4. Cannot play quietly even though he wants to do so
5. Acts like he is driven by a motor even though he wants to stop
6. Talks excessively even though he wants to stop
7. Blurts out answers even though he wants to wait his turn
8. Difficulty waiting his turn even though he wants to wait his turn
9. Interrupts or intrudes even though he wants to wait until invited

Let us assume that you have properly trained your child to know when it is appropriate to run around and play and when it is more appropriate to be quiet and sit still. If he just *cannot* comply, even though he *wants* to cooperate, then he probably has AD/HD.

Other Qualifiers

There are some important situations and exceptions that must be taken into account to confirm the diagnosis of AD/HD. They are:

- There must be clear evidence of *significant* impairment in social, academic, or occupational functioning. These symptoms of AD/HD must cause substantial problems for your child or teenager, not just for other people.
- The impairment that your child experiences as a result of his AD/HD symptoms must be present *in two or more settings*. Your child cannot be diagnosed AD/HD if he only has symptoms while at home but not in school or at soccer practice, for example.
- The symptoms must be present in some form prior to the age of seven. In other words, your child cannot suddenly "catch" or acquire the diagnosis of AD/HD at thirteen years of age, having never shown any sign of the disorder prior to that age.
- The diagnosis of AD/HD does not apply to your child if the symptoms of poor concentration and hyperactivity are better understood as or explained by another mental disorder, such as a depressive disorder, an anxiety disorder, a personality disorder, an autistic disorder, schizophrenia, another psychotic disorder, or the result of substance abuse. *Key point*: this is the qualifier that is most often overlooked.

IMPORTANT

You have to recognize that the symptoms of poor concentration, restlessness, and psychomotor agitation are very common symptoms of many ailments, and in of themselves do not necessarily point to a diagnosis of AD/HD. If your child meets the criteria for Major Depressive Disorder, for example, then his poor concentration and psychomotor agitation or hyperactivity have already been accounted for within that diagnosis. If your child has been diagnosed with depression, adding a diagnosis of AD/HD is like adding the diagnosis of chronic cough to the man who has been diagnosed with lung cancer. Depressed children do not concentrate well and they may be restless and hyperactive. These symptoms can tip off the psychiatrist that your child has anxiety, PTSD, or any number of other diagnoses, and, until these other diagnoses have been eliminated as possibilities, the diagnosis of AD/HD cannot be made.

For a diagram that demonstrates how the symptoms of AD/HD are common to many other disorders, see appendix B.

TREATMENT

Treatment can be divided into three parts: biological, psychological, and social. The biological treatment of AD/HD is psychiatric medication. The psychological treatment of AD/HD is therapy and tutoring, for building organizational skills. The social treatments include making adjustments to the physical arrangement of the classroom, the types of students in the classroom, and the teacher's teaching style.

The temporary use of psychiatric medication is most likely to be successful if your child is also receiving tutoring, is learning organization and study skills, is developing better classroom habits, and is establishing better homework routines, including being provided with an appropriate home study environment.

The prescription medications most often used in the treatment of AD/HD are:

- Strattera (atomoxetine)
- Ritalin or Ritalin LA (methylphenidate), Concerta (methylphenidate), Metadate CD (methylphenidate), Methylin ER (methylphenidate), Dexadrine (dextroamphetamine), DextroStat (dextroamphetamine), Adderall XR (dextroamphetamine), Focalin (dexmethylphenidate)
- Wellbutrin XL (buproprion)
- Effexor XR (venlafaxine), Cymbalta (duloxetine)

- Tofranil (imipramine), Pamelor (nortriptyline), Elavil (amitriptyline), Sinequan (doxepin)
- Catapres (clonidine) or Tenex (guanfacine)
- Risperdal (risperidone), Zyprexa (olanzapine), Seroquel (quetiapine), Geodon (ziprasidone), Abilify (aripiprazole), Haldol (haloperidol)

Case Examples

Sometimes medications can cause more problems than they solve. In the case of a fourteen-year-old boy named David, his problems with a misdiagnosis and inappropriate medicating practices became dangerous for his family. When I evaluated David, his parents were feeling overwhelmed and at a loss. David was violent and terrorizing his entire family, including the family pet. The parents explained that when he didn't want to do something, nothing was going to make him. When he didn't get his way, he became violent. David punched holes in the walls; he hit his parents and his sister. But at school, he was attending gifted classes. The teachers had told David's parents that he occasionally challenged authority but usually backed down. The school staff reported to the parents that they had never seen the kinds of outbursts that occurred at home. At school, David's behavior was manageable and his grades were good.

He had started amphetamine-class medications when he was five years old, for a presumed diagnosis of AD/HD. According to David's parents, he had been disruptive in his kindergarten classroom, where the teacher had diagnosed David with AD/HD. He was promptly started on Ritalin by the pediatrician, based on the teacher's assessment. The drugs appeared to get David to focus a little more on his teacher and his grades were good, although he continued to clown around for the entertainment of the other little boys in his class. At home he was still belligerent, oppositional, and argumentative with his parents. His parents kept complaining to the pediatrician and later to the psychiatrist that David wasn't better yet, so he was switched from one amphetamine to another until I met the family.

I suggested to the family that David might be having violent outbursts due to the eight years of treatment on amphetamines. I explained that David might be experiencing an Amphetamine-Induced Mood Disorder. David's amphetamine treatment was stopped and an antidepressant was used temporarily to treat his irritable, sullen, discontented mood. Because, at home, David's violent behavior was unchanged on or off his amphetamine-class drugs, while always manageable at school, I proposed to the parents that part of David's problem was due to their indulgent style of parenting.

Off amphetamines, David's violence diminished a great deal. Once he had been treated with the antidepressants for several weeks, his angry mood and violent behavior resolved completely. His defiant, belligerent attitude with his parents started to get better as they adjusted their parenting style. He still had a long way to go when our treatment ended, but David and his family were definitely headed down the right track.

In another case, I treated a little girl named Ella, who had been diagnosed with AD/HD by her previous psychiatrist at the military base where her family had been living before moving to Chicago. Ella was seven years old when I evaluated her. Her father was in the military, her mother stayed home with their four children. Ella was the third-born child in the family. Her parents provided a very structured environment for Ella and she was a very cooperative, sweet kid.

She was shy, spoke very little, and made little eye contact during our interview; her mother did all the talking. Ella was a poor student even while taking the many different amphetamine-class medications she had been given for her AD/HD. Ella's teachers told the mother that Ella would just stare out the window during the teacher's presentations. Even when her mother tutored her, Ella found it difficult to grasp concepts, though she appeared to be paying attention. She felt embarrassed when attention was drawn to her by the teacher, especially when she was being questioned about a lesson she did not understand. Her mother confirmed that Ella did not like school, had no desire to succeed in school, and showed little interest in schoolwork.

She preferred to play dolls with her sisters, something she could occupy herself for hours on end. Her family had made multiple moves during her father's tour of duty, and as a result, Ella had been to many different schools. She didn't do well with change; new schools, teachers, and students made her anxious.

In spite of the many failures with amphetamine drugs to make Ella into a good student, her mother could not let go of the diagnosis of AD/HD. When I suggested that the multiple moves may have contributed to Ella's anxiety and school failure, her mother refused to accept my diagnosis, citing a survey she had completed that proved that Ella had the inattentive type of AD/HD. In fact, Ella had taken an abbreviated Conners survey provided by the previous psychiatrist, and the survey did indeed show that Ella had difficulty concentrating. What the survey failed to do was integrate those findings with the rest of Ella's symptoms and clinical history. My involvement in the case ended when the mother took Ella to another psychiatrist who would presumably agree with the diagnosis the mother liked.

An example of a child with AD/HD combined type that I treated was an eleven-year-old boy, Edward, a cooperative child who wanted very much to please his parents and teachers by achieving good grades in school. He was a personable, sweet, and earnest boy who presented no discipline problem for his parents. His teachers loved him, and his parents were proud of their boy though worried about his academic troubles.

Unfortunately, Ed could not attend to his teachers well enough to learn in a classroom setting with thirty other children present. He did much better when tutored one-on-one. Ed was an agile, strong, and athletically inclined boy with good ball-handling skills. Although he loved sports and aspired to succeed in that arena as well, he nonetheless struggled in sports, as he could not always keep his head in the game. He seemed to be hyperactive and always in motion—even when he was trying to sit still, he appeared to be wiggling in his skin. Ed twitched and blinked often, which may have been caused by his hyperactivity, his psychomotor agitation, or possibly the effect of the multitude of different amphetamine-class drugs that he had been prescribed since he was diagnosed with AD/HD at the age of five.

I learned during Ed's assessment that his parents were in the throes of a very vicious, conflicted divorce. Ed's father was a successful real-estate agent who was in recovery from his cocaine and alcohol addiction. Ed's stay-at-home mom was still a practicing alcoholic in complete denial. Ed was in the middle. His parents did a very poor job of hiding their anger and hatred for each other, and one often talked to Ed about what a poor job of parenting the other parent was doing. The kid couldn't win, not at home, not at school, and not on the field. Although Ed denied all symptoms related to anxiety, mood, or trauma, I wonder to this day if he may have had an anxiety disorder.

I recommended couple counseling for these parents, not to patch up their marriage, which seemed beyond repair, but to help this parenting pair learn how to put Ed and his needs first, before their own need to be right. Ed's father agreed with my recommendation and said he wanted help, but never really stopped bashing his son's mother. Ed's mother thought the idea was ridiculous and never returned to my office; his father brought him to see me thereafter.

I treated Ed with a variety of medications from every psychiatric drug class, but with minimal benefit. My counsel on the appropriate approach to parenting through a divorce only reached the father's ears and yet may have been beneficial—this effect was difficult to gauge. Eventually, the father agreed that tutoring—which had produced the best results—was superior to any of the prior med trials and settled on that approach over the use of any medications with Ed. Tutoring and a sober, invested, and devoted father were enough for Ed—he passed his classes and did fairly well on the playing field, something with which both son and father were satisfied and grateful.

7

ODD: Oppositional Defiant Disorder and Conduct Disorder

ODD

Oppositional Defiant Disorder **(ODD)** is a diagnosis that is given to children exclusively. Children with ODD have a pattern of behavior that is defiant, willful, and hostile. This pattern has to be present for at least six months.

Criteria for Diagnosis

As is true of most of the disorders described in the *DSM*, a list of the criteria or symptoms that defines that disease is provided. If your child has at least the minimum number of symptoms established to define that disorder, then the diagnosis applies to him. For ODD, there is a list of eight symptoms. For your child to be diagnosed with ODD, he needs at least four of these, although he may have more. The symptoms of Oppositional Defiant Disorder are:

1. Often loses his temper or has tantrums
2. Often argues with adults at home or at school
3. Often actively and knowingly defies the rules: refuses to comply with the adults' requests

4. Often deliberately annoys others, particularly the adult he is trying to manipulate
5. Unable to take personal responsibility: often blames other people or circumstances for his misbehavior
6. Easily irritated and annoyed by other people and is often touchy
7. Often angry and resents others
8. Often looking for revenge for perceived slights, or is vindictive and spiteful

Oppositional Defiant Disorder is *not* the result of a neurochemical imbalance. You cannot treat this disorder by replenishing neurotransmitters. Unlike mood and anxiety disorders, the symptoms of ODD are not corrected or resolved by treatment with just the right medication. Oppositional Defiant Disorder is caused by a permissive parenting style, poor limit-setting, the overindulging of your child, and a lack of structure in your child's daily routine. Correcting this condition requires healthy doses of the opposite: clear rules, structure, routines, and limit-setting on a regular basis. Many parents insist that they are already adhering to such a schedule in their homes. What typically is learned when a social worker visits such a household, is that the rules and structure are delivered sporadically or only at the time that the child is throwing a tantrum.

Not all anger outbursts and tantrums are the result of a serious psychiatric disorder. It is important to note that sometimes, as is true with ODD, your child's tantrums can be the result of a belligerent child who is simply not getting his way and has learned that tantrums work to get him what he wants.

Again, as with AD/HD, the oppositional behaviors have to be outside of what is typically seen in children the same age and developmental level. For example, any normal two-year-old child will attempt direct disobedience of his parent at least once. Therefore, if you see your two-year-old testing his wings in the defiance arena, don't be alarmed but by all means address his tantrums immediately with behavior-modifying techniques. On the other hand, if your ten-year-old son is still throwing full-fledged temper tantrums on the department store floor, complete with kicking and screaming, then you are looking at behaviors outside of what is normally seen in boys his age.

QUALIFIERS

Along with the four out of eight symptoms, there are a few conditions that must be met as well to confirm the diagnosis of ODD. They are:

- There must be clear evidence of significant impairment in social, academic, or occupational functioning. In other words, the symptoms of ODD must cause substantial problems for your child.
- The diagnosis of ODD does not apply to your child if his symptoms of defiance and oppositional behavior occur exclusively during a psychotic or depressive episode. For example, if your child's depression resolves and he no longer is defiant, then he does not meet the criteria for ODD.
- If your child has the required symptoms for ODD but also meets the extra requirements for the diagnosis of Conduct Disorder, then the diagnosis of ODD does not apply. Conduct Disorder supercedes ODD. (See below.)

Treatment of ODD

Oppositional Defiant Disorder is a truly "behavioral disorder" in that it is not caused by chemical imbalances and *cannot* be cured with medication. ODD is the direct result of your child's early childhood behavioral training or, more precisely, the lack of this training. However, some doctors will still try to treat your ODD child with medications. Psychotropic medications can quiet your child's anger by mildly sedating him. The medications typically used to reduce tantrums are:

- Eskalith, Lithobid (lithium), Depakote (valproate), Tegretol (carbamazepine), Equetro (carbamazepine), Trileptal (oxcarbazepine), Lamictal (lamotrigine), Topimax (topiramate)
- Haldol (haloperidol), Risperdal (risperidone), Zyprexa (olanzapine), Seroquel (quetiapine), Geodon (ziprasidone), Abilify (aripiprazole), Thorazine (chlorpromazine)
- Catapres (clonidine) or Tenex (guanfacine)
- Inderal LA (propranolol) or Tenormin (atenolol)

A sedated child may not give you as much of a fight when he is being oppositional or throwing a tantrum, but with medication treatment alone he will not become cooperative or compliant, either. (For further details on the risks and benefits of each of these medications, refer to part 3.)

The most common cause of Oppositional Defiant Disorder is an ineffective, overindulgent, or even nonexistent parenting style. The best treatment for ODD is effective behavioral training for the parents. The earlier the behavioral program is started, the better the chance for success. Generally, the programs that work best include structure, regular routine, and firm discipline, as outlined in part 4.

CONDUCT DISORDER

THIS IS A much more serious behavioral problem. Like ODD, Conduct Disordered children are also defiant, oppositional, and hostile. Children with **Conduct Disorder** go beyond being simply difficult. Instead, they are breaking laws and violating the rights of others. To make the diagnosis of Conduct Disorder, your child's behaviors must have been present over the last twelve months. For your child to have an active and correct diagnosis, the last Conduct Disordered behavior must have happened within the last six months.

CRITERIA FOR DIAGNOSIS

To qualify for Conduct Disorder, your child has to have demonstrated at least three of the fifteen behaviors listed below. The behaviors are:

Aggression to people and animals
1. Often bullies, threatens, or intimidates others
2. Initiates physical fights often
3. Has used a weapon that can cause serious physical harm to someone, such as a baseball bat, a brick, a broken bottle, a knife, or a gun
4. Has been physically cruel to another person
5. Has been physically cruel to an animal
6. Has stolen while confronting the victim, such as a mugging, purse snatching, armed robbery, or extortion (shoplifting would not meet this criterium)
7. Has forced someone into sexual activity

Destruction of property
1. Has deliberately set a fire with the intention of causing serious damage. A child playing with matches who is remorseful if the fire gets out of control does not qualify.
2. Has deliberately destroyed property using other means aside from arson

Deceitfulness and theft
1. Has broken into another person's home or car to steal or vandalize

2. Often lies to obtain favors and avoid obligations; is a con artist
3. Has stolen valuable items without confronting anyone or breaking into a home, building or car. This would include shoplifting and forgery.

Serious violations of rules
1. Beginning before thirteen years of age, the child stays out at night in defiance of his parents' rules
2. Has run away from home, overnight, at least twice. Once would qualify if your child ran away for a lengthy period of time.
3. Has often been truant from school, starting before the age of thirteen years old.

QUALIFIERS

Along with the three out of fifteen behaviors required to diagnose your child with Conduct Disorder, there are two conditions that must be considered as well to confirm the diagnosis. They are:

- There must be clear evidence of significant impairment in social, academic, or occupational functioning. In other words, the Conduct Disordered behaviors must cause substantial problems for your child or teenager. Your child may be able to break some rules but still maintain good grades, stay out of trouble at school or with the police, and maintain friendships. In this case, he doesn't quite meet the criteria for Conduct Disorder.
- After the age of eighteen, if your son or daughter not only meets the criteria for Conduct Disorder but now also meets the criteria for **Antisocial Personality Disorder**, Antisocial P.D. takes priority over Conduct Disorder.

CLASSIFICATION

The severity of the Conduct Disorder is ranked into one of three levels: mild, moderate, and severe. Also, the age of onset specifies the precise type of Conduct Disorder diagnosed.

- **Mild:** when there is only the minimum number of behaviors demonstrated to meet the criteria for the diagnosis. Also, to assign the severity as mild, it is required that the Conduct Disordered behaviors *cannot* cause significant harm to others. Examples of mild behaviors are: lying, truancy, and staying out after dark without permission.

- **Moderate:** the number of conduct behaviors and the harm caused to others by your child must be between the levels of severe and mild. Examples of moderate level Conduct Disordered behaviors are: vandalism and stealing without confronting the victim.
- **Severe:** many more conduct problems than minimally required to make the diagnosis *or* the specific behaviors cause considerable harm to others. Examples of severe behaviors are: forced sex, physical cruelty, use of a weapon, and stealing while confronting the victim.
- **Childhood-Onset Type:** this applies when your child's first Conduct Disordered behavior was completed before the age of ten.
- **Adolescent-Onset Type:** applies when all of your child's conduct problems started after he turned ten years old.
- **Unspecified Onset:** this designation is used when you are not sure when your child started having problems with conduct.

TREATMENT OF CONDUCT DISORDER

Conduct Disorder, like ODD, is *not* a condition that can be treated effectively with medications. Medications are given to children who have Conduct Disorder with the intention of reducing the degree of the child's aggression and hostility. These medications do not stop the antisocial behaviors of the child, but they can reduce, slightly, the degree of the child's angry aggression, when it does occur. The psychiatric medications used to sedate Conduct Disordered children are:

- Eskalith, Lithobid (lithium), Depakote (valproate), Tegretol (carbamazepine), Equetro (carbamazepine), Trileptal (oxcarbazepine), Lamictal (lamotrigine), Topimax (topiramate)
- Haldol (haloperidol), Risperdal (risperidone), Zyprexa (olanzapine), Seroquel (quetiapine), Geodon (ziprasidone), Abilify (aripiprazole), Thorazine (chlorpromazine)

Even while medicated, these Conduct Disordered children will violate the rights of others. No medication can teach a child the difference between what is right from what is wrong, or give him the motivation to comply with rules. For further details on the risks and benefits of each of these medications refer to part 3.

The best treatment for Conduct Disorder is purely behavioral. The earlier the behavioral program is started, the better the chance for success. Generally, the programs that work best include structure, regular routine, firm discipline, and close supervision.

CASE EXAMPLES

ALTHOUGH THE FOLLOWING case is yet another example of the misdiagnosis of a child thought to have AD/HD who really had ODD, this particular child's evolution—starting from ODD and continuing on through Conduct Disorder and eventually resolving in adulthood—is an excellent example of diagnosis and treatment. I first evaluated Fred when he was fourteen years old. His mother explained to me that, when she became pregnant with Fred, she had not been planning to start her family right at that time, so she and her husband had to put their business plans on hold to have the baby. This was the beginning of the ambivalent bond and attachment between this mother and child. She resented her husband for his freedom to pursue his professional aspirations while she was stuck at home with the newborn. Fred's parents were kind, generous, sweet people but they lacked the resolve or the fortitude to follow through when denying their son the things he wanted or making him do the things he should.

Fred had been diagnosed with AD/HD at five years of age but, regardless of the different medications the doctors treated him with, he continued to be defiant, oppositional, antagonistic, belligerent, and assaultive. He was able to pay attention as long as the subject matter interested him. Fred was a beautiful, tall, blond boy who could be very charming if it suited him. Fred's mood was calm and cooperative as long as he was not being asked to do anything he didn't want to do. Only when he got no for an answer did his parents have problems with Fred. However, he antagonized and taunted the adults at school, which appeared to give him great satisfaction; he often chuckled with impish glee as he watched the disruption he could create in the classroom. His delight at their frustration only irritated his mother and the teachers more. As his behavior evolved with age, Fred became an extremely manipulative teen and thoroughly enjoyed his power to upset and agitate his parents and teachers.

Over the next eleven years, Fred was tried on every possible medication: amphetamines, antidepressants, mood stabilizers, and antipsychotic drugs, but with little change in his core behavior. Certainly he was a little more subdued and sedated with some combinations of drugs, but the core behaviors of belligerence and defiance were never impacted by any medication. The doctors even tried diagnosing him with Bipolar Disorder for a while, until they learned he had discovered street drugs, which he sold and used regularly.

The family lived in constant terror and the police were called to their home on a regular basis to manage his anger outbursts whenever he didn't get his way. Fred eventually required placement in a special school for particularly unruly children. His mother reported to me that many times he had to be physically restrained by the school staff. His mother volunteered in his classroom to help control him during his outbursts. After all, she could not hold a job due to the constant interruptions from the school calling her at work; she'd given up trying to hold a job. His father was a very successful executive and could provide for the family without a second income, so mother made a career out of volunteering at the school and finding services for her son.

Medications did not work for Fred, psychotherapy had no effect, and he had been seen by several different doctors and therapists, when a family friend gave his parents my name. His parents were desperate by the time I met them, because by now their son was running away, ditching school, stealing, and dealing and using street drugs. Starting a new parenting approach with Fred at the age of fourteen after he had already established his dominance in the household seemed a daunting task, but everything else had been tried. His mother was so worn down, she was ready to change her passive parenting approach, but his father was still unable to be tough with his son.

After a couple more years of trying unsuccessfully to regain authority in their home, Fred's parents finally had struggled long enough and they were ready to hand over the day-to-day care and guidance of their son to professionals. I suggested a residential placement for teens with drug and behavioral problems. Their insurance would not pay and the family income was too high to qualify for the free programs provided by their state and county. So Fred was sent to a program out of the country, where teens from the USA are treated. The accommodations were really very nice and most of the staff was American. One and a half years later Fred returned a changed person. He was eighteen years old; he had been off street drugs and psych medications during his entire treatment out of the country. The program had set very firm limits with Fred, which they followed to the letter regardless of how much he disliked it. He did not earn privileges and therefore did not receive them, no matter how he demanded or manipulated the staff.

Once his treatment was completed and he returned to the United States, Fred found his own living quarters, went back to school at the community college, and stayed off drugs. He had not been on medications during his residential treatment, nor did he take them upon his return. When he returned to college, he was motivated to succeed in his studies, as he could finally see the connection between his academic success and his future security. He had no problems attending to his studies even though he was not being medicated. As often happens with unruly, defiant teens once they reach eighteen years old and move out of their parents' home, Fred no longer blamed all his problems on his parents nor was he able to use their "stupid rules and restrictions" as the reason for his failures. The experiences in the residential program along with living independently once he turned eighteen had done more for turning Fred into a responsible, accountable adult than anything medication had been able to do for him. A few years later, his mother informed me that she and Fred had a much better relationship and that he had married and fathered a baby.

In another case of ODD, a girl whose progress I was able to follow from three years old to eighteen, also provides an excellent example of the long-term consequences of a passive parenting style on children. Ginny was three when I met her. Ginny's mother was able to stay home with the children because her husband was a very successful professional. The parents were very happily married and supportive of each other regarding their shared parenting philosophies. Her mother was the sweetest, gentlest lady you could ever hope to meet. Mother simply did not have a mean bone in her body and, when it came to raising Ginny and her two brothers, this soft approach by the mother had some devastating results.

Ginny was, from the time I met her, a girl who did not like to be told no. When she didn't get her way, she would throw herself to the ground, kicking and screaming until her parents relented. Her mother's response was predictable: Mother would try to comfort and soothe Ginny with gentle words of reassurance but this would only cause the girl to escalate until she got what she wanted—and she always did. On one occasion, I witnessed Ginny's tantrum firsthand; a game she had been playing had not gone her way, so she started screaming and crying and stomping her feet—so angry she could hardly get the words out to explain why she was upset. Her mother knelt in front of Ginny, trying desperately to calm and soothe her. Ginny suddenly slapped her mother across the face and continued her tantrum. Her mother's response was to tell the girl, quietly and passively, that this behavior was unacceptable and they were going home. At the announcement that they were leaving, Ginny's tantrum escalated. She threw herself to the floor and continued her tirade even louder than before, adding to her repertoire the kicking and punching of her mother. Her mother spent the next twenty minutes struggling with her child to wrestle her coat and shoes on her to take her home. Scenes such as this were a common occurrence with Ginny.

But her mother's indulgences did not stop there; when Ginny went to her grandparents' home for a holiday meal, if she didn't like any of the dozen different dishes prepared by her grandmother, she would demand that her mother run out and fetch her a fast-food hamburger and fries. Her mother always dutifully delivered. If her mother tried to deny her daughter's demands, the tantrums would start until Ginny got her way.

Her mother often said that her soft, passive approach to parenting was much more appropriate than the strict methods used by her friends. Ginny's mom was critical of tough love and the parents who used this method, citing her own methods as superior because she was not crushing her daughter's creativity and free spirit. By the time Ginny was fifteen, she had started to experiment with alcohol and Internet chat rooms. This led to a late night in her parent's basement, drinking with a man she had met on the Web and had invited into her home. Her parents finally got the message: Ginny was out of control and there was nothing they could do about it.

Again, the help of a residential placement was utilized, this time in Arizona, where Ginny could be kept safe from herself and her parents' permissive, indulgent parenting style. While in residential treatment Ginny got sober and started earning good grades again. To her mother's amazement, Ginny liked her residential placement because, as the girl explained to her mother, she enjoyed the structure, the routine, and the clear-cut expectations of her from her teachers, caregivers, and guidance counselors. With very explicitly declared rules and consequences for violation of them—and almost no opportunities to find trouble—there was, therefore, less temptation to break the rules. Ginny did very well in her residential treatment but all that changed when she returned home. Even though her parents had attended family counseling and parenting education sessions with the counselors from the residential treatment facility, they really didn't change much at all. They announced to all their friends and family that they were changed parents but they were still the sweet, kind, soft, passive, and permissive people they had always been. Great people but poor parents.

Unfortunately, it was Ginny who paid the price for the parents who indulged themselves in the luxury of being the nice guy, the popular parent, the parent who never has to deny their child anything. The last I heard, Ginny was back to drinking and had decided not to attend the college where she had been able to secure an admission after a year and a half of studies and good grades at her placement in Arizona. She planned to live in her parents' home and find a job locally.

8

INTERMITTENT EXPLOSIVE DISORDER

INTERMITTENT EXPLOSIVE DISORDER describes children who have anger outbursts that are so excessive that people get hurt and property is damaged. The anger outbursts of this disorder are more violent than typical tantrums.

CRITERIA FOR DIAGNOSIS

Intermittent Explosive Disorder is a very straightforward diagnosis. There are only two criteria that your child must meet to be diagnosed as having this disorder. The two symptoms are:

1. Several distinct and separate episodes during which your child fails to resist the impulse to be aggressive. To qualify as a symptom, your child's anger outburst must be severe enough that it results in serious assault or the destruction of property.
2. Also, the degree of your child's aggression and the anger expressed during his rage attack must be out of proportion to the event that triggered his anger.

Qualifiers

There are a few situations where another diagnosis would make more sense. They are:

- If your child has other psychiatric symptoms along with his rage attacks, then a different diagnosis may be more appropriate instead. Examples are: Oppositional Defiant Disorder, Conduct Disorder, Borderline Personality Disorder, a Psychotic Disorder, or a Manic Episode, all of which include episodes of anger outbursts. The tantrums your child might display in these other diagnoses generally have the motivation of manipulating you or are of a magnitude more consistent with the severity of the stressor. In Intermittent Explosive Disorder, your child's tantrum would be more extreme and carry on much longer than would be required to simply manipulate you. Generally, doctors try to find a single diagnosis that would account for all of your child's symptoms and problem behaviors. This is not always possible. Sometimes giving more than one diagnosis is the only way to include all of your child's clinically significant issues.
- If your child is intoxicated or withdrawing from street drugs or prescription medications, then your child should not be diagnosed with Intermittent Explosive Disorder alone. The proper diagnosis would be Drug Intoxication or Drug Withdrawal instead of or in addition to Intermittent Explosive Disorder. Furthermore, drug intoxication or the results of chronic street drug use can cause a condition called Drug-Induced Mood Disorder. Note: each of these diagnoses is named specifically for the drug that caused the problem. I will provide you with more information on the subject of drug-related diagnoses in chapter 17.
- There are general medical conditions that can mimic the signs and symptoms of many of the psychiatric disorders. In particular, with Intermittent Explosive Disorder, your doctor would explore the possibility of head trauma or kidney failure, possibly due to juvenile diabetes. This is only a sampling of possible medical issues your child might be experiencing. If there were a general medical disorder that was causing the angry rage attacks, then your child's psychiatrist would refer you back to your pediatrician or primary care doctor for further work-up and treatment.

TREATMENT OF INTERMITTENT EXPLOSIVE DISORDER

The treatment of Intermittent Explosive Disorder is another condition that cannot be cured by medication alone. There are medications that can reduce the degree of volatility expressed by your child, but the medication may not eliminate the rage outbursts entirely. Your child is a creature of habit, as are we all. Once a certain behavioral pattern has been established, breaking the bad habits takes a great deal of work. For your child, stopping his bad habits will require that he be motivated to change, have some self-discipline, and have the perseverance to see his effort through to the successful end. Most adults would find changing a bad habit challenging. So, your child will need *your* help to overcome his behavioral problems.

When you decide that psychiatric medications are the right choice for your child, the prescription medications most often used in the treatment of Intermittent Explosive Disorder are as follows:

- Eskalith, Lithobid (lithium), Depakote (valproate), Tegretol (carbamazepine), Equetro (carbamazepine), Trileptal (oxcarbazepine), Lamictal (lamotrigine), Topamax (topiramate)
- Haldol (haloperidol), Risperdal (risperidone), Zyprexa (olanzapine), Seroquel (quetiapine), Geodon (ziprasidone), Abilify (aripiprazole), Thorazine (chlorpromazine)
- Catapres (clonidine) or Tenex (guanfacine)
- Inderal LA (propranolol) or Tenormin (atenolol)
- Prozac (fluoxetine), Paxil (paroxetine), Zoloft (sertraline), Luvox (fluvoxamine), Celexa (citalopram), Lexapro (escitalopram), Effexor XR (venlafaxine), Cymbalta (duloxetine), Wellbutrin XL (buproprion), Remeron (mirtazapine), Tofranil (imipramine), Pamelor (nortriptyline), Elavil (amitriptyline), Sinequan (doxepin), Anafranil (clomipramine)

For further details on the risks and benefits of each of these medications refer to part 3. The other biological, psychological, and social approaches to treatment are covered in part 4.

CASE EXAMPLES

HANK WAS THIRTEEN when his mother first brought him to my office for treatment. Hank's parents were happily married and his father owned a very successful business so Mom could stay home with the kids. Hank's mom was an extremely nice person. There was nothing she would not do to help family or friend. She volunteered at her children's schools and pitched in to help whenever her family or friends called upon her. She was generous to a fault. Her generous, kindhearted approach to life definitely extended to the way she parented her children. Her children were indulged in every luxury, treat, and toy imaginable. Hank had an entire recording studio in his basement and an assortment of guitars, and his sister was given a red convertible Mustang for her sixteenth birthday, even though they were both failing students.

He wasn't oppositional or defiant, he simply passively refused to do his work. He would tell his mother that he was going to his room to do his homework, and two hours later she would find Hank in his room poring over and studying, very diligently, his skateboard and music magazines. Hank spent hours building elaborate models, which he was very proud of. He could focus and concentrate on activities that he found enjoyable, but school was not one of these activities. The same thing happened at home. He would promise his mother that he would complete his chores around the house at some specified time— just not right now—and inevitably the chores would not get done. Prior to my meeting Hank, he had been treated by a psychiatrist who determined that Hank must have AD/HD. The doctor prescribed every imaginable amphetamine-class drug but nothing changed the boy's behavior—because attention difficulties were not his problem. During this period, Hank also experienced some difficulty sleeping and had little appetite.

After Hank had been indulged for so many years, he had come to understand that he had nothing to lose by not doing his schoolwork or his household chores. Regardless of his performance, his mother could be counted upon to shower him with the best of everything. She would lecture him, scold him, and plead with him to change his ways and be responsible, all of which Hank would sit and listen to respectfully. The lecturing never changed his behavior an iota. Hank had become accustomed to getting everything he asked for, so when his mother tried to stop the steady stream of goodies until the work was done first, he did not take well to this change.

Hank's mother was not comfortable with this new approach either, but she had watched her older daughter ignore her studies and suffer consequences academically that the girl's mom did not want to see repeated in Hank. When the mother finally carried out her threats to stop the treat train, Hank became enraged, which manifested in episodes of destruction with complete abandon. When he could not intimidate his mother into driving him to the mall to purchase the things he wanted—and was used to getting—he would start yelling and screaming, which first escalated into slamming doors and eventually into his destroying property. On one particularly egregious episode, his mother described a scene so out of control that she and her husband feared he would start assaulting them. They sat speechless on the couch while he went about the living room throwing lamps and figurines against the walls to break them and knocking over the bookcases and the china hutch, all the while screaming at his parents that they were unfair cheapskates not to purchase his want of the day.

I suggested to Hank's mom that he did not have AD/HD but rather that he had developed Intermittent Explosive Disorder. I advised that the amphetamines be stopped as they would not be helpful in calming his anger, and in fact these medications had the potential of fueling Hank's anger. The elimination of the amphetamine-class drugs did help Hank sleep better and his appetite returned, but his anger was only slightly improved. In spite of treatment with several different medications, he continued to have bouts of rage—though much less destructive—until he learned that these episodes would not work to manipulate his mother any longer, and then they stopped.

9

MAJOR DEPRESSIVE DISORDER

ONE OUT OF every five Americans will suffer with clinical depression at some time in their lives. The rate at which children experience depression is almost half the rate seen in adults. Because children with depression have very different symptoms than adults, your child's depression could easily be missed.

CRITERIA FOR DIAGNOSIS

To make the diagnosis of **Major Depressive Disorder (MDD)**, your child must have five out of the following nine criteria for at least a two-week period. Furthermore, of the five qualifying symptoms, at least one must be either criterium one or two. The following are the criteria for the diagnosis of depression:

1. Children and adolescents very often express their poor mood as feeling irritated and easily angered. Adults usually will feel sad and empty when they are depressed. Some depressed children feel sadness most of the time, just as adults do. This means that, more than half of the time over a two-week period, your child felt sad or irritable. Your child may not tell you that he feels sad or irritable, but if you observe your child being more tearful and cranky, then this symptom probably applies.

2. Your child loses interest and no longer enjoys the activities and hobbies that once made him happy. If you see this change in your child occurring most of the time, most days, then this symptom applies to your child.

3. A significant increase or decrease in your child's appetite, beyond the typical picky eating that many children engage in, would be the third indication of depression. Watch for unusual weight gain or weight loss in your child. Also, a failure to make expected weight gains in a growing child would be an indication that this criterium applies to your child.

4. There are two ways that sleep is disrupted in depression. Your child can either sleep excessively or have trouble getting and staying asleep. This symptom would need to be occurring almost every day.

5. There are also two ways that your child's level of activity can change during depression. The change has to be present almost every day. He can become lethargic and sluggish. This is referred to as: psychomotor retardation. Alternatively, he can become hyperactive or what is called *psychomotor agitation*. Your child's hyperactive or sluggish behavior has to be observable. That is to say, *you* can see that your child is more or less active than normal.

   Note that it is this hyperactivity that is observed in children with depression that can sometimes lead to the wrong diagnosis. When you tell your doctor that your child is hyperactive, you must also describe the other symptoms listed here. Otherwise, you may give the doctor the idea that your child's only problem is hyperactivity. This misconception can lead your doctor to incorrectly diagnose your child with AD/HD. The medications given for AD/HD can make depression worse in some children. Therefore, it is very important that you provide the doctor with a complete picture of your child's symptoms.

6. Feeling tired and having low energy is another symptom of clinical depression. This fatigue is a subjective symptom, not necessarily something you would observe in your child. This loss of energy is a symptom that your child would have to tell you he was experiencing. Your inability to observe the fatigue in your child is what distinguishes this criterium number six from criterium number five.

7. Your child feels worthless and guilty, without any real reason, during depression. Feeling guilty about being depressed would not be enough alone to apply this symptom to your child. The guilt and poor self-worth your child experiences during depression is excessive and misplaced.

8. Children with depression have difficulty concentrating and trouble thinking. Being inattentive and easily distracted are symptoms that can be misinterpreted by your doctor if not placed in context. If your child has more than just inattention, be sure to explain all of your child's other symptoms as well. Otherwise, the doctor may jump to the conclusion that your child has AD/HD.

Children who have depression often have a hard time making decisions and have problems with their memory. These symptoms make it difficult for your child to get organized or remember his materials for school. Again, these symptoms reported alone to the doctor can lead him to the wrong conclusion. See appendix B for diagrams that show the overlapping symptoms in a number of diagnoses, including depression.

9. Depressed children can have recurrent thoughts of death or suicide. The suicidal thoughts may or may not be accompanied by specific plans, intentions, or attempts. This symptom would not apply to your child if the thoughts of death are just the fear of dying.

Depression is what causes suicide in children, not antidepressant medication. In spite of attempts by some to place blame for completed suicide in children on psychiatric medications, the research does not bear this out. Research shows that the number of children committing suicide has dropped dramatically since the introduction of antidepressant medications. On the other hand, before an antidepressant has a chance to resolve a child's depression, there are times when a child who had been too lethargic from depression to act on his suicidal thoughts may, during initial treatment, gain the energy to act on these thoughts. The new FDA warning specifically warns parents to watch very closely for signs of suicidal ideation when their children are first started on antidepressant medications. Suicidal thoughts in children is a very dangerous and grave situation that should always be taken seriously.

QUALIFIERS

There are a few situations when a different diagnosis than Major Depressive Disorder would be more appropriate. Those conditions are as follows:

- If your child meets less than the five criteria of the nine required for the diagnosis, then your child *does not* have Major Depressive Disorder. If your child still has significant impairment due to the depressive symptoms, then your child may have another diagnosis such as: **Dysthymic Disorder**, Adjustment Disorder with depressed mood, or a Major Depressive Disorder in partial remission.

- When your child *does* meet the criteria for Major Depressive Disorder but has also experienced a manic episode or a psychotic episode, then the more appropriate diagnosis would be Bipolar Disorder or **Schizoaffective Disorder**.

- The symptoms of depression have to cause significant distress and impairment in your child's functioning at home, at school, with friends, or in extracurricular activities.

- To diagnose Major Depressive Disorder, the symptoms of depression cannot be the direct result of drug intoxication. When the depressive symptoms seen in your child are due to the effects of either prescribed medication (such as steroids) or street drugs (such as amphetamines), then MDD is not the appropriate diagnosis. Instead, your child might be diagnosed with Amphetamine-Induced Mood Disorder, for example.

- When your child's depressive symptoms are caused by a general medical condition, then Major Depressive Disorder would not apply. For example, hypothyroidism or diabetes can mimic or appear to have the same symptoms as MDD. This is why it is important to get a physical examination of your child prior to taking him to see a psychiatrist.

- If your child's depressive symptoms can be better accounted for by bereavement, then your child would not appropriately be diagnosed with Major Depressive Disorder.

Major Depressive Disorder Specifiers

The diagnosis of Major Depressive Disorder can be further narrowed into different subtypes by specifying its severity and qualities. The following is a brief outline:

- First episode of depression
- Recurrent episode of depression
- Mild severity
- Moderate severity
- Severe without psychotic features
- Severe with psychotic features (these psychotic symptoms can be hallucinations or delusions)

- Depression is in partial remission
- Depression is in full remission

TREATMENT OF MAJOR DEPRESSIVE DISORDER

Depression can be treated successfully with or without medications. Long before there were antidepressant medications, children recovered from depression. Depression can be effectively treated with therapy alone. Sometimes depression resolves spontaneously without any intervention. Whatever treatment you choose for your child, the first step is accurately identifying depression. When a child who really has the diagnosis of Major Depressive Disorder is *incorrectly* identified as AD/HD or Bipolar Disorder, he may *not* receive the proper treatment for depression. The wrong treatment for your child's Major Depressive Disorder will not bring him relief. The relief of symptoms that comes out of receiving the proper treatment is why correctly identifying the diagnosis is so important.

Once the diagnosis of Major Depressive Disorder has been confirmed, there are several options for treatment: the biological, the psychological, and the social treatments. The physiologically based approaches include psychiatric medications and other approaches such as light therapy or ECT electroconvulsive therapy.

Should you decide that psychiatric medications are the right choice for your child, the prescription medications most often used in the treatment of MDD are as follows:

- Prozac (fluoxetine), Paxil (paroxetine), Zoloft (sertraline), Luvox (fluvoxamine), Celexa (citalopram), Lexapro (escitalopram), Effexor XR (venlafaxine), Cymbalta (duloxetine), Wellbutrin XL (buproprion), Remeron (mirtazapine), Tofranil (imipramine), Pamelor (nortriptyline), Elavil (amitriptyline), Sinequan (doxepin), Anafranil (clomipramine)
- Eskalith & Lithobid (lithium), Depakote (valproate), Tegretol (carbamazepine), Equetro (carbamazepine), Trileptal (oxcarbazepine), Lamictal (lamotrigine), Topamax (topiramate)
- Risperdal (risperidone), Zyprexa (olanzapine), Seroquel (quetiapine), Geodon (ziprasidone), Abilify (aripiprazole), Thorazine (chlorpromazine), Haldol (haloperidol)

If a child has not started to recover from his depression, most parents think that their child is on the wrong psychiatric medication. In actuality, the two most common reasons that psych medications appear not to be working are:

1. Your child was not taking a high enough dose of the antidepressant medication, or
2. He had not been taking his medication faithfully every day for a long enough period of time.

Generally, antidepressant medications require four to six weeks on a full dose to begin having an effect. For further details on the risks and benefits of each of these medications refer to part 3. The other biological, psychological, and social approaches to treatment are covered in part 4.

CASE EXAMPLES

IRIS WAS ONLY six years old when her divorced parents, who both came to the meeting, brought her to my office for treatment. Iris had already been in regular, weekly individual psychotherapy treatment for two years. Her parents explained that they had a very contentious and drawn-out divorce that started with a separation when Iris was only three years old. Both parents agreed that their marriage was hostile and acrimonious, and Iris had been a witness to many screaming matches and domestic violence between the parents. Both of Iris's parents were very successful and therefore busy with their respective businesses. As a result, Iris had spent quite a lot of her early years with different babysitters and nannies. It was Iris's previous therapist who alerted me to the suspicion that Iris may have accidentally seen her father having sex with one of her nannies, a nanny whom the father married immediately after his divorce from Iris's mom and with whom he had a five-month-old child at the time of the assessment.

At the time of my evaluation, Iris was described by each parent a little differently but they could agree that she was easily irritated, cried often, was overeating, slept poorly unless she could sleep in the bed of the parent she happened to be visiting, wasn't concentrating well in class, and talked about hating herself and wanting to die. Iris had asked her mother to kill her because she was fat and no one loved her. The girl told me that her feelings were hurt when her friends criticized her or rejected her. She was wetting her bed seven nights out of ten, which always prompted her parents to allow her to move to their bed as, curiously, Iris never wet either of her parents' beds. Her new stepmom, her former nanny, told me at a later session that Iris was a very manipulative child when there was something she wanted that had been denied her outright, and that she had tried throwing tantrums but they had not been as successful as her manipulations.

Both of Iris's parents were frustrated with the girl's behavior and had not seen any improvement in her in spite of two years of weekly psychotherapy. They asked that I provide their child with both psychotherapy and medication treatment if I thought it would help. Perhaps the one most effective intervention that could have helped Iris was something that was impossible to secure: that the parents would make peace between each other for the sake of their daughter's mental health. I discussed this matter at great length with both parents together and separately in the year that followed. Each one insisted that the other parent was the aggressor, the one who refused to make peace for Iris's sake, while painting themselves as the healthy, mentally stable parent. Throughout the year that I treated the girl, her parents continued their battle with each other over holiday visitations, choices of nannies, and the possession of property and real estate that still remained to be split between them. Their arguments were always nasty, venomous, and vindictive, and sometimes took place in front of Iris.

I treated Iris with antidepressant medications and weekly psychotherapy, focusing mostly on how her parents' anger at each other was in no way a reflection on the love each parent had for her. Iris did admit she had been using suicidal threats early in her treatment, to manipulate her parents to stop fighting. Sadly, this actually worked for a while as both Mom and Dad would drop what they were doing—including fighting with each other—to attend to Iris's suicidal feelings. As often happens with antidepressant medications, the first medication did not work out well enough to treat her depression but luckily the second medication worked very well. Iris had been in therapy for two years prior to coming to me for treatment, but had not been on any psychiatric medication that entire time. Her treatment is another example that shows a combination of medication, applied properly along with effective psychotherapy, can produce the best outcomes.

In another case, I treated a sixteen-year-old girl, Jackie, who had suddenly seen a drop in her academic performance two years prior at the start of freshman year. Unfortunately, Jackie presented herself for assessment and treatment at the height of popularity for the AD/HD diagnosis. Naturally, Jackie's poor academic performance, a great change from many previous years of school success, was immediately seen as a case of AD/HD. The fact that she had also become more easily irritated, more tearful, more tired, less motivated, and more socially withdrawn were all viewed by the doctor as Jackie's emotional reaction to her late-developing AD/HD. The two years that followed that diagnosis were filled with a multitude of amphetamine-class drug trials, deepening depression, and continued academic failures.

When Jackie presented herself to my office, she had started to give up on her dream to study at the small liberal college she had been hoping to attend since a chance visit to their campus, years prior. She was discouraged, and after two years of failed treatment, had lost faith in doctors and their medicines. I diagnosed Jackie with Major Depressive Disorder, stopped her amphetamine-class drugs, and started her on antidepressant medications, which made a huge difference. Her depression lifted, her energy and motivation returned, and she was able to concentrate normally again. By January of Jackie's sophomore year, her grades were back on track and she was thinking about college again.

When she did not get an acceptance from her favorite college, Jackie was afraid that her bad grades during her first two years of high school had been the deciding factor. Thinking that perhaps an explanation from a professional might help, she asked me to write a letter. When I explained to the admission committee about the misdiagnosis that had led to inappropriate medication choices by Jackie's previous doctor and a two-year delay in getting the right treatment, they changed their minds and an acceptance letter was forthcoming.

10

BIPOLAR DISORDER

BIPOLAR DISORDER

THIS DIAGNOSIS HAS recently become one of the most popular diagnoses both in children and adults. In 1995, a child was rarely ever diagnosed with **Bipolar Disorder** under the age of thirteen years old and unheard of under the age of ten years old. Today, psychiatrists are diagnosing Bipolar Disorder in children as young as one year old. Nothing has changed in the *DSM* with regards to the criteria that need to be met to give a child the diagnosis of Bipolar Disorder. One thing that has changed is the way that information is disseminated to the public. With the increased use of the Internet and the use of self-administered diagnostic surveys, parents often arrive at the doctor's office with a preconceived conclusion about their child's diagnosis. Misinterpretation of the diagnostic criteria is one of the reasons why Bipolar Disorder is a diagnosis that is often given incorrectly. Therefore, a careful review of the criteria is an important prerequisite to understanding this very serious mental illness.

CRITERIA FOR DIAGNOSIS

Bipolar Disorder is defined as a mood disturbance with distinct episodes of Depression and episodes of Mania. There can also be episodes during which your child has both Depression and Mania simultaneously. These episodes are called Mixed episodes. In between the episodes of Depression or Mania your child returns to his baseline of normal mood and behavior.

Depressive Episode

For a complete description of a Depressive episode refer to the criteria for diagnosis for Major Depressive Disorder found in chapter 9. In Bipolar Disorder, your child would have episodes of depression for two weeks or longer. Usually a person with Bipolar Disorder has less than four episodes total of mood disturbances, including both Depressive episodes and Manic episodes, per year. Otherwise your child would be further classified as having Rapid Cycling.

Manic Episodes

A manic episode is a cluster of symptoms that occur together over a discrete period of time, usually four to seven days. During a manic episode, the person becomes delusional, bizarre, and out of touch with reality. Even to the untrained eye, a person during a manic episode appears extremely mentally ill. Your child, during a manic episode, will have a distinctly different mood than his normal baseline mood. His mood is abnormally and persistently elevated or euphoric. That is, your child feels excessively excited and abnormally intense.

Along with the elevated mood, your child would also have to have three of the following seven symptoms to qualify for the diagnosis of Bipolar Disorder. The seven criteria are:

1. They lose touch with reality. Typically, a person in a manic state believes she is someone famous or is the close friend of a famous person. These beliefs are termed delusions of grandiosity or inflated self-esteem. A girl in a manic episode might act on these delusions by doing strange, out-of-character things, such as waiting by the window for a famous rock star, her new "best friend," who in reality doesn't know her personally, to arrive in his limo to take her to a concert. Another example of a grandiose delusion in a manic child might be expressed by his trying to make phone calls to a popular video game company to tell the company president about a game that he believes he has just designed himself and is sure will be the next big thing.
2. They require almost no sleep for four to seven days straight. They are awake and hyperactive for the entire episode. This should not be con-

fused with the loss of sleep that occurs in depression or anxiety. Depressed and anxious people are tired, want to sleep, but spend their nights in bed tossing and turning. Manic persons do not desire sleep, they appear not to need sleep, because they just keep moving tirelessly, night and day. Being active and tireless for only fourteen hours and then sleeping, is not the sleep behavior of children with Bipolar Disorder.

3. This symptom of sleeplessness can be easily confused with the dysfunctional yet typical sleep pattern of teenagers. Many teens love to stay up late at night watching TV, playing video games, or talking with their friends on the phone or instant-messaging until 4:00 a.m. If your teenager has adopted this unhealthy sleep habit, her sleep schedule is probably as follows: your daughter may stay awake until 4:00 a.m., the following day she might nap on her desk at school, and then when she arrives home from school, she may sleep for another three to five hours in the afternoon. When she awakens late in the evening, she may get something to eat and then starts this cycle all over again by making a phone call to a friend, turning on the TV or going online. This sleep pattern is *not* the sleeplessness experienced by children in a manic episode, this is an unfortunate outcome of unhealthy sleep routines followed by many teens. Be careful not to confuse the two when reporting your child's sleep habits to your doctor.

4. *Pressured speech* occurs during a manic episode. The afflicted person will talk very rapidly while in the manic state. They speak so quickly and so much that they are impossible to interrupt. Pressured speech is different than the giddy, ramblings of teenage girls on a Friday night. Manics do not pause to allow others to respond. Normal teen girls talk about reality-based events and enjoy exchanging ideas and stories. When a manic person has pressured speech, the content is often delusional, bizarre, or grandiose. The abnormal content is more evidence that your child may be in a manic phase.

5. Flight of ideas or racing thoughts are also symptoms of mania. When a person is experiencing *racing thoughts*, his mind jumps rapidly from idea to idea in what is referred to as a *flight of ideas*. The content of his thoughts is bizarre and disjointed. As your child's mind flies from one bizarre idea to the next, he feels unable to keep up with his own thoughts. Your child will feel unable to slow his thoughts down enough to focus on any one idea. Racing thoughts should not be confused with *ruminating*. See chapter 4 for a full definition of *ruminating* as it compares to *racing thoughts*.

6. During a manic episode, your child's attention would be easily drawn to unimportant or irrelevant items in his surroundings. This distractibility would cause his attention to jump from one trivial detail to the next, with no goal or direction.

7. Manics are involved in multiple activities simultaneously. They are extremely hyperactive and agitated. If your child had this symptom of mania, you would observe her starting (but not usually completing) many different projects at the same time, leaving a series of unfinished projects in her wake while moving on to the next activity. For example, she could start a cooking project and leave it on the stove burning; put a movie in the DVD player and leave the room while it is playing; start washing the dog but leave the animal soapy and wet in the bathroom; or open some oil paints and start painting, then leave all the brushes stuck in the paint while she goes online to chat with strangers.

8. Excessive indulgence in pleasurable activities with a high risk for painful or unpleasant consequences is a symptom seen in a manic episode. Examples of the kinds of indulgent activities seen in mania are unrestrained buying sprees or sexual indiscretions. A person in a manic phase will spend money excessively on items he doesn't need and can't afford. I treated a manic man who tried to buy five cars on the same day. Also, a manic person becomes sexually focused. They are infamous for being out in public, naked and oblivious to the socially inappropriate nature of this behavior. A Bipolar patient may have indiscriminate sexual encounters with multiple partners during a manic episode. In *children*, you are more likely to see hypersexual behaviors more consistent with their age, such as dressing provocatively or flirting with everyone at school, including the teachers. On the other hand, your *teenager* might engage in indiscriminate sexual encounters or may go on wild spending sprees, such as using *your* credit card to purchase electronics, bikes, or music.

QUALIFIERS

THERE ARE A couple of conditions to consider when deciding if your child might be having a manic episode.

- The mood disturbance caused by the manic episode is severe enough to cause significant impairment socially and academically. If the behaviors lead to a psychiatric hospitalization to keep your child safe from his own wild behaviors, then his episode would qualify as Bipolar Disorder.

- Your child is *not* having a manic episode if his behaviors are everyday, consistent, fixed personality traits. For example if your child is hyperactive, distracted, and preoccupied with spending money every day without change or variation, your child is not having a manic episode. By definition, an *episode* has a beginning and an end. To determine if your child is having a manic episode, consider whether the behaviors are fixed, everyday personality traits or do the behaviors come and go. Typical Bipolar patients have no more than four episodes per year. Generally, after experiencing a manic episode your child will be shocked and dismayed at his own behavior. After the episode ends, he will recognize the manic behaviors as a departure from their normal functioning.

- A manic episode occurs in the absence of intoxication. A person bingeing on illicit drugs, especially amphetamines, can resemble someone experiencing a manic episode. If your teen is using drugs or alcohol while acting manic, then he would *not* qualify as having Bipolar Disorder. Likewise, some prescribed medications can cause manic behaviors. Children affected by these medications in this way would not be considered to have Bipolar Disorder.

- Your child would not be considered to have Bipolar Disorder if his mood symptoms are the result of a medical condition. There are a number of medical conditions that cause the patient to have an unstable mood or bizarre maniclike behaviors, such as thyroid imbalances, kidney failure, or lead poisoning, to name a few.

Treatment of Bipolar Disorder

When you decide that psychiatric medications are the right choice for your child, the prescription medications most often used in the treatment of Bipolar Disorder are as follows:

- Eskalith, Lithobid (lithium), Depakote (valproate), Tegretol (carbamazepine), Equetro (carbamazepine), Trileptal (oxcarbazepine), Lamictal (lamotrigine), Topamax (topiramate)
- Haldol (haloperidol), Risperdal (risperidone), Zyprexa (olanzapine), Seroquel (quetiapine), Geodon (ziprasidone), Abilify (aripiprazole)
- Prozac (fluoxetine), Paxil (paroxetine), Zoloft (sertraline), Luvox (fluvoxamine), Celexa (citalopram), Lexapro (escitalopram), Effexor XR

(venlafaxine), Cymbalta (duloxetine), Wellbutrin XL (buproprion), Remeron (mirtazapine)

For further details on the risks and benefits of each of these medications, refer to part 3. The other biological, psychological, and social approaches to treatment are covered in part 4.

CASE EXAMPLES

ALTHOUGH THERE IS little doubt in my mind that many of the cases of Bipolar Disorder being diagnosed in children today are really misdiagnoses, there are of course legitimate cases of Bipolar Disorder. I treated such a child when she had her first episode at thirteen years of age. Kelly's parents reported that she had been experiencing a depressed mood, along with other changes, such as a lowered self-esteem, social withdrawal, poor concentration, excessive eating, and insomnia. I was able to successfully treat her with antidepressants and for many months Kelly did very well; her depression lifted, she was sleeping soundly, her grades improved, and she was enjoying the company of her friends again.

About eight months after her depression resolved her parents returned with Kelly, puzzled and dismayed by the changes in their daughter. Kelly was the oldest child in a family of four children. Her parents had a happy marriage and the mother worked part-time at the Catholic school they all attended to help defray the cost of tuition. Kelly had always been a well-behaved girl; she was a modest girl not given to loud scenes, flamboyant behavior, or dressing in a provocative manner. Kelly had changed overnight, according to her parents, and they were at a complete loss as to what was happening or how to help their daughter. Kelly explained that she no longer felt tired, that she was staying awake all day and almost all night busy in her room, writing in her journal, calling her friends on the phone, singing all hours of the night, watching TV, and doing exercises in her room. She was a little delusional about a special connection she had to God that allowed her to reach fellow students at her Catholic school with His message. Kelly started dressing in very short skirts by rolling up the waistband of her uniform skirt and wearing her blouses with less of the buttons closed. She was very excitable and babbled on incessantly about subjects that seemed disjointed and unrelated to anything going on in her life. This behavior went on for about a week, even though I started a mood stabilizer immediately. When Kelly's mania resolved, she was extremely embarrassed by her behavior during the manic episode and was afraid to return to school for fear of the ridicule she would endure from her peers. On her mood stabilizer, Kelly remained symptom free for several months.

After reading about mood stabilizing medications, her parents decided that the benefits from the medication did not justify the risks. Further, they reasoned that Kelly had been symptom free for six months and therefore probably no longer needed these medications. Her parents never consulted me, nor did they inform me that they were stopping Kelly's medications, they just discontinued the drugs by decreasing the dosage in a pattern that they developed on their own. For the next couple of months, Kelly remained stable and her parents felt reassured that they had done the right thing. Then the family flew to New York City for a vacation, and disaster struck. I received an emergency call from her parents in their New York hotel room. They were frightened and needed guidance and instructions on what to do for Kelly, who was launching into another manic episode. Kelly's medications were restarted and her mania resolved.

In another case that exemplifies the misdiagnosis of Bipolar Disorder, I treated a teenager, Lori, who was hospitalized after a suicide attempt at seventeen years of age. She was diagnosed in the hospital with Bipolar Disorder and started on two medications at the same time, one an antidepressant at a low dose and the other a mood stabilizer—but Lori's history was completely inconsistent with the diagnosis made. She had never had a manic episode and wasn't even having anger outbursts; what she was experiencing were symptoms of depression, anxiety, nightmares of the rape she had experienced four years earlier, flashbacks of the attack, a heightened watchfulness (hypervigilance), insomnia, difficulty concentrating, and social withdrawal. Lori was afraid to leave her home and, after her rape—which had been perpetrated by a boy who attended her high school and had never faced any criminal prosecution—she begged her mother to take her out of school so she could be homeschooled. When I met Lori she reported that she had never received any psychiatric care or counseling prior to her psychiatric hospitalization the week before. Unfortunately, Lori had turned to alcohol and marijuana as an escape to cope with the emotional pain that she carried. The addition of the drugs and alcohol complicated her recovery, because of the depressant effect of the alcohol—her drug of choice by her admission.

My treatment started with the recommendation that Lori stop all drugs and alcohol, and attend Teen-AA. Then I tapered her off her mood stabilizer, which Lori was convinced was responsible for the side effects she had been experiencing, and increased her dose of antidepressant medication. Lori and I started regular psychotherapy sessions thereafter. Probably the greatest improvement in Lori was seen when she stopped drinking alcohol and using marijuana, but I believe it was also very beneficial to Lori to have someone on whom she could unload the emotional burden created by the trauma she had experienced. The antidepressants, I am sure, played their part as well.

The most disturbing feature of the psychiatric care that this child received in the hospital was that her psychiatrist jumped to the conclusion that she had Bipolar Disorder. By making this misdiagnosis he had effectively stopped all the appropriate courses of treatment that would have really helped Lori, including alcohol recovery, psychotherapy, and appropriate doses of an antidepressant for her actual diagnosis of PTSD exacerbated by Alcohol Abuse with possible Alcohol-Induced Mood Disorder.

I have seen numerous cases of children from the age of eighteen months to seventeen years, who had symptoms that were clearly the result of spoiling (ODD); trauma (PTSD); or, drug-induced rages—and all of whom were diagnosed with Bipolar Disorder. This diagnosis is currently so popular that if your child expresses his anger with a temper tantrum or becomes cranky and irritable when he doesn't get his way, then he will likely be diagnosed by someone at some point with Bipolar Disorder. Bipolar Disorder is a very serious psychiatric condition not to be taken lightly, but beware of leaping to this diagnosis without the child's symptoms clearly fulfilling its criteria.

11

BORDERLINE PERSONALITY DISORDER

PERSONALITY DISORDERS

BORDERLINE PERSONALITY DISORDER is one of the ten personality disorders described in the *DSM*. A personality disorder is considered to be a different type of disorder from the rest of the diagnoses in the manual. Personality disorders are thought to be a *trait* or an enduring pattern of inner experience and behavior that deviates significantly from cultural norms. The remainder of the *DSM* diagnoses are considered conditions of *state*. A disorder such as Major Depressive Disorder, for example, is thought to be a condition of *state* because it can be treated, has a discrete period of time during which it affects the patient, and, once resolved, the patient returns to his normal baseline functioning. A personality disorder is thought to be a *trait* because the behaviors are fixed, stable, and can be traced back to childhood.

BORDERLINE PERSONALITY DISORDER

PERSONALITY DISORDERS WERE once only diagnosed in adults. Today, psychiatrists diagnose adolescents with personality disorders as well. If your teen has Borderline Personality Disorder, you and your child are both facing an extremely difficult experience. People who suffer with this personality disorder have excruciating emotional instability, distress, and frustration. Watching your child struggle with Borderline Personality Disorder can leave you feeling helpless and defeated. Females have this condition more often than males.

CRITERIA FOR DIAGNOSIS

BORDERLINE PERSONALITY DISORDER is defined as a long-standing pattern of unstable moods, impulsive behaviors, and conflicted relationships. Like other psychiatric conditions, a list of nine criteria defines the diagnosis. If your teenager has five of these nine symptoms, then she has Borderline Personality Disorder. The criteria are:

1. **Frantic efforts to avoid abandonment:** Even if your child believes there is only a remote possibility of being abandoned, the imagined abandonment strikes fear in her heart. She will pursue these relationships desperately, long after it is clear that the person is not at all interested in a relationship.

2. **Relationships that are intense, unstable, and full of conflict:** Your child may at one time adore and idolize someone who later she may decide is the most evil person on the planet. This change of heart can happen quickly and with little reason.

3. **Unstable self-image:** Your teen frequently changes her identity, group affiliations, belief system, or sense of self. Examples would include switching religions, career paths, or music preferences every few weeks. She might insist one day she was born to be a singer. Then she might decide she hates singing and was really meant to be a painter. A week later, she might change her mind again and insist that all along she is a marathon runner.

4. **Impulsivity in ways that have high potential for self-harm:** Your teen has to engage in two different impulsive behaviors for this criterion to apply. Examples of the risky behaviors are sexual indiscretions, overspending, drug abuse, reckless driving, or binge eating.

5. **Self-mutilating behavior:** Borderline Personality Disordered people cut themselves chronically. They report that the cutting *relieves* pain instead of causing pain. Cutting is not confined to the arms or wrists. Your child may cut anywhere on her body. Some of these children cut with no intention of taking their lives, while others are suicidal. Recurrent suicidal gestures is another manifestation of this symptom.

6. **Unstable mood:** Your child's mood changes very rapidly from happy to angry to depressed in a matter of minutes or hours. Moods that last longer than a day would be more consistent with other mood disorders. Borderline Personality patients are very reactive emotionally. Little slights or hurts can set them into a tailspin of emotions.

7. **Chronic feelings of emptiness:** They may tell you that they feel lonely all the time, isolated, and unfulfilled.

8. **Intense anger:** Your child feels angry most of the time. She has a hard time controlling her anger. As a result, she exhibits frequent anger outbursts, rages, and aggression. Her anger may appear out of place or inappropriate given the event that angered her.

9. **Dissociative symptoms or paranoid feelings related to stress:** A dissociative episode is a brief period during which your child would feel she was not herself. She would tell you she felt as if she were outside herself looking back in, or as if she were existing in a foreign body. These episodes are periodic. If they were constant, another diagnosis would be more appropriate.

Qualifiers

As with other diagnoses, the diagnosis of Borderline Personality Disorder may not apply to your child if the behaviors listed above do not also adhere to the following guidelines.

- The pattern of behavior must lead to significant impairment of your adolescent's social, academic, and occupational functioning.
- The behaviors listed above cannot be the direct result of drug or alcohol abuse alone. This is a subtle distinction when you consider that drug use is a part of criterion 4.
- The Borderline Personality Disorder symptoms listed above cannot be the direct result of a medical illness.
- If your child's behavior corresponds more accurately with a different mental disorder such as Depression, Anxiety, Bipolar, or Oppositional Defiant Disorder (ODD), then Borderline Personality Disorder would *not* be the proper diagnosis.

If you compare the symptoms of Borderline Personality Disorder with those of other diagnoses, such as Bipolar Disorder, you will notice some striking similarities. One of the most important distinctions between these particular two diagnoses is how frequently the symptoms are experienced. If your child is irritable and moody most of the time, as opposed to having discrete episodes of mania, as in Bipolar (see the definition of mania in chapter 4), then Borderline Personality Disorder, Depression, or ODD might be a more accurate diagnosis. You will find, as you review the symptoms for the different mental illnesses listed here in this book, that the same symptom can be found in a number of different disorders. The fact that the same symptoms can be found in a variety of different mental illnesses is why professional guidance is essential in making a correct psychiatric diagnosis in your child.

TREATMENT OF BORDERLINE PERSONALITY DISORDER

ONCE THE DIAGNOSIS of Borderline Personality Disorder has been confirmed in your child, you have several options for treatment. Most patients with Borderline Personality Disorder do require intensive psychotherapy. They are benefited by structure and routine in their lives. One of the theories on what causes of Borderline Personality Disorder is the violation of appropriate *boundaries*. In the mental health profession, we define healthy boundaries as the establishment of appropriate roles and relationships with the people in our lives. For an example of how a boundary can be crossed, consider the inappropriate interaction or relationship created when a mother uses her child as a confidant to vent her frustrations about her troubled marriage or the family's financial crisis. Therefore, one of the psychotherapeutic treatments of your child with Borderline Personality Disorder is to reestablish healthy boundaries with your child by acting like a parent, not like a buddy, pal, confidant, or best friend (more on this topic in chapter 27). Then there is the tragically too frequent and exceedingly inappropriate interaction with children that destroys healthy boundaries that happens when a child is sexually molested. It is of the utmost importance that your child be protected from the perverted elements in our society that draw children into adult situations. These influences can even reach into your home through Internet child porn and the child-molesting predators who search chat rooms looking for children to prey upon. But do not be too complacent—child molesters work in all fields: clergy, teachers, coaches, doctors, and babysitters, and may exist within our own families: uncles, boyfriends, and even spouses. Remember, too, that not all child molesters are male.

When you decide that psychiatric medications are the right choice for your child, the prescription medications most often used in the treatment of Bor-

derline Personality Disorder are listed below. The medications that can be helpful to patients with Borderline Personality Disorder are chosen based on the
symptoms that your child may be experiencing. Antidepressants are given for
depression. Antipsychotics are given for the anger and the transient dissociative symptoms. Mood stabilizers are prescribed for the irritability and impulsive behaviors.

- Prozac (fluoxetine), Paxil (paroxetine), Zoloft (sertraline), Luvox (flu-
  voxamine), Celexa (citalopram), Lexapro (escitalopram), Effexor XR
  (venlafaxine), Cymbalta (duloxetine), Wellbutrin XL (buproprion),
  Remeron (mirtazapine), Tofranil (imipramine), Pamelor (nortriptyline), Elavil (amitriptyline), Sinequan (doxepin), Anafranil
  (clomipramine)
- Haldol (haloperidol), Risperdal (risperidone), Zyprexa (olanzapine),
  Seroquel (quetiapine), Geodon (ziprasidone), Abilify (aripiprazole),
  Thorazine (chlorpromazine)
- Eskalith, Lithobid (lithium), Depakote (valproate), Tegretol (carbamazepine), Equetro (carbamazepine), Trileptal (oxcarbazepine), Lam-
  ictal (lamotrigine), Topamax (topiramate)

For further details on the risks and benefits of each of these medications,
refer to part 3. The other biological, psychological, and social approaches to
treatment are covered in part 4.

CASE EXAMPLE

I TRY NOT to diagnose children with a personality disorder, because it is always
my hope that the personality disordered behaviors I am seeing in a child are
the result of immaturity, and not mental illness. Sheri was a sixteen-year-old
girl that kept coming into the children's psychiatric emergency room for various reasons. Her first visit to our ER was due to an argument with her foster
mother during which there was an exchange of blows and a call for police support. But after that first visit, Sheri became aware that the threat of suicide
would allow her to escape situations and placements with which she was
unhappy. Therefore, whenever she was unhappy with the house rules, had a dis-
agreement with another foster child in the group home, or simply had a personality conflict with a staff member, Sheri would cut on herself or say she was
suicidal, which she knew would earn her a trip to our ER.

Sheri had been raised her first six years by an alcoholic mother who was
unaware of the sexual abuse that Sheri had endured at the hands of the mother's

many boyfriends. Once Sheri was taken into protective custody, her mother disappeared; she never tried to regain custody. The next ten years saw a series of foster and group homes, each representing another broken hope of finding acceptance with a surrogate family. Sheri's unquenchable thirst for attention and affection had driven some caregivers away, while others were pulled into inappropriate relationships with Sheri. She would initially idealize the caregiver, volunteer, or social worker at the beginning of their relationship, but as the relationship developed, and the idealized adult was no longer meeting Sheri's demands adequately, she would suddenly hate, despise, and slander that person to anyone who would listen. Her chronic feelings of emptiness drove her frantic efforts to fill that void by building deeply connected relationships that always deteriorated into enmeshed and unhealthy attachments. She even tried meeting her emotional needs with food, which ultimately led to the development of obesity and more reasons to hate herself and feel inferior and unlovable. If Sheri felt rejected, abandoned, or alone, she responded with anger, self-hatred, and self-mutilation, which she knew would generate a lot of excitement and draw mental health–care professionals to her rescue. When she did not get the approval that she was looking for from her foster parents or the group home staff, she became enraged and had outbursts of anger, which often resulted in assault.

Sheri had been diagnosed with AD/HD, Major Depressive Disorder, Bipolar Disorder, PTSD, Adjustment Disorder, Oppositional Defiant Disorder, and Intermittent Explosive Disorder. She had been treated with antidepressants, amphetamines, mood stabilizers, and antipsychotic medications, none of which seemed to have a great impact on her mood or behavior. She had been provided psychotherapy throughout the years she was in state custody, but always seemed to find fault with the therapist, especially once the counselor had started to get into sensitive issues with Sheri. Unfortunately, Borderline Personality Disorder is an extremely difficult condition to treat and requires many years of a combination of individual therapy, group therapy, a very structured environment, and usually psychiatric medications. Sheri was not ready to work on her recovery when I met her in the ER; she was still in a state of confusion, chaos, and angry agitation, so her ultimate outcome has yet to be seen.

12

Anxiety, Social Phobia, and Panic Disorder

Generalized Anxiety Disorder

A NUMBER OF large studies conducted in the United States, on the prevalence of anxiety in children, have shown that nearly one in ten children meet the criteria for an anxiety disorder. Furthermore, if you have an anxiety disorder, your child is seven times more likely to develop an anxiety disorder as well. Your child's anxiety may range from mild worry and distress to overwhelming incapacitating worry that severely impairs his functioning.

Criteria for Diagnosis

The criteria for **Generalized Anxiety Disorder** requires first that your child has been experiencing excessive anxiety, apprehension, and worry most of the time and that he has had symptoms for a six-month period. Second, your child must find that the anxiety he feels is difficult or nearly impossible to control. In addition, your child must meet at least one of the following six symptoms:

1. Your child feels restless, keyed up, or on edge. You may observe your child acting agitated or hyperactively as a response to this restlessness he feels.

2. Your child becomes easily fatigued or tires more easily since he developed the anxiety symptoms.

3. Children with Generalized Anxiety Disorder find it more difficult to concentrate and pay attention in school. Your child may find his mind goes blank or he is easily distracted by the fears and worries that preoccupy him.

4. He is more easily irritated and angered.

5. Generalized Anxiety Disorder causes children to have increased muscle tension.

6. Sleep disturbance is a symptom of children with anxiety. If your child has difficulty falling asleep or staying asleep or finds his sleep is restless and unsatisfying, then he has the sleep disturbance associated with Generalized Anxiety Disorder.

What may be interesting to note is that, in adults, three of these six symptoms are required to meet the criteria for Generalized Anxiety Disorder. If your child has Generalized Anxiety Disorder, you will find that he is often anxious about how well he performs at school, is overly concerned about punctuality, and worries excessively about catastrophic events such as earthquakes, tornadoes, or terrorist attacks. Your anxious child will require excessive approval and reassurance from you. Of special interest are criteria 1 and 3. You may recognize that these are the very same symptoms that usually have teachers and others jumping to the conclusion that your child has AD/HD. Likewise, children who have the symptoms listed in criteria 4 and 6 will have many jumping to the conclusion that your child has Bipolar Disorder. Here you have more good examples of why it is crucial to have your child carefully and accurately diagnosed prior to proceeding with any treatment.

QUALIFIERS

Generalized Anxiety Disorder shares the same or similar symptoms with a number of other diagnoses. Therefore, it is important to clearly rule out the possibility that another diagnosis doesn't better fit your child's symptoms. There are some important exceptions that must be taken into consideration when making the diagnosis of Generalized Anxiety Disorder.

- The anxiety your child has must cause clinically significant distress and impairment in his functioning at school, at home, or while performing sports, dance, or music.

- If your child's anxiety is only in reference to having the next *panic attack*, then Panic Disorder would be the correct diagnosis, not Generalized Anxiety Disorder.
- If your child's anxiety only occurs when he is being embarrassed in public, then Social Phobia would be the right diagnosis.
- If your child's anxiety is only about being contaminated or not being able to complete his compulsive rituals, then Obsessive Compulsive Disorder would be the more appropriate diagnosis.
- If your child's anxiety is only about being away from home and close relatives, then Separation Anxiety would be the better diagnosis.
- If your child's anxiety is only related to recollections and reexperiencing traumatic events, then Post Traumatic Stress Disorder would be the proper diagnosis.
- When your child's anxiety is due to the side effects of a medication or intoxication with or withdrawal from an illicit drug, then he does not meet the criteria for Generalized Anxiety Disorder. This condition would be referred to as Substance Induced Anxiety Disorder.
- Because there are medical conditions, such as hyperthyroidism, which can create many of the same symptoms as Generalized Anxiety Disorder, it is important to eliminate the possibility that a medical condition is causing your child's anxiety symptoms.

TREATMENT OF GENERALIZED ANXIETY DISORDER

When you decide that psychiatric medications are the right choice for your child, the prescription medications most often used in the treatment of Generalized Anxiety Disorder are as follows:

- Prozac (fluoxetine), Paxil (paroxetine), Zoloft (sertraline), Luvox (fluvoxamine), Celexa (citalopram), Lexapro (escitalopram), Effexor XR (venlafaxine), Cymbalta (duloxetine)
- Tofranil (imipramine), Pamelor (nortriptyline), Elavil (amitriptyline), Sinequan (doxepin), Anafranil (clomipramine)
- Buspar (buspirone)
- Inderal (propranolol), Tenormin (atenolol)
- Benzodiazepines: Xanax (alprazolam), Ativan (lorazepam), Klonapin (clonazepam), Valium (diazepam)

For further details on the risks and benefits of each of these medications, refer to part 3. The other biological, psychological, and social approaches to treatment are covered in part 4.

CASE EXAMPLE

Kevin was fourteen when he and his mother came to my office for his first evaluation by a psychiatrist. His mother was concerned about Kevin's deteriorating mental and emotional state, which included increasing anxiety, tension, and agitation; he was more depressed, more easily irritated, and tearful; and he had insomnia as well. Kevin had been diagnosed by his kindergarten teacher with AD/HD, because at five years of age, he also had symptoms of restlessness and difficulty concentrating, but only at school. At home, Kevin had no problems focusing his attention on his hobby of writing computer code to create Web sites and video game maps. He was also a very successful athlete in both league play and school team sports; he kept his attention on the play of the game easily, and enjoyed playing. For a few years, Kevin's mom tried to manage his poor performance with herbal remedies but with no effect on his school performance.

It was his mother's belief that the root of Kevin's problems started at home, with his relationship with his father. He and his father had locked horns early on and, with his mother's assistance, Kevin had been able to hold his ground in their battle of wills. His father was very critical of everything Kevin did and regularly told him how disappointed he was in his son, how the boy would never amount to anything, and how he was destined for certain failure. This treatment by his father, of course, only exacerbated his poor self-esteem, agitation, and anxiety. Kevin responded with a degree of hostility and disrespect that matched his father's harsh criticisms. No matter what Kevin did, his father found fault with him—with all his poor grades, there was a lot of ammunition for his dad—and, no matter what his father asked him to do, Kevin flatly refused. His mother felt sorry for the boy, but in spite of her lectures, begging, and divorce threats, the father would not back down. To compensate for her husband's criticism and complaints, the mother overindulged Kevin. Of course this did not improve Kevin's emotional health, did not make him a better or more cooperative student, and did nothing to improve his relationship with his father. If anything, Mom's enabling and spoiling intervention caused more resentment in the father and more defiance in Kevin.

After several years of failed herbal treatments, Kevin's mother took him to see a psychologist who also believed, as the teacher did, that Kevin had AD/HD. So on the advice of a psychologist—who lacked the medical degree and license to prescribe medications himself—the pediatrician treated Kevin with an assortment of amphetamines to try and get the boy to be more cooperative with classroom rules and make a greater effort in school. Unfortunately, Kevin started having problems with his medications' side effects, including worsening symptoms of anxiety and agitation. His schoolwork improved a little bit but, by the time I evaluated him, his grades were all D's and F's, even while taking the Ritalin that his pediatrician had gone back to prescribing again.

I stopped the amphetamine drugs, started Kevin on an SSRI antidepressant for his anxiety, and counseled the parents on effective parenting approaches to stop the father's harsh criticism and the mother's indulging. He started feeling better soon after stopping the Ritalin, but the teachers immediately complained to the mother that Kevin was more restless than normal after only two weeks on the new medication. Even though his grades were failing and his emotional health was declining while on the past medications, the teachers put a great deal of pressure on his mother to get Kevin back on Ritalin because he was quieter in their classrooms when he took this drug. I advised the mother to find a school advocate to help her defend her son from the inappropriate medical instructions coming from his teachers and to allow his anxiety medication a chance to work, which usually takes six weeks.

SOCIAL PHOBIA

Social Phobia typically starts in the midteens, although some children begin having symptoms earlier. The symptoms of Social Phobia may begin shortly after a stressful or humiliating experience. If your child has Social Phobia, he will likely cry, freeze, be clingy, remain mute, or throw a tantrum when placed in an anxiety-provoking social situation.

CRITERIA FOR DIAGNOSIS

The following are the criteria for Social Phobia in children:

1. Your child with Social Phobia will experience marked and persistent fear of social or performance situations in which he feels scrutinized by strangers. Your child fears he will humiliate or embarrass himself by doing something foolish or by exposing his anxiety symptoms. Your child would need to have demonstrated that he is *able* to engage in age-appropriate social relationships when he is with familiar people who do not provoke his anxiety. Consequently, his ability clarifies that it is the anxiety that causes your child's avoidance of social interaction not

the lack of social skills. Your child's Social Phobia must occur with peers, not just in interactions with adults.

2. The unavoidable exposure to the feared social situations causes your child great anxiety. He may cry, freeze, panic, cling to you, or even have a tantrum in an attempt to escape the anxiety-provoking environment.

3. Your child may or may not recognize that his fear is excessive or unreasonable. Generally, the younger the child, the less likely he is to have the perspective required to acknowledge his anxiety is excessive.

4. All attempts are made by your child to avoid the anxiety-provoking situations. When required to take part in the feared social experience, your child endures it with intense anxiety and distress.

5. Your child has to have been experiencing symptoms of Social Phobia for at least six months to qualify for this diagnosis.

QUALIFIERS

Beyond the symptoms of Social Phobia listed above, your child must meet a few conditions as well.

- The Social Phobia symptoms must interfere with your child's functioning socially and academically. Your child must also have marked distress about having this uncomfortable condition, which causes such a disruption of his life.
- Your child's anxiety symptoms cannot be the direct result of illicit drug or alcohol intoxication or withdrawal. In such a case, your child would be described as having a Substance-Induced Anxiety Disorder.
- When medication side effects are the cause of your child's Social Phobia symptoms, your child's condition would be termed a Medication-Induced Anxiety Disorder.
- The Social Phobia symptoms cannot be the result of a medical condition that can mimic anxiety.
- If your child's symptoms better fit a different anxiety disorder, then your child would not be diagnosed with Social Phobia.

TREATMENT OF SOCIAL PHOBIA

Once the diagnosis of Social Phobia has been confirmed and you decide that psychiatric medications are the right choice for your child, the prescription medications most often used in the treatment of Social Phobia are as follows:

- Prozac (fluoxetine), Paxil (paroxetine), Zoloft (sertraline), Luvox (fluvoxamine), Celexa (citalopram), Lexapro (escitalopram), Effexor XR (venlafaxine), Cymbalta (duloxetine)
- Tofranil (imipramine), Pamelor (nortriptyline), Elavil (amitriptyline), Sinequan (doxepin)
- Buspar (buspirone)
- Inderal (propranolol), Tenormin (atenolol)
- Benzodiazepines: Xanax (alprazolam), Ativan (lorazepam), Klonapin (clonazepam), Valium (diazepam)

For further details on the risks and benefits of each of these medications, refer to part 3. The other biological, psychological, and social approaches to treatment are covered in part 4.

CASE EXAMPLE

Jason was twelve years old, and should have been starting the eighth grade, when his mother brought him to my office for an evaluation. His mother had been threatened by the school principal and attendance officer that they would refer Jason to the juvenile justice system if he did not return to school promptly, but in spite of her best efforts to get him to attend, he simply refused. He had been attending school up through sixth grade, earning excellent grades, when his parents separated and Jason's emotional state changed. At our assessment, he told me he felt very nervous in crowds, was extremely uncomfortable about meeting new people, and hated to be the focus of his classmates' attention when called upon by the teacher. Jason explained to me that when his classmates were watching him give an answer in class, he felt "a rush of emotions and a great urgency to escape" their scrutiny. He also had difficulty catching his breath, could feel his heart racing and his stomach turning, yet when he was at home or in the company of people with whom he was familiar, he felt none of this fear. Jason wanted to attend school with his friends but the fear of social situations was too much for him to bear.

I recommended that Jason start regular counseling to address his social anxiety by learning techniques and strategies to overcome his discomfort. I also started an antidepressant of the SSRI family that had been particularly helpful to a family member who also had anxiety. The mother was encouraged to request that the school principal have her son assessed for special education services at the school and to determine what changes if any might help Jason feel more comfortable attending school again.

PANIC DISORDER

Panic Disorder is another one of the anxiety group of disorders. Your child can develop any one of the anxiety disorders starting at an early age. Panic Disorder, or *panic attacks*, can develop after a terrifying or traumatic event or can develop without warning. If a parent suffers with any of the anxiety disorders, then their child is seven times more likely to develop an anxiety disorder. Panic attacks are frightening to anyone, but to a child who has a limited knowledge of medical science, the fear can be extreme. The fear experienced during a panic attack can be so consuming, your child may actually believe he is dying.

CRITERIA FOR DIAGNOSIS

Diagnosis with Panic Disorder requires both criteria 1 and 2. Because panic attacks can occur during the course of other psychiatric conditions such as Social Phobia, it is important that your doctor be given all the information you can collect regarding the context and conditions under which your child has panic attacks. Criteria for Panic Disorder are:

- Your child experiences unexpected panic attacks with or without an initiating stressor. The attacks are recurrent. A panic attack consists of a discrete period of intense fear that develops abruptly, usually lasts from 20 to 60 minutes, and peaks in 10 minutes. Along with the intense anxiety your child would also experience four of the following thirteen symptoms:

    - Pounding heart beat or racing heart beat that your child can feel in his chest
    - Sweating
    - Trembling and shaking
    - Sensations of having shortness of breath or smothering, though breathing is normal
    - Feeling like he is choking
    - Chest pains or tightness that feels like a heart attack to your child
    - Nausea, stomachaches, or abdominal distress
    - Feeling dizzy, unsteady, lightheaded, or faint
    - Feeling detached from himself or as if the world around him was unreal
    - Fear of losing control or afraid of going crazy

- Fear of dying
- Numbness or tingling sensations
- Sudden chills or feeling hot flushes

■ Following at least one of your child's panic attacks, he has experienced one of the following three symptoms for a period of time that lasted at least one month, possibly more:

- Your child has a persistent fear that he will have additional panic attacks.
- Your child continues to worry about the consequences of his past panic attack. He may fear that he is actually going crazy or developing a heart condition that might end his life.
- Your child's behavior has changed significantly as a result of the panic attacks. For example, he may quit groups or activities that he once enjoyed, due to fear of future panic attacks or their consequences.

QUALIFIERS

To establish definitively that your child has Panic Disorder, the following conditions must also apply.

■ For Panic Disorder to be the correct diagnosis for your child, his panic symptoms cannot be the direct result of illicit drug or alcohol intoxication or withdrawal. Also, medication side effects cannot be responsible for your child's panic symptoms for the diagnosis of Panic Disorder to apply.

■ Medical conditions, such as hyperthyroidism, cannot be the cause of your child's panic symptoms for Panic Disorder to be the correct diagnosis.

■ Panic Disorder is a condition that can be accompanied by *agoraphobia*. Agoraphobia is the fear of venturing outside of the places your child perceives as safe, such as home. When your child is faced with having to leave "safe" environments, he becomes extremely anxious. Typical situations in which agoraphobic children feel insecure and fearful are being in crowded places, standing in line, leaving the house alone, or traveling on a bus or train. Agoraphobia is not always present in Panic Disorder. Therefore, when making the diagnosis of Panic

Disorder, your doctor will distinguish whether it is with or without agoraphobia.

TREATMENT OF PANIC DISORDER

Once the diagnosis of Panic Disorder has been confirmed and you opt to use psychiatric medications to treat your child's Panic Disorder, the medication treatment usually involves a combination of drugs. The following medications are used for long-term treatment and the control of future panic attacks.

- Prozac (fluoxetine), Paxil (paroxetine), Zoloft (sertraline), Luvox (fluvoxamine), Celexa (citalopram), Lexapro (escitalopram), Effexor XR (venlafaxine), Cymbalta (duloxetine)
- Tofranil (imipramine), Pamelor (nortriptyline), Elavil (amitriptyline) and Sinequan (doxepin)

For the treatment of Panic Disorder, doctors usually supplement the above drugs with a fast-acting medication for the immediate relief of the panic attack in progress. The medications used to stop a panic attack can be very addicting. Therefore, the following must be used with caution, on an intermittent basis and only as needed. These are the medications that bring a patient the security of knowing he has the power to control the attacks.

- Benzodiazepines: Xanax (alprazolam), Ativan (lorazepam)

My patients have carried their benzodiazepines with them for years, never actually having to take them, because the Panic Disorder was under good control. But they have explained to me that, having the medication on hand, they no longer fear the onset of an attack, and rarely find the attacks occur. To a child with Panic Disorder, benzodiazepines are like the safety net under the tightrope walker. With the medication, they can go about their business without worry. Without the benzodiazepines, they are afraid to leave their homes. Unfortunately, some children have a paradoxically opposite reaction to benzodiazepines. Some children become more anxious and agitated on these medications. Therefore, proceed with caution if benzodiazepines are prescribed.

For further details on the risks and benefits of each of these medications, refer to part 3. The other biological, psychological, and social approaches to treatment are covered in part 4.

CASE EXAMPLES

I treated a boy, Mike, who at nine years old developed panic attacks after his parents' friends, a man and his wife, died in a car accident and left their children orphaned. Mike was close friends with the orphaned children, so after their parents' death, he lived in constant fear that harm would come to his own parents. Mike was extremely worried about his own parents' welfare to the point that he needed to know their whereabouts at all times; he had panic attacks at school if he could not reach his mother or father by phone. The anxiety attacks so upset him that he feared the next attack as they were unpredictable; sometimes he did *not* have an attack when he was worried about his parents' safety, sometimes he did. Mike was anxiety free when he was at home or while he accompanied his parents anywhere else; as long as he was with them, he did not fear having a panic attack.

Prior to the tragedy, Mike was a very happy, easygoing boy who enjoyed school and sports, and was a very independent person with no separation issues or anxiety. But after the accident, he lived in constant fear of his next panic attack. Once during a visit to my office, before his medications started to work, he had been asked to wait in the waiting room while his mother and I spoke privately about her concerns for Mike. After ten minutes, he knocked on the door; unfortunately, my secretary had stepped out momentarily, so his knocking was not answered promptly. This really worried Mike; after knocking repeatedly on the door without a response, he had a panic attack complete with yelling and crying that could be heard throughout my office suite. Mike began refusing to go to school so he could keep an eye on his mother.

Mike had already started psychotherapy with an independent therapist in town prior to his evaluation with me, which left only the biological aspect of care to address. I treated Mike with an SSRI antidepressant for long-term coverage of his Panic Disorder and, with plenty of warning, I also prescribed a benzodiazepine for the immediate relief of his attacks. Both treatments helped a great deal and after a year of stable recovery while taking the medication and attending his therapy sessions, I was able to stop Mike's meds without a recurrence of his symptoms.

In another case of Panic Disorder, I treated a fourteen-year-old boy, Aaron, who had developed panic attacks over the twelve months prior to his assessment with me. Aaron was an excellent student, taking honors courses at the public high school. He loved playing his saxophone and wanted to join the marching band, he had many friends, and was well respected by the faculty. Aaron's fear was that he might not make it to the bathroom before he soiled his pants accidentally, so the location and the accessibility of the nearest bathroom was always on his mind. Prior to developing his fear of public humiliation, he had not experienced any anxiety or panic; he had actually been very well adjusted. But since the panic attacks had started, he had difficulty getting ready for school in the morning, as he anticipated the amount of time he would have to spend waiting at the bus stop and riding the school bus—a time during which he would not have access to a bathroom. He feared taking part in the marching band because of the involved process of getting in and out of the uniform and the extended period of time he would be required to stay on the field in formation. He did march in the band and wait at the bus stop, occasionally, without actually having a panic attack, but never without experiencing the constant fear and dread that at any moment he might have an episode. His panic attacks included symptoms of intense anxiety, tearfulness, and such severe fear of humiliation—that he might become incontinent—that he experienced a sense of derealization, which is the sensation that nothing in one's surroundings feels real or normal as if in a dream.

Aaron was treated with an antidepressant in the SSRI class for long-term coverage and a benzodiazepine for more immediate relief. Unfortunately, Aaron did not do well on the benzodiazepine; it actually appeared to make his anxiety worse. I replaced the benzodiazepine with a nonaddicting anxiety aid that is not quite as effective for most individuals' panic symptoms but it is generally very well tolerated. On this combination, Aaron did very well and was able to march in the school band and wait at the bus stop comfortably and with confidence that his panic attacks were no longer going to control his life.

13

Obsessive Compulsive Disorder

Obsessive Compulsive Behavior

OBSESSIVE COMPULSIVE DISORDER (OCD) is another one of the anxiety group of disorders. The average age for the onset of OCD is ten years old. Children as young as five have been identified as having OCD. The prevalence of OCD is estimated to range from 1 to 3.6 percent in adolescents. For children, the most common symptoms of OCD are fears of contamination, compulsive washing, and avoidance of "contaminated objects." Another common OCD symptom in children is repetitive checking for such things as unlocked doors, or for the safety of family members.

The rituals and compulsions of children with OCD can take many unusual and sometimes bizarre forms, and can absorb a great deal of a child's time, making it difficult for them to be productive. For example, I treated a six-year-boy who could not go to school except in a very specific outfit that he insisted on wearing every day. If his mother tried to confiscate the outfit so she could wash it, he would have a meltdown and would try to sneak this special, but very dirty, outfit out of the laundry basket to wear again.

CRITERIA FOR DIAGNOSIS

IF YOUR CHILD HAS Obsessive Compulsive Disorder, he may have either obsessions or compulsions or both.

OBSESSIONS

Criteria for obsessions include all of the following symptoms:

- Your child has recurring thoughts or impulses that are felt by him to be intrusive, unwanted, and inappropriate. The intrusive thoughts and impulses are distressing to your child and cause him significant anxiety.
- These unwanted thoughts and impulses are not just excessive worries about real-life problems, such as the ruminations that depressed children often have. The intrusive thoughts of OCD are often strange, unreasonable, and inappropriate, as perceived by your child.
- Your child with Obsessive Compulsive Disorder attempts to ignore or suppress these thoughts and impulses. Additionally, he tries to neutralize these unwanted, distressing thoughts with another thought or action intended to eliminate them.
- There is the realization by your child that these distressing impulses are simply a product of his mind. When children believe that some entity outside of themselves, such as aliens or ghosts, are placing these thoughts in their heads, this represents an entirely different disorder and this symptom is referred to as *thought insertion*.

COMPULSIONS

Criteria for compulsions include both of the following:

- Your child feels driven to repeat specific behaviors or mental acts in response to his obsessions. Your child with OCD would have very specific, self-scripted, self-imposed, rigidly applied rules governing how his ritualistic compulsions are carried out. Examples of the typical rituals or compulsions that OCD patients have are hand washing, ordering, checking, tapping, touching, counting, repeating, or praying obsessively.
- You would not include the arranging, counting, and organizing of trading cards as proof that your child has OCD. His compulsions have to

be behaviors that serve no real purpose. Straightening and cleaning, for example, are not OCD behaviors in themselves. But, if your child cleans and recleans something that he has already cleaned perfectly well, then this would apply. An example of how a normal behavior becomes an OCD symptom was demonstrated in an eleven-year-old boy I treated. This boy took four hours to shower and get ready for bed every night. If during his showering ritual he did not complete one of the steps properly, he would have to start over from the beginning.

- Your child feels very uncomfortable and anxious until he is able to complete his rituals. Completing his rituals will bring your child some temporary relief until the next compulsion starts. The compulsions can recur repeatedly one right after the other. This can leave your child exhausted, still unfulfilled, and ashamed of his powerlessness to stop these behaviors.

- Your child's compulsions are aimed at preventing or undoing some dreaded event he has decided will befall him or his family if he is unable to complete his ritual. The ritual and the disaster he is attempting to prevent are not necessarily logically connected.

- A good example of how the compulsions of OCD are not necessarily connected to the feared disaster can be seen in the case of a twelve-year-old boy I treated. He was compelled to walk in and out of his front door exactly five times prior to allowing anyone else in his family to enter the home. He believed that if the ritual were not done each time the family entered the home, his family would be gravely harmed or even killed. When returning from a family outing, if a sibling had to rush into the house for a bathroom emergency before he was able to complete his ritual, he would become hysterical and collapse on the ground in tears.

Qualifiers

In determining the diagnosis of Obsessive Compulsive Disorder several qualifiers need to be considered.

- Your child may or may never recognize that his obsessions and compulsions are excessive and unreasonable. At some point during the course of their illness, most adults *are* able to realize how counterproductive and unreasonable their behaviors are. Children do not necessarily come to this insight.

- The obsessions and compulsions cause your child significant distress. The rituals consume a significant amount of time each day, that is more than an hour per day. These behaviors interfere with your child's normal activities and impair his functioning at home, socially with friends, or academically at school.
- To make a diagnosis of OCD, your child's obsessions cannot be restricted to one specific topic or activity that would make a different diagnosis more accurate. For example, if your child is only obsessed with her weight and what she eats, and nothing else, then an Eating Disorder would be a more appropriate diagnosis.
- Obsessive Compulsive Disorder is *not* the correct diagnosis if your child's symptoms of obsessions and compulsions are caused by drug abuse or a prescribed medication.
- If a general medical illness is causing your child's symptoms, then OCD would *not* be the right diagnosis.

TREATMENT OF OBSESSIVE COMPULSIVE DISORDER

ONCE THE DIAGNOSIS of Obsessive Compulsive Disorder has been confirmed and you decide that psychiatric medications are the right choice for your child, the prescription medications most often used in the treatment of Obsessive Compulsive Disorder are as follows:

- Prozac (fluoxetine), Paxil (paroxetine), Zoloft (sertraline), Luvox (fluvoxamine), Celexa (citalopram), Lexapro (escitalopram), Effexor XR (venlafaxine), Cymbalta (duloxetine)
- Anafranil (clomipramine)

In general, for the treatment of OCD, your child will require much higher doses of medication than are usually given for depression or anxiety. I usually need to provide a child with double, even triple the dose typically taken for depression. At a lower dose, my child patients may still be suffering with obsessions and compulsions, while at a higher dose their symptoms are well controlled.

For further details on the risks and benefits of each of these medications, refer to part 3. The other biological, psychological, and social approaches to treatment are covered in part 4.

CASE EXAMPLES

PETER WAS TEN years old when he came to my office for his first psychiatric assessment. His parents explained that for most of his life he had been an anxious child with some obsessive qualities but, over the past year, his symptoms had become much more serious. The year before I met Peter, he had had a very rough year in Catholic school due to a punitive teacher who taught his fourth-grade class. His grades fell from A's and B's to C's and D's, he tried to avoid attending school altogether, and at times he had to be dragged to school crying and screaming.

By the end of fourth grade, Peter was having symptoms consistent with the diagnosis of Obsessive Compulsive Disorder (OCD). He was obsessed with cleanliness and germs. He could get so anxious that he would become nauseous to the point of almost vomiting. He so feared germs that he refused to eat from any plate or with silverware from outside of his home, which required his mother to carry these supplies from home whenever the family ate out or was invited for a meal at the home of a friend. Already a picky eater, now Peter could not eat food if anyone other than his mother had touched the food prior to serving it to him, and he flatly refused to eat food that was left over, even if he was the only person to have eaten from the left-over dish. If anyone took a sip from a glass from which he had been drinking, he did not want to continue to drink from that same glass and would pour the remaining liquid down the drain. Wearing socks was only possible for Peter if he placed his shoes on his feet immediately after his socks were on, otherwise he became too anxious to continue wearing his socks. Years earlier, Peter had viewed a TV program about a boy who had been locked in a closet. After seeing this show, he became obsessed with sleeping with his lights on in the bedroom, with all the closet doors shut completely. He was very anxious about being picked up at school on time by his parents, and he obsessed over his and his family's schedules repeatedly asking his mother for reassurance about her plans and their schedule. In spite of his extreme fear of germs, Peter was *not* a child who needed to wash his hands frequently. Nonetheless, he struggled with a number of symptoms, including difficulty concentrating when he was anxious, ruminating, easy irritability, low self-esteem, and social isolation; eventually he was refusing to do his homework at all.

Peter's symptoms did resolve on antidepressant medications but only after several trials of different medications and only once I arrived at an effective combination of an SSRI and another nonselective serotonin reuptake inhibitor. On psychiatric medications, Peter was not completely symptom free but he was functioning a great deal better than he had been prior to the start of medications.

Julie was a little more complicated diagnostically; as is often the case, she had developed a second psychiatric diagnosis before the first disorder had been resolved. Julie was ten years old when her mother brought her to me for treatment because the counseling she had been receiving was not doing enough to treat her anxiety, especially since the emergence of the second disorder. Julie had a history of anxiety, obsessions, and compulsions since she was four years old, which included the symptoms of washing her hands repeatedly until they were raw and bleeding; pulling out the hair on her head and eyebrows and lashes; and obsessing about how her clothing—especially her socks—were fitting; also, she would blow her nose continually until it was bleeding.

Her parents were trying to get help from a therapist for Julie's problems when her baby sister died a crib death at four months old. With her sister's death, Julie developed panic attacks—episodes of intense fear, shaking, difficulty catching her breath, chills, nausea, pounding heartbeat, and dizziness—on top of her OCD symptoms. Initially, her parents tried to address her anxiety, panic, and OCD with counseling alone but, over the intervening six years before I met her, Julie's symptoms continued unabated and became more ingrained as habits. Eventually, her fear became so great that she was afraid to go to school and in the morning she would beg, cry, and plead with her mother to allow her to stay home from school. Julie had even resorted to sticking herself with a sewing needle, believing that the injury would provide an excuse to stay home from school. Surprisingly, she was a gifted student, earning straight A grades in her fifth-grade class; and her mother volunteered in her classroom as well.

I recommended that Julie continue to receive psychotherapy to address her anxiety and to learn coping strategies, but I also told the mother that it would be helpful for the parents to get some counseling of their own, specifically to learn parenting strategies for coping with Julie's anxiety and refusal to attend school. Luckily, the same class of psychiatric medication that treats OCD also treats Panic Disorder, and Julie's symptoms did respond to the medications in time. For the immediate relief of panic attacks, Clonidine helped her a little bit until the SSRI had a chance to start working.

14

PTSD:
Post Traumatic Stress
Disorder

Post Traumatic Stress Disorder

Post Traumatic Stress Disorder (PTSD) develops after your child is exposed to a traumatic event. Your child can be traumatized by an injury or abuse he experiences directly, or by a frightening event that he witnesses. PTSD describes the characteristic set of symptoms that develop in your child following such a trauma.

Criteria for Diagnosis

The criteria for Post Traumatic Stress Disorder include some or all of each of the following four categories of symptoms. The symptoms that are present from categories 2, 3, and 4 have to be present in your child for at least one month. If your child has been traumatized and is having symptoms, but they are not severe enough to qualify for PTSD, he may be more appropriately diagnosed as having an Adjustment Disorder. The four categories of criteria and the symptoms in each are as follows:

1. Your child must meet both of the following conditions for the diagnosis of Post Traumatic Stress Disorder to apply.

- Your child has experienced a traumatic event that either was directly injurious to him, or he witnessed an event so disturbing that he believed that he or a loved one could have been killed or seriously injured. Children can be traumatized by a variety of frightening events that might not be as disturbing to an adult, such as sexual molestation, physical abuse, early childhood neglect and abandonment, the death of a parent, witnessing a rape, watching parents being arrested, or witnessing domestic violence between parents.

- Your child's response to the trauma he has witnessed or experienced is to feel intense fear, horror, and helplessness. Alternatively, some children behave in a disorganized, agitated manner, as their expression of the horror they have experienced.

2. The traumatic event is reexperienced by your child in at least one of the following ways (your child may have more than just one of these symptoms).

   Your child's thoughts are repeatedly intruded upon by distressing recollections of the traumatic event. These memories can take the form of images, thoughts, or emotional reactions that your child experienced at the time of the trauma. Also, your child may express these recollections through their play. For example, she might reenact the events as she plays out the scenario repetitively with dolls that take on the roles of the persons involved in the trauma.

   - Recurring, distressing dreams about the trauma start to torment your child. Within several weeks, for younger children with PTSD, the event specific dreams may be replaced by generalized nightmares of monsters and other frightening themes.
   - Your child has episodes during which he feels as if he were reliving the traumatic incident. These episodes, which are often referred to as a *flashback*, can include illusions, hallucinations, and dissociative experiences of reliving the event. In some younger children, the original trauma is reenacted by the child as the manifestation of his flashback.
   - Your child experiences intense emotional distress after encountering anything that resembles or symbolizes any aspect of the past traumatic event.

- After encountering something that resembles or symbolizes an aspect of the trauma, your child becomes a great deal more emotionally sensitive and overreacts to minor stressors.

3. Children with Post Traumatic Stress Disorder consistently avoid anything that reminds them of the trauma or anyone who was associated with the event. Your child experiences a general numbing in response to the people and activities that once brought him joy. These symptoms in your child must be exhibited by having three or more of the following seven criteria.

- Your child makes a concerted effort to avoid thoughts, feelings, or conversations that remind him of the trauma.
- Your child also makes a great effort to avoid activities, places, and people that remind him of the disturbing incident.
- Children with PTSD are unable to recall an important aspect about the traumatic event.
- Child victims lose interest and stop participating in the activities they once enjoyed prior to the trauma.
- Your child feels detached and estranged from people who were once close to him.
- The range of emotions that a traumatized child feels is restricted. For example, he may not be able to have loving feelings or feelings of trust.
- A trauma victim does not have a vision of his future. He does not imagine a life ahead in which he can fulfill his dreams. To your child with PTSD, the world is not a safe place and he does not expect to have a normal life span.

4. Children with Post Traumatic Stress Disorder are in a persistent state of heightened arousal or overstimulated hyperactivity. Your traumatized child would have two, possibly more of these following symptoms:

- Children with PTSD have a difficult time falling asleep. They also have trouble staying asleep and often are awake all night, tossing and turning.
- Your child is easily irritated, what you might describe as being moody or having mood swings. Your child with PTSD has anger outbursts or rage attacks.

- If your child has been traumatized, he has a very difficult time concentrating and paying attention.
- PTSD victims are *hypervigilant*. Hypervigilant children are in a state of constant, fearful watchfulness. Your child with PTSD is always on the lookout for approaching danger.
- Your child has an exaggerated startle response. That is to say, your child jumps out of his skin when confronted with the unexpected.

This last set of symptoms represents another of the common pathways for the misdiagnosis of children. Here among these five symptoms are the same symptoms for AD/HD (poor attention), Major Depressive Disorder (irritability, poor sleep, poor concentration), and even Bipolar (irritability, sleeplessness). The reality that the same symptoms reappear in several different diagnoses is exactly why it is so important to get a careful, thorough evaluation by a trained specialist.

QUALIFIERS

THE SYMPTOMS OF Post Traumatic Stress Disorder must have caused the child significant distress or impaired his ability to continue functioning normally, as he had prior to the traumatic event.

Post Traumatic Stress Disorder is sometimes exhibited a little differently in children than it is in adults:

- Young children develop what is referred to as *omen formation*. They come to believe that there had been signs that, had they been more observant, they would have caught, which would have warned them of the coming trauma. They start to watch for these omens to avoid future disasters.
- Really young children, toddlers, have more generalized anxiety symptoms, such as separation anxiety or stranger fears, and fears of animals or monsters.
- The situations the children try to avoid may not have an apparent connection to the trauma.
- The symbols and items they fixate on may not have a clear relationship to the disaster.

Treatment of Post Traumatic Stress Disorder

ONCE THE DIAGNOSIS of Post Traumatic Stress Disorder has been confirmed and you decide that psychiatric medications are the right choice for your child, the prescription medications most often used in the treatment of Post Traumatic Stress Disorder are as follows:

- Prozac (fluoxetine), Paxil (paroxetine), Zoloft (sertraline), Luvox (fluvoxamine), Celexa (citalopram), Lexapro (escitalopram), Effexor XR (venlafaxine), Cymbalta (duloxetine)
- Tofranil (imipramine), Pamelor (nortriptyline), Elavil (amitriptyline) and Sinequan (doxepin)
- Catapres (clonidine) or Tenex (guanfacine)
- Desyrel (trazadone) for nightmares and insomnia

For further details on the risks and benefits of each of these medications, refer to part 3. The other biological, psychological, and social approaches to treatment are covered in part 4.

Case Examples

KRISTEN CAME TO my office with her mother for an evaluation when she was thirteen years old. Initially, she was too ashamed and embarrassed to tell her story, so her mother told me that Kristen had been sexually abused by her second stepfather from age eight to eleven, and that the first stepfather had physically and verbally abused both mother and child from the time her daughter was two years old until she was eight. Of course, her mother was aware of the physical abuse that Kristen had endured but did not learn of the sexual abuse until the girl told her mother one year after the mother's divorce from the abuser. The perpetrator had convinced Kristen that if she revealed the truth about the sexual abuse to her mother or anyone else, great harm would come to her and her mother.

Kristen was eventually able to share with me that she was worrying all the time that someone would break into her house or follow her home and hurt her, so she was afraid to be home alone. She said she had problems sleeping, nightmares, and intrusive recollections of the trauma, and trouble concentrating and that lately she did not feel like being with her friends. Furthermore, she felt confused, depressed, tearful, and easily irritated most of the time. In spite of all that she had to cope with, she was still earning good grades but finding it more and more difficult to do so.

Kristen had started to have anxiety and depressive symptoms, which prompted her mother to enter her into psychotherapy. The diagnosis of PTSD was initially made based on the physical abuse, because the history of the sexual abuse did not come out until the year after therapy had begun. During that first year of counseling, Kristen was not ready to work on her recovery and she cried throughout many of the sessions, never revealing the more painful secret that she carried. Without a complete history, the therapist concluded that all of Kristen's symptoms were the result of the known physical abuse. Once Kristen was able to talk about her abuse in its entirety, her therapy started to progress but then her symptoms also amplified; as a result her therapist thought it best if Kristen were evaluated for treatment with medications.

I started Kristen on antidepressants, and after some adjustments she felt much better. With the relief that she found on the psychiatric medication, she was able to engage more fully in her psychotherapy and thus move forward in her recovery. Though no amount of medication or counseling can completely erase the painful memories of child abuse, with the proper combinations of treatments and the judicious use of medications, children like Kristen can enjoy a full and happy life again.

At the request of the fourth-grade teacher, a woman brought her nine-year-old granddaughter, Sara, to my office for treatment of the girl's AD/HD. Sara's teacher had provided the grandmother—Sara's legal guardian—with a report card and the results of standardized testing that showed that her granddaughter was doing very poorly in school and that she was having trouble concentrating in the classroom.

The grandmother explained that the girl's mother had lost custody multiple times to Child Protective Services due to the mother's use of methamphetamine and neglect of Sara and her little brother. Although it was not known with certainty, it was presumed by her guardian that the girl had been exposed to various street drugs during gestation. While her mother was high on drugs, Sara had been exposed to severe domestic violence and had witnessed her mother doing drugs and having sex. While living with their mother, Sara and her brother had missed many meals and were often unsupervised. In fact it was Sara who, starting when she was only five years old, tried to take care of her younger brother. Sara's mother had played the courts for nine years, repeatedly going before the family court judge and promising to complete drug rehab, begging for another chance, regaining custody, only to fail again. Every time that the mother would be awarded custody of Sara and her brother, she would return to using drugs, and yet her parental rights were never terminated. Every time that the mother lost custody, Sara's grandmother would be given temporary guardianship until the mother had completed the next course of drug rehab.

Her grandmother explained that Sara was suffering from severe anxiety and had a constant dread of being returned to her mother only to suffer the consequences of the parent's next broken promise. Sara bit her nails, sucked her thumb, had motor twitches, was easily startled, cried often and easily, and had nightmares about being abducted. She hoarded food and could not tolerate any kind of discord among family members in her grandmother's home. When there was an argument, Sara would weep and curl up in a ball on her grandmother's lap.

Though Sara had failing grades in fourth-grade, her grades in third had been much better and she had never been a behavior-problem child at school in any grade. The diagnosis, as I saw it, was clearly PTSD, but the fourth-grade teacher believed that Sara had AD/HD, to explain Sara's poor marks, and had convinced the grandmother of the same at the teacher-parent conferences. This misconception about Sara's diagnosis, which had been planted by the teacher in the grandmother's mind, required a great deal of time and effort on my part to re-educate the grandmother about the correct diagnosis and the criteria for the diagnoses of both AD/HD and PTSD, including the fact that trouble concentrating is a symptom of PTSD as well, not just exclusively of AD/HD.

Once she better understood the girl's condition, I had the grandmother's support and cooperation for treatment. Sara started seeing a therapist to work on the issues surrounding her personal trauma, not just the court-appointed counselor whose job it was to work on the family reunification with the mother. I did not prescribe an amphetamine-class drug, as her teacher had wanted me to; instead I gave Sara an antidepressant medication. After a couple of trials and failures due to side effects, I was able to identify an antidepressant that, at the right dose, brought her great relief. I wish I could say that Sara's case was an oddity and that rarely do I see patients whose teachers have diagnosed and sent them to the doctor for a prescription of one of the amphetamine-class drugs, but the truth is that Sara's case is illustrative of a very common scenario that takes place in my office frequently.

15

SCHIZOPHRENIA

SCHIZOPHRENIA

SCHIZOPHRENIA RARELY OCCURS in children. Most people develop the first signs of Schizophrenia between the ages of seventeen and twenty-five. Therefore, if your child develops psychotic symptoms as he reaches late adolescence, the diagnosis of Schizophrenia is increasingly more likely. Of course, there are other disorders aside from Schizophrenia that can cause psychotic symptoms, such as severe depression or a drug-induced psychosis.

Psychotic symptoms are beliefs and perceptions that do not conform to reality. An example of a psychotic perception is hearing the voices of people who are not really there. Because the side effects of the medications that treat Schizophrenia have a great potential for causing severe and permanent damage, it is of critical importance to be sure about the diagnosis.

CRITERIA FOR DIAGNOSIS

THE DIAGNOSIS OF Schizophrenia is based on the presence of two or more of the following symptoms. An exception can be made to the two-symptom rule if your child's one symptom includes either (1) a delusion that is really bizarre, or (2) a hallucination of a voice that keeps up a running commentary on

everything your child is doing and thinking, or the hallucination is of two people having a conversation. The criteria of Schizophrenia are:

1. **Delusions:** These are beliefs that do not conform with reality. An
   example of a common delusion experienced by people with Schizophrenia is believing that they are a religious figure, such as Jesus or the
   Virgin Mary. Another delusion common in Schizophrenia is the belief
   that you are visited by aliens or that you communicate with aliens
   through some device implanted in your body. These would be examples
   of bizarre delusions. A less bizarre but common example of delusions
   is the belief that you can read other people's minds or that, conversely,
   your thoughts are being broadcast to everyone around you.
2. **Hallucinations:** These are perceptions (hearing or seeing things)
   that are not really present. In Schizophrenia, the hallucinations that
   are experienced most often are the auditory hallucinations, hearing
   things that are really not there. If your child tells you he is hearing the
   voices of people that are not real, then you should suspect either
   Schizophrenia or a psychotic depression. Whereas, your child's reports
   of visual hallucinations (seeing things that are not real) should raise
   your suspicions that drugs may be involved. Visual hallucinations are
   more common in drug-induced psychosis.
3. **Disorganized Speech:** People with Schizophrenia often cannot carry
   on a coherent conversation. Their thoughts and ideas are expressed in
   a disorganized, disjointed manner. It is often difficult to understand what
   they are trying to say even though their words may be articulated sufficiently. In midsentence, they suddenly seem to just stop their train of
   thought and jump to an entirely unrelated topic without even pausing.
4. **Grossly Disorganized or Catatonic Behavior:** Disorganized behaviors include unpredictable agitation or strange, odd activities that
   have no purpose. One example of a typical disorganized behavior of
   Schizophrenia is collecting plastic bags out of the public trash bins and
   pushing them around town in a shopping cart, while looking for more
   trash to store at home. Another example is wearing multiple overcoats,
   scarves, and gloves on a hot day. Sometimes the bizarre behaviors of
   Schizophrenia include sexual acts, such as masturbating in public.
   However, this is usually done in an oblivious, self-absorbed way rather
   than as an act of exhibitionism.
       Catatonic behavior usually includes extreme slowing of movement
   to almost a standstill. Your child with catatonic behavior might be

mute or barely responsive while still appearing to hear what you are saying to him. Sometimes catatonic persons hold odd body positions or
gestures for hours at a time. They actively resist attempts to be moved.

5. **Negative Symptoms:** *Affective flattening, alogia,* and *avolition* are all
examples of the negative symptoms of Schizophrenia. Let us define
them one at a time.

If all expression appears to leave your child's face, he seems to be
emotionally unresponsive, and he makes no eye contact, then you are
looking at affective flattening. Although a person with affective flattening can smile or show emotion at times, the range of expression is
very limited. A flattened affect is seen in other disorders as well, such
as severe depression or complicated grief.

Alogia is simply a reduced amount of speech, also referred to as a
poverty of speech. This is not the same as a refusal to speak.

Avolition describes the lack of activity seen in Schizophrenia. A person with
avolition may sit for hours at a time showing little interest in participating in
any kind of social, recreational, or productive endeavors. Be aware that some
of the medications used in psychiatry can cause your child to be extremely sluggish or appear like a "zombie," as parents have described it to me. For your
child's behavior to be considered one of the negative symptoms of Schizophrenia, the behaviors should develop independently of any treatment with
medications. When in doubt, discuss your concerns with your doctor, the
drugs may be to blame.

SOCIAL DYSFUNCTION OF SCHIZOPHRENIA

ALONG WITH THE criteria listed above, children with Schizophrenia struggle
at school both socially and academically. They cannot even take care of their
own hygiene. For older children, they lose gains made in self-care and inde-
pendence. When Schizophrenia strikes in younger children, they simply fail
to make the developmental achievements in socialization skills and self-care.
You may notice your child lacks the awareness and the insight to make and keep
friends. Your child may lose interest in his hobbies and lose all his ambition.

Remember that drugs can cause a condition that resembles Schizophrenia.
Most notably, amphetamines and hallucinogens can cause Substance-Induced
Psychotic Disorder, which looks just like Schizophrenia.

Schizophrenia can keep your child from completing his education or staying gainfully employed. Your child may never marry. Up to 70 percent of people with Schizophrenia never do. As your child becomes increasingly more socially withdrawn, losing interest in all fun activities, being less talkative, and spending the bulk of his day in bed, you may feel as if your child is "gradually slipping away."

QUALIFIERS

THE FOLLOWING ADDITIONAL conditions need to be considered when making the diagnosis of Schizophrenia.

- Duration of the symptoms should be at least six months. An exception can be made when your child met the criteria adequately but then he was successfully treated and the symptoms stopped before the six-month period required.
- Major Depressive Disorder with psychotic features and Schizoaffective Disorder have been ruled out as possible diagnoses.
- Substance-Induced Psychotic Disorder has been eliminated as a possibility whether that substance was a prescribed medication or an illicit drug.
- Autism cannot better account for your child's behaviors.

TREATMENT OF SCHIZOPHRENIA

ONCE THE DIAGNOSIS of Schizophrenia has been confirmed and you decide that psychiatric medications are the right choice for your child, the prescription medications most often used in the treatment of Schizophrenia are as follows:

- Haldol (haloperidol), Risperdal (risperidone), Zyprexa (olanzapine), Seroquel (quetiapine), Geodon (ziprasidone), Abilify (aripiprazole), Thorazine (chlorpromazine), Clozaril (clozapine)
- Eskalith, Lithobid (lithium), Depakote (valproate), Tegretol (carbamazepine), Equetro (carbamazepine), Trileptal (oxcarbazepine), Lamictal (lamotrigine), Topamax (topiramate)

For further details on the risks and benefits of each of these medications, refer to part 3. The other biological, psychological, and social approaches to treatment are covered in part 4.

CASE EXAMPLES

A BOY I treated in the psychiatric emergency room was a tragic example of how Schizophrenia can rob a child of his future. Just six months before I met him, at seventeen years old, Justin had been a very successful and ambitious basketball player for the high school team and, academically, a good student as well. Colleges were recruiting him with offers of full scholarships for playing basketball for their school. Justin had never exhibited behavior problems either at home or at school. He had no history of drug abuse and his mother insisted he had not so much as a sip of beer because he was such a dedicated athlete.

Then Schizophrenia hit. When I first met Justin, he had not bathed himself or groomed his hair for days. When he did shower, it was only because his mother had fought with him to get him into the tub. He had been arrested, but released due to his obvious mental illness, for repeatedly urinating off his mother's third-floor apartment's balcony. He had stopped going to school and was failing all his classes. Justin had been dropped from the basketball team and, of course, the college offers had been taken off the table. All but one of his friends had stopped pursuing his company. His mother reported to us that Justin had become socially withdrawn, had stopped seeking her company and counsel, and would not give her direct eye contact when responding to her questions with anything more than a grunt of yes or no. He had developed strange paranoid ideas about the neighbors and conspiracies against him, which kept him home.

While in the ER he sat with a blank expression, staring off into space, and vocally responding to some hallucinated voice inside his head. Occasionally he would giggle to himself and then return to mumbling his responses to what he alone heard. The nursing staff had to continually remind him to keep his pants pulled up, as he kept slowly pulling them down and allowing himself to be exposed while touching his own genitals. He was not exposing himself in a sexual or exhibitionist way, he just appeared completely unaware of himself and the impact his bizarre behaviors had on the people around him. Tests done in our ER confirmed that he had not been using any drugs, which helped to establish that Justin did indeed have the diagnosis of Schizophrenia. Tragically, only six months earlier, he had been the picture of health with a promising future in basketball.

16

Asperger's Disorder, Autistic Disorder, and Mental Retardation

Asperger's Disorder, Autism, and Mental Retardation represent a body of information that is too broad to cover adequately in any detail here. Instead, I will present to you enough basic information to determine if these are diagnoses you need to consider for your child. Because these disorders, particularly Asperger's, have become so popular recently, I thought it important to include them in this book.

Although not all three of these diagnoses are classified together in the *DSM*, they often do occur together. Asperger's and Autism are grouped together. Both are included in the group of disorders called Pervasive Developmental Disorders (PDD). Fifty percent of children with autism have severe or profound Mental Retardation (MR), 30 percent have mild to moderate MR, and only 20 percent of autistic children have an IQ in the normal range. All three of these disorders are apparent by the age of three and are conditions that are continuous and lifelong.

Autistic Disorder and MR can be profoundly disabling. These children usually require considerable school resources, extensive social skills education, personal care training, and almost constant supervision by adults. Children with Asperger's Disorder have a little better prognosis, given their verbal abilities and relative lack of IQ deficiency. There is a much lower incidence of MR associated with Asperger's than with Autism.

ASPERGER'S DISORDER

CRITERIA FOR DIAGNOSIS OF ASPERGER'S DISORDER

Asperger's Disorder (1) hinders your child's ability to engage in normal interpersonal relationships, and (2) causes him to engage in repetitive odd mannerisms and restrictive abnormal obsessions with parts of an object instead of using the entire object for its intended purpose.

The deficit in social interactions is demonstrated by at least two but possibly more of the following symptoms:

1. **Significant lack of the use of nonverbal social cues:** Your child with Asperger's Disorder does not use facial expressions, does not make eye contact, does not use body language, nor does he use gestures while communicating with others. Though Asperger's Disordered children will point at objects to indicate there is something they want, they do not use gestures to enhance or embellish their messages to other people.

2. **Failure to develop peer relationships:** This should not be confused with the child who desires social contact and seeks out friendship but is simply too socially awkward to attain friends and keep them. If your child has Asperger's Disorder, he has no friends and is not interested in social play, games, or having friends. He prefers solitary play. Your child will involve other children in his activities only as a tool or "mechanical" aid.

3. **Lack of any desire to share joy with others:** Children with Asperger's Disorder are not interested in and do not seek out other people with whom to share their achievements, discoveries, or interests. Your child will not bring you his artwork or school project for your inspection, approval, or praise. If your child has Asperger's Disorder, he will not point out items of interest that caught his eye for you to marvel at with him.

4. **Lack of social and emotional reciprocity:** Asperger's Disordered children lack the ability to empathize. In other words, they are completely unable to understand how other people might be feeling. If your child is not interested in spending time with you, does not want to play with you, and does not try to please you with gifts at Mother's Day, he

lacks normal social and emotional reciprocity. Your child with Asperger's Disorder may be instructed by his schoolteacher to produce a Mother's Day gift for you, but he will not be interested in your delight with the project when you open it, if he remembers to give it to you. If your child is affectionate and loving, he may have MR but probably not Asperger's Disorder.

The criteria that demonstrate an Asperger's Disordered child's repetitive odd mannerisms, stereotyped patterns, and restrictive abnormal obsessions with parts of objects and activities are listed below. Your child needs only one of the following symptoms to qualify for this portion of the diagnosis:

- **Encompassing preoccupation with one or more restrictive activities or interests that is abnormal in intensity:** An example of the restrictive obsessive activities of Asperger's Disorder is a thirteen-year-old boy who rides a large tricycle back and forth from one point in his backyard to a second point, over and over again without variance for hours. Another example is a sixteen-year-old boy who is obsessed with collecting paper fliers, pamphlets, and junk mail that he never reads but just stores at home. Everywhere this teenager went, he obsessed and pursued his pamphlets relentlessly. If denied access to the pamphlets he wanted, he would have an angry outburst.

    An Asperger's Disordered child might have an obsessive interest in one particular animal, frogs for example, about which he spends every waking minute talking about, reading about, and collecting to an abnormal overly obsessive extent.
- **Inflexible routines:** Children with Asperger's Disorder require sameness to feel comfortable. They like everything in their world to follow predictable routines upon which they can depend. They become distraught when even the smallest part of their world or routine changes. If your child has Asperger's Disorder, he will become upset when you acquire new furniture or change the curtains at his window. Your child will want meals, bedtime, and even nonfunctional routines he has developed on his own, to be followed the same way every day.
- **Stereotypies:** The repetitive motor mannerisms that children with Asperger's Disorder display have been called *stereotypies* or stereotyped movements. Typical stereotypies are hand flapping, flicking their ears repeatedly, wringing their hands repeatedly, twisting their fingers, or complex whole-body movements, such as rocking themselves.

- **Preoccupation with parts of objects:** Asperger's Disordered children do not understand or engage in representative play. This means that they do not use a toy to represent a character in the script of their imaginative play. For example, instead of driving a toy car around the playroom, pretending that the car represents a car and driver in his imagination, your child with Asperger's Disorder will spend long periods of time sitting and just spinning a wheel of the car over and over again.

QUALIFIERS

Children with Asperger's Disorder can be distinguished from other autistic disorders by two important features:

1. Asperger's Disordered children do not have the language delays that the children with other autistic disorders have. Single words will be used by two years of age and phrases by three years, to communicate. However, if your child has Asperger's, he will miss inferences and nuances in conversation. He will not understand humor and he will want to talk about his topic of obsession without regard to what others are talking about.
2. A child with Asperger's Disorder usually has a normal IQ, unlike children with the other Pervasive Developmental Disorders, the majority of whom have mild to profound MR.

The qualifying feature that all autistic spectrum disorders, including Autistic Disorder and Asperger's Disorder, share is the impact on the child's ability to function successfully socially or academically. Asperger's Disorder causes significant impairment in social, academic, and occupational functioning.

This seems to be forgotten when sensational speculations start circulating that perhaps Albert Einstein and Marie Curie had Asperger's Disorder. Both of these people were happily married and involved with political movements related to their scientific endeavors and achievements. Suggesting that these two great scientists could possibly have Asperger's Disorder is quite a stretch of the diagnosis. Even more shocking is the suggestion that Jane Austen, author of many successful romance novels about love and relationships, had Asperger's Disorder. The author of these ideas, Simon Baron-Cohen, declines to give the full description of Asperger's Disorder. Instead, he minimizes this serious psychiatric disorder by describing it as "finding social situations confusing, difficulty making small talk, good at picking up on details, and being able to focus for a long time," according to an interview with the BBC (British Broadcasting Company) reporter Megan Lane. Others he has included on his list of autistic patients are: Socrates, Michelangelo, Charles Darwin, Isaac Newton, Andy Warhol, and Bill Gates.[1]

The above-described distortion of the diagnosis of Asperger's Disorder by individuals who present themselves to the public as experts, is exactly how your child can be first misdiagnosed as having and then overmedicated for this condition. The rationale given by such experts as these, is that your child can be just "a little bit autistic." This is like describing a person with a potbelly as being "a little bit pregnant." There are some essential features missing in this sort of analysis. Children with autistic disorders, such as Asperger's, are not just a little socially awkward and passionate about a single area of study, such as the theory of relativity (Einstein) or the discovery of a new element (Curie). Asperger's Disorder involves a significant shift in your child's ability to engage in meaningful relationships with other people or to have an in-depth understanding of the world around him. Children with Asperger's are obsessed with the parts and pieces of their own little worlds. They are drawn into themselves and are generally oblivious to the wants, cares, and needs of others. Autism is the complete lack of social interrelation that leads to significant impairment in functioning.

Asperger's Disorder is not a new way to label brilliant scientists and artists who are passionate about their field of study and a little socially awkward. A more honest and realistic example of Autistic Disorder is the character played by Dustin Hoffman in the movie *Rainman*. Rent the movie and decide for yourself if Einstein and Michelangelo could have been diagnosed with Asperger's Disorder, which is Autism but with almost normal speech.

TREATMENT OF ASPERGER'S

Once the diagnosis of Asperger's Disorder has been confirmed, there are several options for treatment, but it should be clarified that there is no cure for Asperger's Disorder. When you decide that psychiatric medications are the right choice for your child, the prescription medications most often used in the treatment of the symptoms associated with Asperger's Disorder are as follows:

- Eskalith, Lithobid (lithium), Depakote (valproate), Tegretol (carbamazepine), Equetro (carbamazepine), Trileptal (oxcarbazepine), Lamictal (lamotrigine), Topamax (topiramate)
- Prozac (fluoxetine), Paxil (paroxetine), Zoloft (sertraline), Luvox (fluvoxamine), Celexa (citalopram), Lexapro (escitalopram), Effexor XR

(venlafaxine), Cymbalta (duloxetine), Wellbutrin XL (buproprion)
- Tofranil (imipramine), Anafranil (clomipramine)
- Eskalith, Lithobid (lithium), Depakote (valproate), Tegretol (carbamazepine), Equetro (carbamazepine), Trileptal (oxcarbazepine), Lamictal (lamotrigine), Topamax (topiramate)
- Inderal (propranolol), Tenormin (atenolol)
- Benzodiazepines: Xanax (alprazolam), Ativan (lorazepam), Klonapin (clonazepam), Valium (diazepam) (Proceed with caution with this class of drugs.)

For further details on the risks and benefits of each of these medications, refer to part 3.

CASE EXAMPLES

An Asperger's Disordered child should not be confused with a socially awkward one who is anxious, lonely, and frustrated. I treated a ten-year-old boy, Ben, who had been abandoned by his drug-addicted mother at five years of age. He was rescued by Child Protective Services and placed with a caring foster mother. Ben was angry and frustrated a good deal of the time. He had never been nurtured or given guidance and discipline. Adjusting to parental rules, learning to share with and engaging in social interactions with other children was all new territory for Ben. He had a very difficult time accepting no for an answer but he was slowly learning under the guidance of his foster parents.

He was socially awkward with his peers, was afraid to be separated from his adoptive mother, and complained that he had no friends though he wanted them desperately. Ben's loneliness frequently moved him to tears but, between his anxiety and his lack of social skills, he was locked out of the friendships he desired. Yu-Gi-Oh trading card collecting was his one great joy and passion. His hobby made him feel a little closer to the boys in his class who also valued the activity highly—a fact not lost on Ben. He had hopes that his collection would draw the interest of his peers, which indeed it did, but Ben drove the other boys away because he was unable to share or be a good sport.

The fact that he had taken a great deal of care to arrange his trading cards in a special folder, along with his lack of friends, was interpreted by a doctor as proof that Ben had Asperger's Disorder. In all the years that doctors had treated him with psychiatric medications, prior to my assessment, he had only received antipsychotics and mood stabilizers, which of course did little to help Ben with his anxiety. In fact, his anxiety had never been addressed with medications appropriate for anxiety; instead his previous doctors focused on the one or two symptoms that confirmed the trendy diagnosis of Asperger's and treated him accordingly. I wish I could tell you that this was a rare phenomenon—tragically, it is not. I see children misdiagnosed with Asperger's Disorder all the time, it has become one of the newest, most fashionable disorders to be identified. Parents, be careful.

Once Ben had been taken off of the sedating antipsychotics and mood stabilizers he was much more alert, and his symptoms of anger, frustration, defiance, social awkwardness, and anxiety were no worse. On serotonin antidepressants, his anxiety and anger reduced considerably but his defiance continued. Ben's foster parents required a great deal of education to help them understand his diagnosis, and the benefits and limitations they could reasonably expect from the psychiatric medications. I recommended that they join a parent support group and attend parent-education classes to address Ben's defiance; also, I advised that Ben take part in social clubs at the parks and recreation department or with Boy Scouts to build his social skills, now that his anxiety was under better control.

Austistic Disorder

Criteria for Diagnosis of Autistic Disorder

Autistic Disorder hinders your child's ability to engage in normal interpersonal relationships. This disorder also causes your child to engage in repetitive odd mannerisms and restrictive abnormal obsessions with parts of objects instead of using the entire object for its intended purpose. Finally, Autistic Disorder causes significant speech impairment in your child. The criteria for making a diagnosis of Autistic Disorder requires that your child have at least six, total, of the following twelve symptoms. Your child must have at least two symptoms from the first group, the social impairments, and at least one from the other two groups, the communication impairments and the stereotypies.

1. The deficit in social interactions is demonstrated by at least two but possibly more of the following symptoms:

    - **Significant lack of the use of nonverbal social cues:** Your child with Autistic Disorder does not use facial expressions, does not make eye contact, does not use body language, nor does he use gestures while communicating with others. Though Autistic Disordered children will point at objects to indicate there is something they want, they do not use gestures to enhance or embellish their messages to other people.

- **Failure to develop peer relationships:** This should not be confused with the child who desires social contact and seeks out friendship, but is simply too socially awkward to attain friends and keep them. If your child has Autistic Disorder, he has no friends and is not interested in social play, games, or having friends. He prefers solitary play. Your child will involve other children in his activities only as a tool or "mechanical" aid.

- **Lack of any desire to share joy with others:** Children with Autistic Disorder are not interested in and do not seek out other people with whom to share their achievements, discoveries, or interests. Your child will not bring you his artwork or school project for your inspection, approval, or praise. If your child has Autistic Disorder, he will not point out items of interest that caught his eye for you to marvel at with him.

- **Lack of social and emotional reciprocity:** Autistic Disordered children lack the ability to empathize. In other words, they are completely unable to understand how other people might be feeling. If your child is not interested in spending time with you, does not want to play with you, and does not try to please you with gifts at Mother's Day, he lacks normal social and emotional reciprocity. Your child with Autistic Disorder may be instructed by his schoolteacher to produce a Mother's Day gift for you, but he will not be interested in your delight with the project when you open it, if he remembers to give it to you. If your child is affectionate and loving, he may have Mental Retardation (MR) but probably not Autistic Disorder. It is extremely rare for a person with Autism to marry.

2. Your child must have at least one but may have more of the following symptoms that demonstrate his impairments with communication:

- **Delay or lack of speech:** Your child has a severe and sustained delay in the development of spoken language. Some children with Autistic Disorder never develop verbal communication skills. This criterion would not apply to your child if he attempted to compensate for his inability to speak by developing alternative methods of communication, such as gesturing or miming.

- **Inability to sustain or initial conversation:** Autistic Disordered children have marked difficulty in initiating or sustaining verbal exchanges with other people. You would not include people who are shy and socially awkward with people they hardly know. If your child has Autism, he will have the same communication struggles with the people whom he is closest, as well as with strangers.

- **Lack of language comprehension:** Autistic children make little use of word meaning in their memory and thought process. Normal children learning language understand more than they can say. They can use a word once and then not use it again for up to a year. Some autistic children with normal intelligence can teach themselves to read at an early age (*hyperlexia*), due to their obsession with letters. Even though these children can read surprisingly well, they do not comprehend anything they are reading.

- **Stereotyped or idiosyncratic language:** As infants, autistic children may have reduced or abnormal babbling. If they do make sounds, they emit noises, such as clicks, screeches, nonsense syllables, over and over again, but with no apparent attempt to communicate. Children with Autistic Disorder repeat back what is said to them, sometimes immediately, sometimes much later. Doctors call this *echolalia*. They will repeat incessantly a phrase or word out of context, or what doctors call *stereotyped language*. They may use appropriate words but without meaningful order, such as "You can eat" when what they want is for you to get them something to eat. About 50 percent of children with Autistic Disorder never develop useful speech.

- **Lack of make-believe play:** Autistic kids do not play out roles, or pretend to be someone else as a part of a game. Their play is not spontaneous or creative. Instead children with Autistic Disorder will spin wheels of toy cars or manipulate some part of a toy repeatedly to entertain or stimulate themselves.

3. The criteria that demonstrate an Autistic Disordered child's repetitive odd mannerisms, stereotyped patterns, and restrictive abnormal obsessions with parts of objects and activities are listed below. Your child

needs at least one but may have more of the following symptoms to qualify for this portion of the diagnosis:

- **Encompassing preoccupation with one or more restrictive activities or interests that are abnormal in intensity:** An example of the restrictive obsessive activities of Autistic Disorder is a sixteen-year-old boy who is obsessed with collecting paper clips that he never uses but just stores at home.
- **Inflexible routines:** Children with Autistic Disorder require sameness to feel comfortable. They like everything in their world to follow predictable routines upon which they can depend. They become distraught when even the smallest part of their world or routine changes. If your child has Autistic Disorder, he will become upset if you switch brands of breakfast cereal or even if the box of the same brand has been redesigned. Your child will want meals, bedtime, and even nonfunctional routines he has developed on his own, to be followed the same way every day.
- **Stereotypies:** The repetitive motor mannerisms that children with Autistic Disorder display have been called *stereotypies*, or stereotyped movements. Typical stereotypies are hand flapping, flicking their ears repeatedly, wringing their hands repeatedly, twisting their fingers, or complex whole-body movements, such as rocking themselves.
- **Preoccupation with parts of objects:** Autistic Disordered children do not understand or engage in representative play. This means that they do not use a toy to represent a character in the script of their imaginative play. For example, instead of engaging multiple action figures in mock-combat, your child with Autistic Disorder will spend long periods of time swinging a single figure's leg back and forth.

QUALIFIERS

The qualifying feature that all autistic spectrum disorders, including Autistic and Asperger's Disorders, share is the impact on the child's ability to function successfully socially or academically. Autistic Disorder causes significant impairment in social, academic, and occupational functioning.

- Autistic disorder is associated with Mental Retardation in 80 percent of cases. Fifty of children have severe to profound MR, and 30 percent have mild to moderate MR.
- Some autistic children have sudden mood changes with outbursts of laughing or crying or anger, but without expressing thought behind the demonstration of emotion.
- Autistic Disordered children can be extremely sensitive to some noises but may be fascinated by the ticking of a watch. Many love music and will hum along. Their pain response can either be extremely sensitive or completely oblivious. Autistic children can injure themselves and not even be aware of it.
- Aggressiveness and tantrums can occur for no apparent reason or because their routine was altered.
- Autistic children cause self-injury by banging their own head repeatedly, biting, scratching, and pulling out their own hair.
- Hyperactivity can be a problem or, less frequently, they are very slowed down and sedentary, which is always accompanied by episodes of the hyperactivity.
- Autistic Disordered children often have feeding problems and they are not always continent of their bowel or bladder.

Treatment of Autistic Disorder

Once the diagnosis of Autistic Disorder has been confirmed, there are several options for treatment, but it should be clarified that there is no cure for Autistic Disorder. When you decide that psychiatric medications are the right choice for your child, the prescription medications most often used in the treatment of the symptoms associated with Autistic Disorder are as follows:

- Haldol (haloperidol), Risperdal (risperidone), Zyprexa (olanzapine), Seroquel (quetiapine), Geodon (ziprasidone), Abilify (aripiprazole), Thorazine (chlorpromazine)
- Prozac (fluoxetine), Paxil (paroxetine), Zoloft (sertraline), Luvox (fluvoxamine), Celexa (citalopram), Lexapro (escitalopram), Effexor XR (venlafaxine), Cymbalta (duloxetine), Wellbutrin XL (buproprion)
- Tofranil (imipramine), Anafranil (clomipramine)
- Eskalith, Lithobid (lithium), Depakote (valproate), Tegretol (carbamazepine), Equetro (carbamazepine), Trileptal (oxcarbazepine), Lamictal (lamotrigine), Topamax (topiramate)

- Inderal (propranolol), Tenormin (atenolol)
- Benzodiazepines: Xanax (alprazolam), Ativan (lorazepam), Klonapin (clonazepam), Valium (diazepam) (Proceed with caution when benzodiazepines have been prescribed.)

For further details on the risks and benefits of each of these medications, refer to part 3.

CASE EXAMPLE

Jimmy was thirteen years old when he was brought to our clinic for assessment. He was physically normal but he rarely spoke; mostly he grunted and pointed without giving eye contact, though he did have a vocabulary of two dozen words. Jimmy would sit cross-legged on the floor for long periods of time and rock his upper torso back and forth, often while also flapping his hands in the air or flipping his ears. He had very rigid routines that, if not followed to the letter, sent him into a screaming fit, during which he could become violent. Explanations by his parents seemed to make no difference to him. Jimmy was oblivious to the feelings, needs, or cares of his family members—he did not seek them out or miss them when they were gone, as long as they were not required to play a part in his regular routines.

What baffled his parents was that in school, particularly in math, he was performing near grade level. Based on his poor social functioning, Jimmy's parents thought that he must have very low intelligence, but his competence in math mystified them. No, he could not write poetry and could not capture the nuances or themes in a novel, but he could spell, and diagram a sentence. Jimmy did have problems functioning normally in the classroom because he was so sensitive to environmental stimuli, and the noise and activity in the classroom bothered him.

His parents brought him in for assessment for his violent behavior. Jimmy had always been difficult to redirect, both at home and in the classroom. But since he had started to enter puberty, he had become even more aggressive when his routines were disturbed. His parents were hoping to learn that prior doctors had missed something and that our team at the Children's Hospital would find there was some treatment or medication that would restore their son to normal functioning. Sadly, we had to explain to the parents that Jimmy's condition, Autistic Disorder, was not one that could be reversed with medication and, in fact, it would remain mostly unchanged throughout his life— barring some miraculous cure discovered by scientists in the future. The unfortunate contribution that his puberty was making to increase his aggression seemed to answer their questions, though it hardly came as any reassurance. Jimmy was offered blood pressure medications that can reduce anger and they seemed to help, albeit moderately.

MENTAL RETARDATION

CRITERIA FOR DIAGNOSIS OF MENTAL RETARDATION

Mental Retardation (MR) is based on your child's Intelligence Quotient (IQ). On a scale where 100 is average intelligence, the criteria for a diagnosis of MR is an IQ of less than 70. All other problems that are associated with Mental Retardation are a result of your child's diminished cognitive ability. MR is separated into degrees of severity based on the IQ level. You will notice that there is a little overlap in the IQ scores at the boundary between each level. The following outlines this designation:

MILD MENTAL RETARDATION   IQ level approximately 50 to 70
MODERATE MENTAL RETARDATION IQ level approximately 35 to 55
SEVERE MENTAL RETARDATION   IQ level approximately 20 to 40
PROFOUND MENTAL RETARDATION IQ level below approximately 25

The deficits and impairments that are associated with Mental Retardation affect your child's functioning in a number of areas. He will be unable to reach the normal milestones of childhood development, such as walking, talking, toileting, dressing himself, riding a bike, or reading. These skills and abilities are referred to by doctors as adaptive functioning. You can expect problems in at least two, possibly more, of the following areas to be affected:

- Communication
- Self-care
- Home living (managing a household)
- Social/interpersonal skills
- Use of community resources
- Self-direction
- Academic skills
- Work
- Leisure

- Health
- Safety

Qualifiers

Children with Mental Retardation have a three to four times greater likelihood of having another psychiatric disorder. MR children have the same symptoms as any other normal person when suffering with another psychiatric or medical condition, though it may be harder to assess due to the deficits in communication. Your child with MR may also have mood disorders, anxiety disorders, autistic disorders, AD/HD, movement impairments, seizure disorders, schizophrenia, and conduct disorders.

A multitude of diseases and conditions can cause Mental Retardation. In 30 to 40 percent of individuals, no clear cause can be identified. The causes of MR can be divided into six categories:

- **Heredity:** Errors in the parents' genes that cause metabolism dysfunction in the child. Examples of this pathway to Mental Retardation are: Fragile X, Tay-Sachs disease, and Down syndrome caused by translocation of a gene.
- **Early alterations of embryonic development:** damage to your baby's genes (DNA) during fetal development. This can be caused by the mother's consumption of drugs or alcohol during pregnancy, infections during pregnancy, or Down syndrome caused by *trisomy*.
- **Environmental influences:** The lack of stimulation can cause Mental Retardation. When infants do not receive sufficient nurturing and activity, they can fail to develop cognitively or intellectually. If your infant does not hear enough spoken language, is not visually stimulated by a diverse environment, and does not experience adequate physical activity by being held, rocked, and played with, he may not develop normally.
- **Mental disorders:** Autism and the other Pervasive Developmental Disorders, including Asperger's, can cause MR.
- **Pregnancy and prenatal problems:** difficulties experienced by your baby during or before birth. If your baby does not receive enough oxygen during delivery (hypoxia), this can lead to MR. Trauma during delivery or during pregnancy can also cause problems with cognitive development. Any premature baby is at risk for Mental Retardation.

Also, children who are malnourished or exposed to viral infections (rubella/German measles, herpes, or HIV) or a syphilis infection during gestation can develop MR.

- **General medical conditions acquired during early childhood:** head trauma, hypoxia from near drowning, infections, and lead poisoning during first years of life can cause Mental Retardation in your child.

Your child's Mental Retardation can be caused by any combination of the above factors but in 30 to 40 percent of cases, no clear cause is ever identified.

TREATMENT OF MENTAL RETARDATION

Mental Retardation cannot be cured with medication. Nonetheless, psychiatric medications are used regularly to treat children with Mental Retardation, though not to treat the disease itself. Medications are used to address associated symptoms of anger, aggression, poor impulse control, and inattention. Children with MR are just as prone to develop other psychiatric disorders as are children with normal IQs. Therefore, the diagnosis of other psychiatric illnesses, such as depression or anxiety, is another justification to treat MR children with medications.

The ideal treatment of Mental Retardation consists of developing an educational and socialization plan to help your child learn the skills required to be as independent and self-sufficient as possible. This may include special education classes, speech therapy, and occupational therapy. An effective ADL (Activities of Daily Living) training program will teach your child basic personal grooming proficiency, shopping skills, meal preparation, and how to take public transportation. The behavior modification your child receives in psychosocial therapy can provide him social skills and help him manage his anger and aggression.

Caution should be used when treating your mentally retarded child with any psychiatric medications. Children with MR may have a paradoxically opposite reaction or hypersensitivity to the side effects of many of these drugs. Unfortunately, some children become more instead of less anxious, aggressive, and agitated on these medications. Proceed with caution if such treatment is prescribed for a child with MR.

For further details on the risks and benefits of each of the different medications, refer to part 3.

Case Example

Tim was seventeen when I met him; he was very tall, six foot three inches, and strong as an ox. He had been identified early in life as having an IQ of 50 points, and a diagnosis of mild to moderate Mental Retardation was made. Tim had been placed in special education classes from the age of five and monitored throughout his life by a series of psychiatrists, to address both his educational needs and his behavioral problems. His mother was a very attentive advocate for her son. She made sure that Tim was receiving every resource and service from every available program and activity for children with MR. She probably spent more than half of her waking hours at his school, meeting with teachers and principals to address his needs academically and vocationally.

At seventeen, Tim functioned at about the level of a six-year-old child. He was friendly, playful, and engaging, though his vocabulary was very limited. He was always starting up conversations with complete strangers everywhere he went. More often than not, Tim wanted praise for some feature about himself or for a task he had just completed, such as his great height, a new word he had learned, or for being able to tie his own shoes. He loved to laugh with people, and his feelings could be easily hurt if people he was trying to engage did not respond. When he became angry he could escalate into a tantrum, but those who knew him best were able to distract him fairly easily to calm him down.

Tim's behavioral problems were fairly well managed by his teachers and his parents while he was younger, but as he reached his later adolescence his size made it more difficult for his caregivers. Hoarding and collecting items that hold little to no value is not unusual for children with MR, and Tim was no exception. He wanted to take home pamphlets and fliers from every office, store, and clinic he ever visited. His mother could curtail his collecting obsession until he became too big for her to forcibly take by the hand and lead away. Once Tim realized his strength was more than his mother could handle, he was no longer as compliant with his mother's directives as he had been previously. To make matters worse, he developed a fascination with girls at this same time, which drove him to grab and grope the girls in school and at his sheltered workshop job. Their jewelry fascinated him and many incidents occurred at school, on the special education transport bus, and at work when he tried to touch the jewelry of the girls and women with whom he worked and studied.

Because Tim's mother had already exhausted every behavioral technique known and enlisted the help of every available professional but was still having problems controlling her son's aggressive behaviors, she came to me to see if psychiatric medications might play a role in helping him. Tim's obsessions with pamphlets responded only moderately to the serotonin antidepressants (SSRI) typically used for Obsessive Compulsive Disorder. His aggressive and impulsive touching of girls was harder to treat. The SSRI used to treat his obsessions did appear to have a slight affect on his aggression but not substantially. I discussed medication alternatives and Tim's mom wanted to try antipsychotics. On these, Tim was definitely less aggressive but also more lethargic, less lively and vivacious than he normally was—his mom was not pleased with the results. Nonsedating antipsychotic medications were not yet on the market at that time, so I added an antihypertensive, which seemed to help a great deal. Tim's mother was much happier with the results on this combination and at the same time relieved that she did not have to concern herself with the side effects that go along with the antipsychotic medications.

17

ADDICTIONS TO DRUGS AND ALCOHOL, AND RELATED DISORDERS

ADDICTIONS TO DRUGS AND ALCOHOL

THE ABUSE OF drugs and alcohol in children causes numerous mental health problems, too many to cover adequately in one chapter. My goal in this chapter is to familiarize you with the types of mental illnesses that can develop from the abuse of substances and to introduce you to the treatment options. Your child can have all the signs and symptoms of a psychiatric condition simply due to the drugs he is abusing. Most of the time, the only treatment needed is for your child to get clean and sober. This chapter will provide you with some insight into the diagnoses that can emerge from using drugs and alcohol.

CRITERIA FOR DIAGNOSIS

IN THE DSM, all the disorders related to substance abuse are organized by the specific substance being abused. The *Diagnostic and Statistical Manual* lists the following substances of abuse:

- Alcohol (beer, wine, liquor)
- Amphetamines (speed, meth, crystal, ice, diet pills, Ritalin)
- Cannabis (THC, marijuana, pot, weed, reefers, joints, hash, chronic)

- Cocaine (coke, crack, rock, free base)
- Hallucinogens (LSD, acid, psilocybin, mushrooms, mescaline, peyote, MDMA, ecstacy)
- Inhalant (glue, permanent markers, correction fluid, gasoline, paint thinner, aerosol spray paints and cleansers)
- Opioids (heroin, morphine, methadone, oxycodone, codeine, fentanyl)
- Phencyclidine (PCP, hog, angel dust)
- Sedative-Hypnotics (Valium, Xanax, Ativan, Klonapin, Ambien, Sonata, barbiturates)
- Nicotine (cigarettes, cigars, pipes, chewing tobacco)
- Caffeine (coffee, tea, many types of carbonated drinks)

Under the heading for each drug of abuse, the disorders are first divided into either Drug Use Disorders or **Drug-Induced Disorders**. Each group of Drug-Induced Disorders is then further subdivided by the type of mental illness the substance abuse caused.

Following is an example of how each of the substances listed above can be further subdivided. Instead of naming each of the specific substances abused, I will simply substitute the word "Substance." In other words, instead of naming Cocaine Dependence specifically, I will substitute the term Substance Dependence; likewise, Substance-Induced Mood Disorder will replace Alcohol-Induced Mood Disorder. Why? Most of the substances named above can cause any of the mental illnesses described here, though not every substance abused by teens can cause every type of drug-related mental illness listed here. The obvious exceptions are Nicotine and Caffeine.

SUBSTANCE USE DISORDERS

- Substance Dependence (withdrawal symptoms and cravings occur when drug is stopped)
- Substance Abuse (use of drugs have caused dysfunction but *not* withdrawal or cravings)

To make a diagnosis of Substance Abuse or Dependence, your child must have experienced significant impairment in functioning due to the use of drugs or alcohol. Occasional use would not be considered Abuse or Dependence, by *DSM* terms. It should be noted, however, that even the occasional use of drugs or alcohol by teenagers should be taken seriously. Any recreational use of substances by your child or teen should be considered potentially dangerous. No child starts off as a heavy user. They all start off using occasionally and then escalate.

The abuse of drugs and alcohol has a very recognizable pattern. Typically, children who abuse drugs or alcohol develop problems in three areas of functioning: their behavior, their reasoning abilities, and their mood.

Behavioral Problems
- Hyperactivity
- Agitation
- Lethargy (loss of motivation or ambition)
- Sleepiness
- Insomnia
- Loss of inhibitions (greater risk taking)
- Hypervigilance

Cognitive Problems (loss of reasoning abilities)
- Poor concentration
- Shortened attention span
- Delusions
- Paranoia
- Hallucinations

Mood Problems
- Depression
- Euphoria
- Mania

The problems that your child develops as a result of using drugs are dependent on which substance he has abused, the amount he has taken into his body, and the amount of time he has been using drugs. Regardless of how your child's abuse of drugs affects his mental health, the results will be a loss of functioning. Teens show their impairment through two basic avenues.

1. **Interpersonal Relationships:** Your teenager will have a great many more conflicts with you and other family members. While adolescence is a time of turmoil and conflict anyway, once your teen starts using drugs the conflicts become much more hostile and irrational.
2. **Academic Functioning:** Almost without exception, when your teenager's grades make a dramatic drop, you should suspect that substance

abuse is involved. Academic failure is a hallmark of substance abuse. School failure can also be caused by a traumatic event or by enduring a major life change. If your child has not experienced anything devastating, then you should suspect drugs.

SUBSTANCE-INDUCED DISORDERS

SUBSTANCE-INDUCED DISORDER are categorized as the following:

- Substance Intoxication
- Substance Withdrawal
- Substance Intoxication Delirium
- Substance Withdrawal Delirium
- Substance-Induced Persisting Dementia
- Substance-Induced Persisting Amnestic Disorder
- Substance-Induced Persisting Perception Disorder (flashbacks)
- Substance-Induced Psychotic Disorder, with Delusions
- Substance-Induced Psychotic Disorder, with Hallucinations
- Substance-Induced Mood Disorder
- Substance-Induced Anxiety Disorder
- Substance-Induced Sexual Dysfunction
- Substance-Induced Sleep Disorder
- Substance-Induced Disorder Not Otherwise Specified (NOS)

Substance-Induced Disorders do not only derive from the heavy use of drugs or alcohol. Even the occasional use of marijuana, for example, can affect how well your child is able to focus, concentrate, and attend to his studies. I have treated many teenagers who were using marijuana only a few times each month with their friends at weekend parties. They had been good students previously but, after starting to use marijuana, they were no longer paying attention in class. As a result, their parents, having researched attention problems on the Internet, took the teen to the pediatrician for a prescription of Ritalin and a presumed diagnosis of AD/HD. Amphetamines will help anyone study better. Therefore, some children are able to stumble along getting passing grades while using marijuana on the weekends and prescribed amphetamines on school days. These sorts of solutions are not ideal, as your child may escalate his use of drugs.

The symptoms associated with any of the Substance-Induced Disorders are defined by the description of the standard disorder, the only difference being that the abuse of drugs has led to the condition. For example, if your child is a binge drinker, or gets drunk at high school weekend parties but does not have withdrawal symptoms, he would be diagnosed with Alcohol Abuse. If your child develops the signs and symptoms of Major Depressive Disorder, then he probably has the second diagnosis of Alcohol-Induced Mood Disorder. Therefore, to determine if your child has Major Depressive Disorder or Alcohol-Induced Mood Disorder, your teen would first have to stop drinking completely for a long enough time for the effects of the alcohol on his mental health to be resolved. That can take months, for some children.

Treatment of Substance Use Disorders

The cornerstone of all successful substance abuse treatment programs is *complete abstinence*. Teens that try the *controlled use* approach are doomed to failure. Complete abstinence has repeatedly proven to be the only effective way to treat substance abuse. Once you have accepted the need for your child's sobriety, you and your team of therapists and doctors need to decide where and for how long your child will need drug rehab treatment. This depends on the severity of his addiction, of course. The following is a list of the considerations and elements needed in a successful substance-abuse treatment plan:

- **Intensity:** Treatment needs to be intense enough and continue on for a long enough period of time to change your child's attitudes and behaviors toward his drug of choice.
- **Education:** Treatment needs to provide your teen with extensive education on the impact of drugs and alcohol on his mental and physical health, along with the effects on his social and academic functioning.
- **Meetings:** Treatment should encourage your teen to take part in Alcoholics Anonymous (AA) or Narcotics Anonymous (NA) above and beyond whatever ongoing treatment he is receiving. Twelve-step program attendance will help provide your child a sober peer group and reinforce what he is learning in his treatment program. Families can benefit by attending Al-Anon or Families Anonymous (FA) meetings as well. These meetings can provide you and the rest of the family a support group of people who understand what you are going through.
- **Therapy:** Treatment should include a comprehensive psychotherapy element, including individual psychotherapy, group therapy to work on interpersonal skills, and family therapy.

- **Family:** Treatment should include the family members who interact most directly with the addicted teen. The goals in the family therapy sessions are to (1) improve communications, and (2) help parents provide better guidance and limit setting for the substance-abusing child.
- **Sober living:** Treatment should teach the family and the teen how to live a drug-free and alcohol-free lifestyle. This element would include educating the family about eliminating the pervasive presence of alcohol at family celebrations, holidays, and recreational activities. The goal here is to teach the family that they can enjoy life without alcohol.
- **Mental health:** Treatment of any psychiatric condition that requires medication needs to be addressed. Your child should receive medication as deemed appropriate by a psychiatrist. Medications should not be started until your teen has been sober between three to four weeks, and should be monitored very closely.
- **Aftercare:** Treatment needs to include an aftercare plan that outlines what treatment follows the intensive phase of your child's substance-abuse treatment program. Good aftercare should provide your teen with enough contact with therapists, drug counselors, and twelve-step meetings such as AA and NA that the insights and gains he has made during the intensive phase can be sustained.

Case Examples

One of the best examples of the problems that can develop when a teen with Cannabis-Induced Disorder NOS is treated with psychiatric medications can be illustrated by the case of a sixteen-year-old boy, Steve, whom I treated in 1998. His regular use of marijuana had led to symptoms of inattention, apathy, and a lack of motivation. Because he was unmotivated and had no desire to succeed academically, he made no effort at school and thus was failing most of his classes, which didn't seem to bother Steve at all. Even though prior to eighth grade he had been a good student, his previous psychiatrist had diagnosed him with AD/HD based on his failures in high school. His mother was frustrated with his poor progress on the Ritalin, which had been prescribed for two years. His previous psychiatrist had started Steve with 20 mg. of Ritalin, but at each visit over the two years his mother would report that absolutely nothing had changed, so the new doctor raised the dose until he was taking three times the dose usually prescribed, 40mg., three times per day. In spite of these high dosage Steve continued to be unmotivated to study, was not paying attention in class, and had no interest in succeeding in school.

Steve was a pleasant, agreeable, and relaxed teenager. There were no signs of hyperactivity. After several sessions with the boy, I suggested to his mother that he may not be taking the Ritalin at all and that he appeared to me to have a condition more consistent with drug abuse. I suggested she investigate. A search of his room turned up a bag of two hundred tablets of Ritalin. When his mother confronted him with the evidence, he admitted to her that he had been deceiving her for two years by not taking his Ritalin and that instead, all along, he had been smoking marijuana regularly. He had started using drugs just before he was diagnosed with AD/HD. Furthermore, Steve explained to his mother, the Ritalin in the bag was not all that had accumulated; he had used some of the pills for the past two years to finance his drug habit, by paying for his marijuana with the proceeds made from selling his Ritalin to the students at school who abused amphetamines.

Jill had been prescribed Adderall for her AD/HD because she was another teen whose use of marijuana had led to a poor performance academically. Unfortunately, Jill liked amphetamines as much and eventually even more than she liked marijuana. She was very resistant to drug rehab treatment, insisting that she could kick the habit on her own. She repeatedly failed, relapsing on Adderall that was readily available at her high school from the other teens who had been diagnosed with AD/HD and were being treated with Adderall, too. She was hopelessly addicted to the Adderall and simply could not stop herself. Jill felt frustrated and humiliated by the whole ordeal and held the doctor, who first prescribed the Adderall to her, personally responsible for getting her hooked on speed. Her anger and rage at the previous doctor was so great that she had fantasies of murdering him, though she assured me she would never actually do such a thing. The one feature about Jill's case that has remained with me through the years was her question about the doctor who first gave her Adderall: "Why would he give me a drug he knew was addicting, without telling me first?" Why indeed?—Jill, that is a very good question.

While I was the medical director at the Hazelden for young adults, I met a sixteen-year-old girl named Tammy. She was a beautiful girl from a very nice family with loving supportive parents. She was an excellent student, and active in campus sports and clubs. Tammy did enjoy an active social life and attended high school parties, but held herself to the standard that she would never, ever use drugs no matter what, especially not heroin. When she did drink alcohol or beer at a party, she held herself to a limit of three, which she thought was very responsible. Then one night at a party a high school student had brought heroin to the party and offered it to Tammy. Initially she declined, but after three drinks and a little more pressure from the boy who brought the heroin, she thought, "Oh well, what the heck, trying it just once couldn't hurt, then I can see what the whole heroin hype is all about." She didn't use a needle she simply snorted it up her nose, which seemed innocent enough to her at the time.

Tammy developed a heavy addiction to heroin shortly after that night. When her grades fell and she dropped out of her activities at school, her parents became suspicious and brought her to Hazelden for treatment. She did well initially, embracing the program fully, including all of its philosophies. During her rehab, Tammy realized that had she not been drinking alcohol in the first place, she would never have tried the heroin that fateful night, not even once. Unfortunately, after a year of successful recovery from drugs, she relapsed. Addictions in general are extremely difficult to overcome, but heroin in particular is the most gripping addiction of them all. Tammy's case is a perfect example of how easy it is to start but how painfully difficult it is to stop.

An example of a boy with Substance-Induced Disorder, Zach was a sixteen-year-old who had been raised by parents both of whom had very heavy methamphetamine addictions during his entire childhood. His parents stopped using and started their drug rehab treatment when Zach was fourteen but, two years prior, at twelve, he had begun using methamphetamine himself, initially dipping into his parents' stash of drugs. He was using meth almost daily soon after he got started and continued to do so long after his parents quit. His parents, who were racked with guilt about their own use of drugs during Zach's formative years, were oblivious to their son's addiction because they were completely absorbed with their own drug rehabilitation and recovery. After four years of almost daily use of meth, Zach became psychotic—he hallucinated snakes and monsters writhing out of the walls and ceilings. He became extremely paranoid, believing that he had special powers and insights that allowed him to be omnipotent, controlling the future and the minds of others. Zach refused to go to school, as he was certain that there were conspiracies afoot on campus.

Treatment with antipsychotic medication had all failed, but still his parents remained more focused on getting Zach psychiatric medications for the treatment of what they presumed to be a purely psychiatric diagnosis, completely unrelated to the boy's use of methamphetamines, rather than focusing on getting him into drug rehab. Their feelings of guilt about their own role in the development of Zach's addiction and the consequential psychosis, prohibited them from seeing the part that street drugs had played in causing their son's mental illness, so they minimized the affect of the meth on his mind, and refused any drug rehab treatment that I offered to their son. His parents would not allow us to confirm their assertion that Zach was no longer using methamphetamine. Zach refused to provide us with a urine sample to test him for drug use and the parents did not want to press the issue with their son because this might upset the boy. The parents simply continued to insist that Zach had simply been unlucky to have developed Schizophrenia and rationalized their belief that his use of methamphetamine was unrelated to his psychosis because they themselves had used more meth and had not developed psychotic symptoms. Of course neither parent was as young as Zach was when he had started on street drugs. Zach's care was transferred to a different psychiatrist by his parents who did not want to hear about the addiction issues from me anymore. This was a clear-cut case of Amphetamine-Induced Psychotic Disorder that our clinic was unable to address because of uncooperative parents too consumed with guilt to get their son the help he really needed. To my knowledge, Zach may still be using meth to this day.

PART 3

DOES YOUR CHILD *REALLY* NEED MEDICATION?

Introduction

Medications, while often very helpful, are not always required to treat mental illness effectively. If your child is prescribed psychotropic drugs, be sure to complement his medicines with the psychological and social treatments outlined in part 4 of this book.

- Remember, should you do choose to medicate your child, the best results will be achieved by combining medication with other psychological and social interventions. Psychotherapy can help him by addressing the troubles he has in his interpersonal relationships, in his thought patterns, and his concepts about life. You can help your child by making adjustments in other problem areas of his life, such as his school, his neighborhood, or his family environment. Medicating your child without addressing these underlying issues is like placing a Band-Aid on a wound without cleaning and treating the injured tissue first.

- If drugs are to be administered, it is important to understand one important principle: medications do not target the *disorder*, they target the *symptom(s)*. Any medication chosen to treat your child should address a particular symptom, regardless of the disorder in which that symptom may occur. Thus, the same medication may be used in a number of different psychiatric diagnoses. This explains why children with Major Depressive Disorder with Psychotic Features, for example, would be treated with an antipsychotic medication. Your child, in this example, might be treated with an antidepressant for the depressed mood and an antipsychotic for the psychotic symptoms (hallucinations or delusions.)

- In general, for the treatment of any of the anxiety disorders, your child will require a higher dose of medication than is usually given for depression. For anxiety, I usually need to provide a child with double the dose typically taken for depression and, for Obsessive Compulsive

Disorder, some children need even more than would be needed usually for anxiety disorders in general. At a lower dose, many of my child patients would still be suffering with their anxiety or OCD, but if I increased their dose of the antidepressant, then their symptoms would be well controlled.

- Caution should be used when treating your child with a benzodiazepine. Benzodiazepines are very addicting when taken every day. Withdrawal from an addiction to this class of drug can be both painful and dangerous. Additionally, some children have a paradoxically opposite reaction to benzodiazepines. Unfortunately, on these medications, they may become *more* anxious and agitated instead of less. Proceed with caution.

- As your child's parent and health advocate, it is your responsibility to decide if the potential benefits to your child of psychiatric drugs outweigh the risks associated with them. After you have informed yourself sufficiently about the benefits and relative risks of each type of treatment, including addiction to some types of medications, you need to work with your child's doctors and therapists to develop a treatment plan that best suits your child. Ultimately, the choice of which treatments your child receives is always yours.

- The potential benefits of any medication has to be weighed against the potential risks associated with it. In the chapters that follow, you will find a list of the medications most commonly used today. They represent a wide variety of very different chemical compounds. Both the most common and any of the dangerous side effects, will be listed under each class of medication. This is not an exhaustive list of every single possible side effect. Complete information on medication side effects can be found in the *Physician's Desk Reference* or from your pharmacist. It is always a good idea to obtain such information about the medications your child is taking as soon as they're prescribed, to be able to compare it against any symptoms of side effects that your child may develop.

- It is worth repeating that the information in this book should not be considered a replacement for an appropriate assessment and treatment by a trained professional.

18

ANTIDEPRESSANTS

REALISTIC EXPECTATIONS OF ANTIDEPRESSANTS

ANTIDEPRESSANT MEDICATIONS CAN be used for a number of different disorders because the symptoms that antidepressants treat can occur in a variety of psychiatric conditions. Therefore, regardless of what his *diagnosis* may be, if your child has one of the following *symptoms*, antidepressant medication may be helpful in bringing him relief.

- Sad or depressed mood
- Anxiety, nervousness, or fearfulness
- Panic attacks
- Obsessions, including eating obsessions
- Compulsions
- Anger
- Irritated mood
- Agitation
- Sleep problems
- Nightmares due to trauma
- Appetite problems
- Low energy and fatigue

- Poor concentration associated with depressed or anxious moods
- Hopelessness
- Suicidal thoughts

How Antidepressant Medications Can and Cannot Help Your Child

ANTIDEPRESSANT MEDICATIONS ALONE cannot cure depression if other psychosocial issues have not been addressed. Such drugs can alleviate some of the symptoms listed above but if the underlying causes of your child's depression remain, then he cannot really recover. Imagine the man who continually hits his head all day, complaining to his doctor that the aspirin he is taking has brought no relief to his headache. If a child's depression arises out of a negative experience at school, where he is failing classes and being teased by peers, all the antidepressant medication in the world is not going to address his depression. At the same time that this child is being treated with medications, he should also be receiving psychotherapy, getting academic assistance, and making changes to his social life that address his isolation and alienation from his peers.

Your child may be experiencing several symptoms or problems that medications cannot address. For example, one of the key features of Major Depressive Disorder is low self-esteem. Antidepressants cannot treat low self-esteem. Good self-esteem develops from one thing: accomplishment. To help your child build self-esteem, you need to find a way for him to feel successful at something. A few of the other childhood difficulties that parents often hope might be cured with antidepressants are: learning difficulties, belligerence, and defiance. Unfortunately, these problems cannot be treated with medications, either. These issues have to be treated with psychosocial interventions.

As a general rule, antidepressant medications need roughly four to six weeks, on a full dose, to take effect. This waiting period requires a lot of patience because results may not even begin until after at least six weeks have passed. A common misconception is that improvements with antidepressants will be seen in small increments throughout the six-week waiting period. This is not true. It is quite possible that your child will see no improvement in his symptoms until after the entire waiting period has passed. If you are not aware of this property of antidepressant medications, you can quickly lose faith in the medication and in the doctor who prescribed it to your child.

No doctor can predict with absolute certainty which antidepressant medication will be the right one for your child. Doctors make an educated guess about the type of antidepressant that might be beneficial. After choosing a medication, all you and your doctor can do is wait. If your child can tolerate the potential side effects, you will have to wait the necessary four to six weeks before you can determine that the medication your child is taking is the one that will treat his symptoms. Even after waiting six weeks, your doctor may likely tell you that the dose of the medication needs to be increased before abandoning that medication for a different one. If your child has not started to recover from his depression, you may assume that your child is on the wrong psychiatric medication. In actuality, the two most common reasons that psychiatric medications appear not to be working are:

- Your child was not taking a high enough dose of the antidepressant medication, or
- He had not been taking his medication faithfully every day for a long enough time.

Antidepressant medication can be a lifesaver. When your doctor finds the right medication at the right dose for your child, the difference can be dramatic. Once your child's symptoms are under control on antidepressants, your doctor will typically want to keep your child on the medications for at least one year. This allows your child to stabilize emotionally, socially, and neuro-chemically. Depending on his diagnosis and the severity of his condition when treatment started, your child may therefore be a candidate to be weaned off his medication after a year has passed. This is a decision that must be discussed with your doctor.

The best outcomes are possible when every aspect of treatment is applied to his problem. This means engaging all the psychosocial interventions as well as psychiatric medications. The key to success is finding a good doctor and therapist who can work with each other, and with you and the school staff, as a team, for the benefit of your child.

THE RISKS OF MEDICATING YOUR CHILD WITH ANTIDEPRESSANT MEDICATIONS

No medication is without some sort of risk. It is important to know that most of the side effects from antidepressant medications usually resolve on their own after one to two weeks. If your child is being treated for anxiety, antidepressant medications, especially the **SSRI** class, can cause him to feel *more* anxious initially. Parents who are not aware of this effect while using antidepressants to treat anxiety, may become confused and disheartened. Trust that, once the right antidepressant has had time to take effect, your anxious child should feel a great deal of relief.

SELECTIVE SEROTONIN REUPTAKE INHIBITORS (SSRI)

Drug Names
- Prozac (fluoxetine)
- Paxil (paroxetine)
- Zoloft (sertraline)
- Luvox (fluvoxamine)
- Celexa (citalopram)
- Lexapro (escitalopram)

Common Side Effects of SSRI
- Nausea
- Stomach upset
- Diarrhea
- Dry mouth
- Insomnia
- Sleepiness
- Decreased appetite

For rare but potentially permanent or serious side effects of antidepressants, see pages 162–163.

COMBINED SEROTONIN AND NOREPINEPHRINE REUPTAKE INHIBITORS

Drug Names
- Effexor XR (venlafaxine)
- Cymbalta (duloxetine)

Common Side Effects of Serotonin and Norepinephrine Reuptake Inhibitors
- Nausea
- Stomach upset
- Sleepiness
- Dry mouth

- Dizziness
- Constipation
- Decreased appetite

Rare but Potentially Permanent or Serious Side Effects of Serotonin and Norepinephrine Reuptake Inhibitors
- increased blood pressure

Also, for rare but potentially permanent or serious side effects of antidepressants, see pages 162–163.

Dopamine Reuptake Inhibitors

Drug Name
- Wellbutrin XL (buproprion)

Unique Qualities of Wellbutrin
- Wellbutrin does not treat anxiety, panic, or obsessive compulsive disorder.
- Wellbutrin has been shown to be effective in AD/HD.

Common Side Effects of Wellbutrin
- Headache
- Nausea
- Insomnia
- Restlessness
- Dry mouth
- Constipation
- Decreased appetite

Rare but Potentially Permanent or Serious Side Effects of Wellbutrin
- At doses over the recommended range of 300 mg. to 450 mg., there is an increased incidence of seizures.

Also, for rare but potentially permanent or serious side effects of antidepressants, see pages 162–163.

PRESYNAPTIC ALPHA ADRENERGIC ANTAGONIST

- Remeron (mirtazapine)

Common Side Effects of Remeron
- Nausea
- Stomach upset
- Increased appetite
- Weight gain
- Sleepiness, fatigue
- Dry mouth
- Dizziness
- Constipation

Rare but Potentially Permanent or Serious Side Effects of Remeron
- Agranulocytosis, a condition in which the body is not producing enough white blood cells

Also, for rare but potentially permanent or serious side effects of antidepressants, see pages 162–163.

TRICYCLIC ANTIDEPRESSANTS

Drug Names
- Tofranil (imipramine)
- Pamelor (nortriptyline)
- Elavil (amitriptyline)
- Sinequan (doxepin)
- Anafranil (clomipramine)

Common Side Effects of Tricyclic Antidepressants
- Nausea
- Stomach upset
- Increased appetite
- Weight gain
- Sleepiness, fatigue
- Dry mouth
- Blurred vision
- Urinary retention (unable to urinate) or urinary hesitation

- Constipation
- Dizziness

Rare but Potentially Permanent or Serious Side Effects of Tricyclic Antidepressants
- Heart complications, especially those with preexisting cardiac conditions
- Overdoses intended as a suicide attempt can be fatal; other antidepressants are safer in overdose.

Also, for rare but potentially permanent or serious side effects of antidepressants, see pages 162–163.

SEROTONIN REUPTAKE INHIBITOR

Drug Names
- Desyrel (trazadone)
- Serazone (nefazodone) This medication is no longer on the market due to adverse reactions.

Unique Qualities of Desyrel
- Desyrel (trazadone) is effective for the treatment of insomnia and nightmares in children who have been traumatized. Though this medication is not often used as an antidepressant alone, it is still popular as a treatment for insomnia with or without depression.

Common Side Effects of Serotonin Reuptake Inhibitor
- Nausea
- Stomach upset
- Sleepiness, fatigue
- Dry mouth
- Dizziness, especially when first standing up from a sitting or lying-down position
- Headache

Rare but Potentially Permanent or Serious Side Effects of Serotonin Reuptake Inhibitor
- Priapism, a condition in which an erection of the penis will not reduce or relax

- Heart complications, especially those with preexisting cardiac conditions

Also, for rare but potentially permanent or serious side effects of antidepressants, see pages 162–163.

Monoamine Oxidase Inhibitor (MAO-Inhibitor, or MAO-I)

Drug Names
- Parnate (tranylcypromine)
- Nardil (phenelzine)
- Eldepryl (selegiline)

Common and Serious Side Effects of MAO-Inhibitors
- **Tyramine-Induced Hypertensive Crisis:** Due to this potentially fatal reaction, great care must be taken when treating with **MAO-Inhibitors**. Although this class of antidepressant is thought to be very effective, it is rarely, if ever, used anymore because of this potential reaction. Children taking a MAO-Inhibitor cannot eat any foods rich in tyramines, such as certain cheeses, meats, beans, pickled products, packaged soups, orange pulp, or alcohol. There are many other foods that can only be eaten in small amounts. Also, many medications cannot be taken with MAO-Inhibitors. When a package warning on over-the-counter medicine warns it cannot be taken at the same time that you are taking an antidepressant, the MAO-Inhibitor is the antidepressant to which the warning refers. Upon combining a forbidden food or medication with an MAO-I, your child's blood pressure would rise to a level that could cause a stroke.

Common Side Effects of MAO-Inhibitors
- Increased appetite
- Weight gain
- Insomnia
- Dizziness, especially when first standing up from a sitting or lying-down position
- Muscle pain and stiffness

Rare but Potentially Permanent or Serious Side Effects of MAO-Inhibitors
- Tyramine-Induced Hypertensive Crisis (see above)

- Caution must be exercised when treating with MAO-I in children with kidney problems, seizure disorders, or hyperthyroidism because of the interaction between the MAO-I and most of the medications that are required to treat these diseases.
- Heart complications, especially those with preexisting cardiac conditions
- Overdoses intended as a suicide attempt can be fatal; other antidepressants are safer in overdose.

Also, for rare but potentially permanent or serious side effects of antidepressants, see pages 162–163.

SPECIAL ISSUES CONCERNING ANTIDEPRESSANTS

SUICIDE

In 2004, a great controversy was stirred up in Congress by parents who claimed the Selective Serotonin Reuptake Inhibitors (SSRI)–class antidepressants that their teenage children were taking for depression had caused the adolescents to attempt or commit suicide. As a result, the U.S. Food and Drug Administration (FDA) required that a warning label be added to all antidepressant prescriptions.

In the February 2005 issue of *Nature Reviews: Drug Discovery*, Dr. Julio Licinio, professor of psychiatry at the University of California–Los Angeles (UCLA) School of Medicine, published the results of his study on SSRI medication use in children over the last forty-five years.[1] Licinio's results show that the suicide rates in the United States and Europe steadily climbed every year from 1960 until 1988. Then, there was a dramatic change. In 1988, when the first SSRI medication ever developed, Prozac, was introduced to the market, the suicide rate declined substantially and continued to do so. According to the U.S. Center for Disease Control and Prevention, suicide has fallen in the United States from the eighth leading cause of death in 1998 to the eleventh in 2002.[2]

What is well known to most psychiatrists about SSRI medications and verified by Licinio, is that when patients' energy is restored to its normal level from before their depressed mood, their feelings of hopelessness and thoughts about ending their lives have resolved. This energy gives them the boost they need to act on their thoughts of suicide. This is why it is important to watch children and adults closely during the early part of their treatment on any antidepressant. Eventually, after approximately six weeks, antidepressants will treat all these symptoms of depression, including the suicidal feelings.

VIOLENCE

Jeff Weise was the Native American teen from the Red Lake Indian Reservation in Minnesota who went on a shooting spree at his high school and killed ten people, including himself, on March 21, 2005. This sixteen-year-old boy had been in trouble with the police and had been suspended from his high school, for reasons that remain confidential. He was known to be a heavy drinker and he used marijuana. His father committed suicide when Jeff was eight years old and, the following year, his mother was placed in a nursing home due to permanent brain damage caused by an auto accident. Jeff frequented Nazi Web sites, and claimed an allegiance to Hitler and a belief in racial cleansing. He created movie shorts online with violent, murderous themes. One year prior to the March 2005 killings, a threat of a school shooting had been made at this same high school, a threat Jeff was suspected of making but for which he was later cleared. His two aunts, with whom he had been living at the time, reported that they realized that he was a very troubled boy. Because of his emotional problems, his aunts had taken him for help. Whether the boy received any psychotherapy, counseling, or drug rehabilitation is unknown but probably unlikely, based on the absence of such reports. In spite of all of this evidence, there are people who are trying to place the responsibility for these killings on the antidepressant medication Jeff was taking at the time of the shootings.

19

AMPHETAMINES

REALISTIC EXPECTATIONS OF AMPHETAMINES

AMPHETAMINES ARE VERY effective medications that work almost immediately, within twenty minutes of ingestion. Just as you will find with any psychiatric medication, amphetamines treat *symptoms* not a *diagnosis*. This means that even though amphetamines are most often prescribed for AD/HD, your child does not have to be diagnosed with AD/HD to benefit from the effects of amphetamines. The old wives' tale that only children with AD/HD will benefit from amphetamine medications, is completely false. Amphetamines can help almost anyone with the symptoms that this drug class targets. The exception is a child with anxiety. Anxious children find that amphetamines cause them increased anxiety and agitation. The following symptoms respond to amphetamines:

- Poor concentration
- Inattention
- Easy distraction
- Low energy
- Fatigue
- Sleepiness

- Excessive appetite and unwanted weight gain
- Hyperactivity. Amphetamines can help to reduce hyperactivity as a secondary result of the child's improved concentration and attention; when a child is paying more attention to his teacher or his schoolwork, he is not as hyperactive.

HISTORY OF AMPHETAMINES

A GERMAN CHEMIST first synthesized amphetamines in 1887. In 1937 Charles Bradley used amphetamines clinically for the first time in a child and was able to demonstrate that these drugs were capable of improving the child's concentration. Later, amphetamines were used extensively during World War II by Japan, Germany, and the USA to help soldiers stay awake longer, maintain more sustained attention, and reduce their need for food and sleep while in combat. Although amphetamines did indeed have all these intended effects, the downside was that amphetamines also caused soldiers to become angrier, depressed, irritable, agitated, anxious, paranoid, and even psychotic. The project was scrapped because military doctors found that the benefits did not outweigh the ill effects.

In the United States in the 1950s, legally manufactured tablets of amphetamines became readily available and were used non-medically by college students, truck drivers, and athletes to improve attention and performance. Amphetamines were readily available without a prescription and became a cure-all for such things as weight control and treating mild depression. As the use of amphetamines spread, so did their abuse. Amphetamine abuse became popular with cocaine addicts after cocaine became illegal in 1914 because amphetamines produced a very similar effect as cocaine. By 1965 amphetamines were only available with a prescription. Again, the patients taking these amphetamines had the same side effects that had stopped their use in soldiers. The problems caused by amphetamine treatments used as diet pills created a lot of negative press at that time. Subsequently, doctors stopped prescribing amphetamines as a weight-loss drug.

By the 1980s, amphetamines were being used extensively to help children with attention-deficit problems and the number of new cases increased dramatically and continues to climb today. Amphetamine-class medications have enjoyed great popularity with parents and teachers. Despite the negative reports in the media about amphetamines through the years, this class of drug continues to be widely prescribed. The DEA reported that from 1990 to 95, Ritalin prescriptions increased sixfold.

How Amphetamine Medications
Can and Cannot Help Your Child

THE CONTINUED POPULARITY of amphetamines is due to the fact that they are very effective at improving concentration and academic performance. Children with AD/HD are helped tremendously by these drugs. Furthermore, unless your child has some sort of anxiety disorder, amphetamine medications can improve your child's attention even if he does *not* have AD/HD. In my clinical practice, I have become aware of parents who purposely deceive their child's pediatrician into believing that the child has AD/HD, so that the doctor will prescribe amphetamines. They create this deception to give their children what they believe is a "competitive edge" in school. These parents know that the improved powers of attention and concentration that amphetamines can provide, will allow their child to score higher on tests and get better grades in school. Ritalin and the other amphetamines truly are performance-enhancing drugs.

Amphetamines can improve an AD/HD student's poor performance enough to allow him to earn average scores and grades. When given to an average student, one who is bored or unmotivated, amphetamines can help boost his scores to the excellent range. Today on college campuses across the United States, and unbeknownst to their parents, students are acquiring prescription amphetamines, referring to such amphetamines as Ritalin, Adderall, and Concerta as "study drugs," because these medications improve academic performance across the board. Several college students interviewed on ABC's *Prime Time Live* on June 2, 2005, admitted that they fool their doctor into believing they have the diagnosis of AD/HD so they can be prescribed amphetamines. If that does not work, these students said, they could always illicitly purchase amphetamines on campus, where these drugs are readily available from fellow students.

Like most other psychiatric conditions, AD/HD is best treated with more than just medications. Children with AD/HD do best when there is a comprehensive treatment plan that includes adjustments to their educational and home environments. This plan can include changes to the teaching approach, seating arrangement in the classroom, and the teacher-to-student ratio; implementation of a behavior-modification program in the classroom for the student; and changes to the homework study space and routine at home.

Many parents are disappointed to learn that amphetamines cannot make a child behave himself. If your child is not paying attention in class because he does not want to pay attention, then amphetamines will not help him very much. I treated a boy who explained to me that he did not *want* to pay attention in class. He told me that he could "overpower the focusing effect" of his

Ritalin, so he could carry on with his own goal to entertain his classmates with his silly antics.

Drug Names
- Ritalin LA (methylphenidate)
- Concerta (methylphenidate)
- Metadate CD (methylphenidate)
- Methylin ER (methylphenidate)
- Dexadrine (dextroamphetamine)
- DextroStat (dextroamphetamine)
- Adderall XR (dextroamphetamine)
- Focalin (dex-methylphenidate)

The Risks of Medicating Your Child with Amphetamines

Common Side Effects of Amphetamines
- Insomnia
- Loss of appetite
- Weight loss
- Stunted growth
- Irritability, anger, and agitation
- Depression
- Anxiety
- Increased heart rate
- Increased blood pressure

Rare but Potentially Serious or Permanent Side Effects of Amphetamines
- Addiction has become a serious problem with amphetamine medication. In 1996, the DEA found that 30 to 50 percent of teens in drug treatment centers were using Ritalin for recreational purposes. Prescription amphetamines are crushed and snorted to achieve the very same "high" that drug users get from cocaine or street speed. Some drug abusers even dissolve the amphetamine medication and inject it into their bloodstream. This causes complications with blockage of vessels, due to some of the fillers found in the pill form.

- These medications are very addicting when abused. They are being bought and sold by students from junior high school through college and beyond. These amphetamines are also used for performance enhancement when students want to cram at the end of the semester at the college level. A 1994 University of Michigan study showed that more high school seniors were abusing Ritalin than were seniors taking Ritalin with a legitimate prescription. In 1998, Indiana University found that almost 7 percent of high school freshmen had used Ritalin illicitly. In a 2004 study by Partnership for a Drug-Free America, more teens were abusing prescription amphetamines (10%) than were abusing crack or cocaine (9%), ecstasy (9%) street speed (8%) LSD (6%), or heroin (4%).

- Motor tics can develop after a brief period of treatment on amphetamine medication, but more often tics develop after many years on amphetamines. Sometimes this condition will resolve once the amphetamine is discontinued. Sometimes the motor tic disorder remains a permanent condition.

- Seizures can develop as a result of treatment with amphetamine medication. It appears that the threshold for having a seizure is lowered by amphetamines. Once the medication is discontinued, the seizures resolve.

- Psychosis (delusions, paranoia, and hallucinations) can be caused by long-term treatment with prescription amphetamines, just as it can occur with street amphetamines (albeit much faster). In every way, your child will appear to have paranoid schizophrenia. There is no absolute proof of the connection, as defenders of prescription amphetamines will claim that the child treated with these drugs for ten years would have developed Schizophrenia anyway. There is no way to prove or disprove this association. This is information that can only be acquired through clinical practice. There are no controlled studies longer than six weeks on most of these prescription amphetamines. Therefore, it is necessary to rely on the observations of doctors who have been treating children with these medications for years.

- Agitation, anger, and violence can develop as a result of long-term treatment with prescription amphetamines. Again, these cases of agitated, irritable, violent children are only seen in the clinical setting, after the child has received many years of treatment with prescription amphetamines. I treated a fifteen-year-old boy who had been taking Ritalin or some other prescription amphetamine for ten years. Initially, at five years of age, he had appeared much improved on the Ritalin. This emboldened his parents and doctors to assume that, because he concentrated better on amphetamines, he must have had AD/HD. After the boy had spent ten years on prescription amphetamines, his doctor sent the family to me for a second opinion on the teen's violent behavior. No matter how many adjustments were made to his amphetamine prescriptions, the boy was still violent. He would behave well enough at school to be on the honor roll and had no behavioral problems in the classroom yet, when he got home, he beat up his parents and siblings, tortured the family dog, punched holes in the walls, and even set small fires in the house to entertain himself. When I stopped his amphetamine prescription and started him on an SSRI antidepressant, he changed into an entirely different boy. He was no longer agitated or violent. He continued to earn good grades.

Special Issues Concerning Amphetamines

IF YOUR CHILD has any kind of cardiac condition, extreme caution should be used when choosing to put your child on a prescription amphetamine. Adderall XR (dextroamphetamine) was pulled off the market in Canada early in 2005 after researchers there concluded that this drug had some causal link to twenty deaths in adults and children. The FDA followed with a posting of its own results, concluding that of the twenty, twelve cases of sudden death between 1999 and 2003 in boys aged seven to sixteen, *may* have been related to Adderall. Upon autopsy, five were shown to have had preexisting cardiac conditions but seven of the boys had normal hearts. By October 2005, the makers of Adderall were able to convince the pharmaceutical regulatory body in Canada to lift its ban on their drug.

What Is Strattera?

STRATTERA (ATOMOXETINE) IS a new approach to the treatment of AD/HD. Instead of using an amphetamine-class drug, this drug uses a similar mechanism of action as the medications that treat depression. Strattera is really more like an antidepressant in the Tricyclic class, because Strattera is a selective norepinephrine reuptake inhibitor. Therefore, children treated with Strattera do not face the same risks associated with the treatment of amphetamines (see page 167).

Strattera, unlike the amphetamines and more like an antidepressant, can need up to six weeks to take effect. This waiting period requires a lot of patience because results may not even begin until after at least six weeks have passed. A common misconception is that improvements with antidepressants will be seen in small increments throughout the six-week waiting period. This is not true. It is quite possible that your child will see no improvement in his symptoms until after the entire waiting period has passed. Parents who are not aware of this reality of antidepressant medication, can quickly lose faith in the medication and in the doctor who prescribed it.

Strattera is most effective at quieting your child's hyperactivity, but also has some benefit for improving attention.

Common Side Effects of Strattera
- Nausea
- Stomach upset
- Decreased appetite
- Insomnia
- Dry mouth
- Constipation
- Dizziness

Rare but Potentially Serious Side Effects of Strattera

Strattera can cause increases in blood pressure and heart rate. Regular monitoring is advised. Caution should be exercised when considering Strattera for any child who has a preexisting cardiac condition that would be adversely affected by an increase in blood pressure.

20

ANTIPSYCHOTICS

REALISTIC EXPECTATIONS OF ANTIPSYCHOTICS

ANTIPSYCHOTIC MEDICATIONS ARE very effective at treating a number of different symptoms regardless of your child's diagnosis. Just as you will find with any psychiatric medication, antipsychotics treat a *symptom* not a *diagnosis*. Antipsychotics have benefits that are experienced minutes after ingesting the medication. These medications can also provide additional symptom relief as much as six weeks later (when taken daily.) The newer antipsychotics, called **atypicals**, are much improved and have fewer side effects than the older members of this class of drug. The following symptoms can respond to antipsychotics:

- Hallucinations: hearing and seeing things that do not exist
- Delusions: believing impossible or bizarre things to be true
- Paranoia
- Disconnected thinking: being unable to keep a train of thought
- Agitation
- Anger and irritability
- Violence and aggression
- Hyperactivity

- Impulsivity
- Mania
- Insomnia
- Motor or vocal tics
- Stereotypies: the flapping and self-stimulating behaviors of autistic children
- Obsessions and compulsions
- Vomiting

HOW ANTIPSYCHOTIC MEDICATIONS CAN AND CANNOT HELP YOUR CHILD

ANTIPSYCHOTICS ARE VERY effective medications. For a child who develops psychotic symptoms, these medications can be a lifesaver. Due to the improvements found in the new generation of antipsychotics, long-term treatment with these medications is much more easily tolerated.

There are immediate and long-term benefits with antipsychotics. In the short term, these medications can reduce or eliminate hallucinations, agitation, and mania. In the long term, they can help schizophrenic patients come out of their deep social and emotional withdrawal. Furthermore, antipsychotics taken on a daily basis can prevent the recurrence of another psychotic episode.

What these antipsychotics can do for children with Schizophrenia, they can do for anyone, regardless of the diagnosis. Antipsychotics can treat any of the target symptoms listed earlier for this class of medication. Therefore, whether your child is agitated due to Schizophrenia, Bipolar Disorder, Post Traumatic Stress Disorder, or Oppositional Defiant Disorder (ODD), antipsychotic medications can reduce agitation. Even though antipsychotics do not have FDA approval for the treatment of all psychiatric diagnoses, it has become common practice to use them whenever they can be helpful.

It is important to keep in mind that, just because antipsychotics can treat one symptom in a diagnosis, this does not mean that these medications can treat *all* the symptoms of that diagnosis. With a diagnosis such as ODD, for example, a child would have the following symptoms: often angry, often touchy, easily annoyed, often losing his temper, blaming others, and defiant. Antipsychotics will not eliminate all these symptoms. On the other hand, these medications can appear to be at least partially effective for ODD by reducing your child's anger and temper outbursts.

Antipsychotics are strong sedatives and can create an illusion of successful treatment by resolving some of the symptoms of ODD. This partial progress can give the false impression of being able to provide a complete cure for such a child. Yes, they would be able to reduce the anger and the extent of his temper tantrums. However, though the ODD child's anger might show improvements while treated with antipsychotics, he would still be touchy, annoyed, and defiant. In the case of ODD, successful treatment cannot be achieved by simply reducing the child's anger with sedating medication. Other psychotherapeutic interventions must also be included for complete success. It is important to bear in mind that antipsychotics can be useful up to a point, but for many diagnoses they would only play a small role.

Drug Names
- Thorazine (chlorpromazine), an older antipsychotic with low potency
- Haldol (haloperidol), an older antipsychotic with high potency
- Clozaril (clozapine), an original atypical
- Risperdal (risperidone), a newer antipsychotic-atypical
- Zyprexa (olanzapine), a newer antipsychotic-atypical
- Seroquel (quetiapine), a newer antipsychotic-atypical
- Geodon (ziprasidone), a newer antipsychotic-atypical
- Abilify (aripiprazole), a newer antipsychotic-atypical

The Risks and Benefits of Medicating Your Child with Antipsychotics

THE POTENTIAL BENEFITS of antipsychotic medication have to be weighed against its dangerous, irreversible, and permanent side effects. Because antipsychotic medications are very powerful, they can have extreme consequences. Consider your options and the ramifications for your child before making the choice to start antipsychotics.

> Treating your child with antipsychotic medications
> is not something to be taken lightly.

Some of the side effects of antipsychotic medications are permanent and can affect your child for the rest of his life. Though the serious and dangerous side effects are a possibility, they are not common. Conversely, the common side effects are not as dangerous. An example of one of the less serious but very common side effects of antipsychotics is weight gain. Most children treated with antipsychotics gain a significant amount of weight. When the drug is combined with a mood stabilizer, as antipsychotics often are, a teen typically gains between 50 and 100 pounds.

COMMON SIDE EFFECTS OF ANTIPSYCHOTICS

- Weight gain (not as common with Geodon or Abilify)
- Sedation, sleepiness, and fatigue (less so with Abilify)
- Muscle stiffness
- Dry mouth
- Constipation
- Blurred vision
- Urinary retention (inability to urinate) or urinary hesitation
- Nausea
- Stomach upset
- Dizziness
- Sun sensitivity of skin; burns and rashes can result

SERIOUS BUT LESS COMMON SIDE EFFECTS OF ANTIPSYCHOTICS

- Locked, stiff, rigid muscles (acute dystonia)
- Twisting spasms of body and neck (torticollis)
- Jaw locked open (can cause jaw dislocation)
- Tongue protrudes involuntarily
- Development of female breasts in males (gynocomatia)
- Milk excreted from breast (galactorrhea)
- Irregular menstrual periods (amenorrhea)
- Seizures
- Rigid muscles, shuffling walk, tremors, stooped posture, and drooling (parkinsonism)
- Muscle discomfort, relentless pacing, agitated, repeatedly sitting and standing (akathisia)

RARE BUT POTENTIALLY PERMANENT OR LETHAL SIDE EFFECTS OF ANTIPSYCHOTICS

- **Tardive Dyskinesia (TD)** is a delayed effect of antipsychotic medications. This side effect rarely occurs until after your child had been taking the antipsychotics for at least six months. TD can be sustained and permanent even after the antipsychotics are stopped. Tardive dyskinesia includes:

- Constant, involuntary writhing and moving of limbs, torso, and neck
- Lip puckering and smacking
- Facial grimacing
- Tongue muscle spasms that cause the tongue to tremor, twist, dart, and protrude
- Involuntary chewing movements of the jaw
- Finger writhing and fist clenching
- Irregular muscle spasms; jerking and twisting of the body, neck, and head
- Hip thrusting

Tardive dyskinesia is more likely to develop, the longer your child takes these medications. Children are more at risk of developing TD than adults. The atypical antipsychotics cause TD less often than the older antipsychotics. Twenty percent of patients treated for more than one year on antipsychotics develop TD. Between 5 and 40 percent of all TD cases voluntarily resolve on their own. The approach to TD includes prevention, diagnosis, and management.

> **Prevention of TD is best achieved by not taking antipsychotics unless absolutely necessary.**

Unfortunately, the success with the newer atypical antipsychotics has created a rather lax attitude on the part of the doctors who are prescribing them to children. Diagnosis of TD is achieved by carefully, constantly watching for the signs of the disorder. Management requires stopping, switching or lowering the dose of the antipsychotic.

- **Neuroleptic Malignant Syndrome (NMS)** is a potentially fatal condition that can develop at any time while taking antipsychotics. Neuroleptic malignant syndrome can develop over a 24- to 72-hour period. If untreated, it can last up to fourteen days. The death rate can reach 30 percent in patients receiving their antipsychotics by injection.

The signs of NMS are: fluctuating alertness from mute and deeply sedated to agitated with muscle rigidity. Vital signs fluctuate as well. NMS can cause your child's temperature to rise to as high as 107 degrees Fahrenheit, as well as sweating, and increased blood pressure and heart rate. Treatment involves the immediate discontinuation of the antipsychotics, and emergency services to stabilize the child's fever and unstable vital signs. Medications that can treat NMS should be administered as soon as possible and include:

- Parlodel (bromocriptine)
- Dantrium (dantrolene)

SPECIAL ISSUES CONCERNING ANTIPSYCHOTICS

ANTIPSYCHOTICS CAUSE A number of movement disorders, including dystonia, parkinsonism, akathisia, and torticollis. The atypical antipsychotics cause these movement disorders less often than do the older antipsychotics. Some doctors wait to see signs of a movement disorder before starting one of these treatments. Others prefer to start one of the anticholinergic medications at the same time that the antipsychotic is begun as a prophylaxis. These movement disorders can be treated with the following anticholinergic medications:

Drug Names
- Cogentin (benztropine) anticholinergic
- Artane (trihexyphenidyl) anticholinergic
- Benadryl (diphenhydramine) antihistamine

CLOZARIL

CLOZARIL (CLOZAPINE) IS a unique antipsychotic that requires special consideration. Clozaril was the first atypical antipsychotic to be developed. It was the first antipsychotic to have significantly fewer side effects than is typical with the older antipsychotics. Also, Clozaril offered an alternative to patients who were not recovering on the standard antipsychotics. These "treatment-resistant" schizophrenic patients had a viable option for treatment with Clozaril, when everything else failed.

Unfortunately, Clozaril has serious side effects of its own in spite of its excellent clinical effectiveness. Patients taking Clozaril must be monitored on

a regular basis to watch for a potentially fatal condition called agranulocytosis. Agranulocytosis refers to the body's inability to produce white blood cells.
This condition is a rare side effect, only affecting 1 to 2 percent of people who
take Clozaril. However, in the early days, one-third of the patients who developed agranulocytosis died. Today, close monitoring has eliminated all casu-
alties from this side effect.

21

MOOD STABILIZERS

REALISTIC EXPECTATIONS OF MOOD STABILIZERS

THE TERM **MOOD** stabilizer refers to a diverse group of medications. With the exception of lithium, all the other mood stabilizers were originally developed as seizure medication. Mood-stabilizing medications are very effective at treating a number of different symptoms regardless of your child's diagnosis. Just as you will find with any psychiatric medication, mood stabilizers treat a *symptom* not a *diagnosis*. Mood stabilizers have some benefits that are experienced the same day you start the medication. Additional benefits are not seen until days to weeks later, if the medication is taken daily. The following symptoms can respond to mood-stabilizing medications:

- Mania
- Agitation
- Anger and irritability
- Violence and aggression
- Hyperactivity
- Impulsivity
- Depression
- Insomnia

- Headaches
- Seizures

How Mood Stabilizers Can
and Cannot Help Your Child

THERE ARE IMMEDIATE and long-term benefits with mood stabilizers. In the short term, these medications can reduce or eliminate agitation, aggression, insomnia, or headaches. In the long term, they can help Bipolar Disorder patients stabilize their mood and control their mania. Furthermore, mood stabilizers, taken on a daily basis, can prevent the recurrence of another manic episode.

Mood stabilizers are also used to augment the effects of other medications. Augmentation is simply boosting the benefits of another medication, such as an antipsychotic in the treatment of schizophrenia, or an antidepressant in the treatment of depression.

What these mood stabilizers can do for children with Bipolar Disorder, they can do for anyone, regardless of the diagnosis. Therefore, whether your child is agitated due to Bipolar Disorder, Asperger's Syndrome, Post Traumatic Stress Disorder, or Oppositional Defiant Disorder (ODD), mood-stabilizing medications will reduce his agitation. Mood stabilizers can treat any of the target symptoms listed earlier for this class of medication, regardless of the diagnosis. Even though mood stabilizers do not have FDA approval for the treatment of all psychiatric diagnoses, it has become common practice to use them whenever they might be helpful.

It is important to keep in mind that, just because mood stabilizers can treat one symptom in a diagnosis, this does not mean that these medications can treat all the symptoms of that same diagnosis. With a diagnosis such as ODD, for example, mood stabilizers will not eliminate your child's behaviors of defiance of your rules, arguing with you all the time, and blaming everyone else for his mistakes. On the other hand, these medications can be at least partially effective for ODD by reducing the child's anger and temper outbursts.

Mood stabilizers are strong sedatives. They will be able to reduce an ODD child's anger and the extent of his temper tantrums. This partial progress can give the false impression of being able to provide a complete cure for the diagnosis of ODD. Mood stabilizers can create an illusion of successful treatment by resolving some of the symptoms. However, though the child's anger may show improvements while treated with mood stabilizers, he would still be touchy, annoyed, and defiant. In the case of ODD, successful treatment cannot be achieved by simply reducing the child's anger with sedating medication.

Other psychotherapeutic interventions must also be included for complete success. It is important to bear in mind that mood stabilizers can be useful up to a point, but for many diagnoses they only play a small role.

Drug Names
- Eskalith, Lithobid (lithium)
- Depakote (valproate)
- Tegretol (carbamazepine)
- Equetro (carbamazepine)
- Trileptal (oxcarbazepine)
- Lamictal (lamotrigine)
- Topamax (topiramate)
- Neurontin (gabapentin). Research has now shown that Neurontin has no psychiatric benefit in treatment of such mood disorders as Bipolar Disorder or Major Depressive Disorder.

THE RISKS AND BENEFITS OF MEDICATING YOUR CHILD WITH MOOD STABILIZERS

MOOD STABILIZING MEDICATIONS can benefit your child by controlling his manic episodes or reducing his anger outbursts, but there are risks. Mood stabilizers are a very diverse group of medications. Each one of these medications has a unique set of side effects and safety issues. Although mood stabilizers are very powerful and effective medications, there are potentially severe consequences to this treatment. The possible benefits of mood-stabilizing medications have to be weighed against their dangerous, irreversible, and possibly permanent side effects. Consider your options and the ramifications for your child before making the choice to start mood stabilizers.

> **Treating your child with mood-stabilizing medications is not something to be taken lightly.**

Some of the side effects of these medications are permanent and can affect your child for the rest of his life. Though they are not common, the serious and dangerous side effects are a possibility. Conversely, the common side effects are not as dangerous. An example of one of the less serious but very common side effects of mood stabilizers is weight gain. Most children treated with mood stabilizers gain a significant amount of weight. When such drugs are administered alone or when combined with an antipsychotic (as mood stabilizers often are), a teen typically gains between 50 and 100 pounds.

LITHIUM

Lithium is a salt, an element. Unlike most medications, it is not a compound of chemicals. It was the first mood-stabilizing medication ever developed. Unlike all the other mood stabilizers, Lithium has never been used to treat seizures.

Common Side Effects of Lithium
- Sedation, fatigue, and lethargy
- Excessive weight gain
- Nausea and vomiting
- Fine tremors
- Diarrhea
- Excessive thirst
- Frequent urinating
- Dehydration
- Headaches
- Dizziness

Rare but Serious and Potentially Lethal Side Effects of Lithium
- **Lithium toxicity:** Symptoms of lithium toxicity include: persistent vomiting, unsteadiness, stumbling walk, muscle weakness, slurred speech, blurred vision, ringing in the ears, confusion, seizures, and coma. When lithium toxicity is severe enough, your child can have generalized convulsions, his kidneys could shut down, and he could die. Toxicity occurs when the lithium level gets too high. The lithium level in the body must be maintained very carefully within a narrow range to be safe. Also, not consuming enough salt or adequate water will cause toxic levels to develop. Sweating excessively can cause higher concentrations of lithium to develop in your child's body, so he must avoid activities that require a great deal of sweating. To monitor his lithium level, your child will have to go to the lab to have his blood drawn every week to every six months, depending on how long he has been taking lithium. If not maintained carefully, the lithium level in your child could become toxic.

- **Kidney failure:** Although excessive thirst and urination are common problems with lithium, permanent damage can occur. This is a rare complication. Still, it is important to monitor kidney function through regular blood testing. These tests can be included with the regular testing of the lithium levels.
- **Thyroid compromise:** Over time, lithium can suppress the thyroid. Lithium can compromise the functioning of the thyroid, causing it to produce less thyroid hormone. The impact lithium has on the thyroid gland is thought to be benign and temporary. Careful monitoring of thyroid functioning is also required and can be included with the other blood tests for lithium levels.
- **Cardiac affect:** Because of lithium's ability to replace potassium in the body, lithium can impact the heart function. The effect of lithium on the heart is thought to be temporary and disappear after lithium is stopped. Nonetheless, it is wise to get an ECG (electrocardiogram) at least once, just prior to starting lithium. In rare cases, lithium has caused arrhythmias and congestive heart failure.

Depakote

Depakote was originally developed to control seizures. It has also been found to be a very effective medication to treat Bipolar Disorder, reduce anger and aggression, treat headaches and migraines, supplement antidepressants in the treatment of depression, and supplement antipsychotics in the treatment of schizophrenia.

Common Side Effects of Depakote

- Sedation, fatigue, and lethargy
- Excessive weight gain (as much as 100 pounds in one year, in a teen)
- Dizziness
- Nausea and vomiting
- Diarrhea
- Confusion
- Tremor
- Unsteadiness walking

Less Common but Serious and Potentially Lethal Side Effects of Depakote

- **Liver failure:** Depakote can cause serious liver failure, which can be fatal. Symptoms of liver failure are: fatigue, weakness, feeling sick as if with flu, swelling of the face, vomiting, loss of appetite, yellowing of the whites of the eyes, and black tarry stools. If your child develops the symptoms of liver failure, you should seek *immediate* medical attention for him. Great care must be taken to monitor liver function with regular blood testing. The testing should occur weekly to once every six months, depending on how long your child has been taking Depakote.

- **Pancreas failure:** Depakote can cause failure of the pancreas as well. This condition can also be fatal. Pancreatic failure is not dependent on how long your child has been taking Depakote. This condition can develop during the initial phase of treatment. The failure of the pancreas can develop rapidly and progress to death quickly. Symptoms of pancreatic failure are: abdominal pain, nausea, and vomiting. If your child develops the symptoms of pancreatic failure, you should seek *immediate* medical attention for him. Again, blood tests of pancreatic enzymes are required on a regular basis and can be combined with the liver tests.
- **Thrombocytopenia:** decreased production of platelets in the body. Platelets are responsible for allowing blood to clot at a wound site. Without platelets, an injury would cause a person to bleed uncontrollably, and blunt trauma would cause excessive bruising. Depakote can cause a decrease in the platelet count but not to a dangerous level.
- **Aplastic anemia:** a condition in which the body is unable to produce any blood cells, white or red. Symptoms of aplastic anemia are: weakness, fatigue, difficulty fighting infections, and slow healing of wounds. Again, blood tests for the levels of red and white cells are required on a regular basis and can be combined with the liver tests.
- **Hair loss** is rare but usually reversible once the Depakote is stopped.

Tegretol and Equetro

Tegretol and Equetro are two different brand names for the generic drug called carbamazepine. Tegretol has been available for many years and was originally developed to treat seizures. Equetro is an extended-release version of carbamazepine, also a seizure treatment medication. Both Tegretol and Equetro are approved for use for Bipolar Disorder.

Common Side Effects of Tegretol and Equetro
- Sedation, fatigue, and lethargy
- Excessive weight gain
- Dizziness

- Nausea and vomiting
- Diarrhea
- Constipation
- Confusion
- Tremor
- Unsteadiness walking

Rare but Serious and Potentially Lethal Side Effects of Tegretol and Equetro
- **Aplastic anemia and agranulocytosis:** conditions in which the body is unable to produce any blood cells, white or red. Symptoms of aplastic anemia and agranulocytosis are: fever, sore throat, weakness, fatigue, difficulty fighting infections, and slow healing of wounds. These symptoms are an indication that your child may have developed aplastic anemia and agranulocytosis in reaction to Tegretol or Equetro. If your child develops the symptoms of aplastic anemia and agranulocytosis, you should seek immediate medical attention for him, as this condition can be lethal. Great care must be taken to monitor the levels of red and white blood cells with regular blood testing. The testing should occur weekly to once every six months, depending on how long your child has been taking Tegretol or Equetro.
- **Thrombocytopenia:** decreased production of platelets in the body. Tegretol and Equetro can cause a decrease in the platelet count. Platelets are responsible for allowing blood to clot at a wound site. Without platelets, an injury would cause a person to bleed uncontrollably, and blunt trauma would cause excessive bruising. Signs of thrombocytopenia are: easy bruising and easy bleeding. These symptoms are indications that your child may have developed thrombocytopenia in reaction to Tegretol or Equetro. If your child develops the symptoms of thrombocytopenia, you should seek immediate medical attention for him, as this condition can be lethal. Your child's platelet levels should be monitored regularly. These blood tests can be combined with the tests of the blood cells.
- **Hepatitis:** Tegretol and Equetro can cause serious liver conditions, which can be fatal. Symptoms of hepatitis are: fatigue, weakness, feeling sick as if with flu, swelling of the face, vomiting, loss of appetite, yellowing of the whites of the eyes, and black tarry stools. Great care must be taken to monitor liver function with regular blood testing. These blood tests can be combined with the tests of the blood cells.

- **Exfoliative dermatitis:** Tegretol and Equetro can commonly cause a benign rash. Unfortunately, some of these medication-induced rashes can develop into a serious, life-threatening rash. For this reason, should your child develop a rash of any kind, your doctor will likely want to discontinue the Tegretol or Equetro. You should seek immediate consultation with your doctor before continuing with the treatment.
- **Cardiac complications:** There have been rare instances of Tegretol or Equetro causing heart conditions that can lead to death. Children with heart conditions should probably not be started on Tegretol and Equetro. Discuss this with your doctor.

TRILEPTAL

Trileptal was developed to treat partial seizures by itself or in conjunction with other seizure medications. It has approval for treatment in children as young as four years old. Trileptal is clinically similar to Tegretol and Equetro but with a much less dangerous side-effect profile.

Common Side Effects of Trileptal
- Confused or slow thinking
- Slurred speech
- Sedation, fatigue, and lethargy
- Unsteadiness walking
- Headaches
- Dizziness
- Nausea and vomiting
- Blurred or double vision
- Tremor

Rare but Serious and Potentially Lethal Side Effects of Trileptal
- **Hyponatremia:** Trileptal can cause sodium levels in the blood to lower below normal levels, which is called *hyponatremia*. Signs that your child might be developing hyponatremia are: increased nausea, headache, confusion, severe sedation, and difficulty awakening. The Trileptal dose must be adjusted or the medication discontinued, but always consult with your doctor first.
- **Exfoliative dermatitis:** Trileptal can commonly cause a benign rash. Unfortunately, some of these medication-induced rashes can develop

into a serious, life-threatening rash. These lethal forms of rash are very rare, as few as one in a million. Still, should your child develop a rash of any kind, your doctor will likely want to discontinue the Trileptal. You should seek immediate consultation with your doctor before continuing with the treatment.

LAMICTAL

Lamictal was originally developed to treat seizures, but now has approval for the treatment of Bipolar Disorder. Lamictal has been tested and is approved for use in children with seizure disorders as young as three years old.

Common Side Effects of Lamictal
- Insomnia
- Sedation
- Fatigue and lethargy
- Nausea and vomiting
- Constipation
- Diarrhea
- Rash (nonlethal)
- Unsteadiness walking
- Headaches
- Dizziness
- Weight Gain

Rare but Serious and Potentially Lethal Side Effects of Lamictal
- **Exfoliative dermatitis:** Lamictal can cause a benign rash in 7 percent of patients. Unfortunately, some of these medication-induced rashes can develop into a serious, life-threatening rash. Unlike other medications with this side-effect risk, Lamictal has a much greater frequency of causing a rash. One in 1,000 to 2,000 patients taking Lamictal may develop one of the deadly forms of rash. In comparison, serious or deadly rash occurs only in one in a million patients taking Trileptal. For this reason, should your child develop a rash of any kind, your doctor will likely want to discontinue the Lamictal. You should seek immediate consultation with your doctor before continuing with this medication. Unfortunately, there are no tests that can warn you that your child might be developing this dangerous condition. You must simply be very watchful for any changes in your child's skin while he is taking Lamictal.

- **Status epilepticus:** Seven of 2,000 patients being treated for a seizure disorder with Lamictal, during the clinical trials, developed *status epilepticus*, a life-threatening seizure episode. The patients who developed status epilepticus were not being treated with Lamictal for a psychiatric condition. There were cases of status epilepticus in the patients who were taking Lamictal for Bipolar Disorder.
- **Sudden unexplained death in epilepsy (SUDEP):** There were twenty cases of sudden unexplained deaths in the 4,700 patients treated with Lamictal for seizure disorder. The 4,700 were *not* being treated with Lamictal for a psychiatric condition. There were *no* deaths in the patients who were taking Lamictal for Bipolar Disorder.
- **Accumulation in the eye:** Lamictal can bind to melanin, a protein found in the eye. After taking Lamictal for an extended period of time, the accumulated medication in the eye can cause toxicity to eye tissues. This condition can affect vision and should be monitored by a specialist.

Topamax

Topamax was originally developed to treat seizures and, though it does not have approval for the treatment of Bipolar Disorder, it has shown promise in several studies. Topamax has been tested and is approved for use in children with seizure disorders as young as two years old.

Common Side Effects of Topamax
- Confused or slow thinking
- Difficulty with memory
- Sedation, fatigue, and lethargy
- Unsteadiness walking
- Headaches
- Dizziness
- Weight loss
- Slurred speech
- Nausea
- Burning or prickling sensation on the skin (paresthesia)
- Blurred or double vision
- Tremor
- Nervousness

Rare but Serious and Potentially Lethal Side Effects of Topamax

- **Acute glaucoma:** Symptoms usually develop in the first month that a patient is taking Topamax. People who develop this acute glaucoma suddenly experience poor vision and pain in their eyes. This condition can cause the eye's pupil to dilate, but not always. Should your child develop these symptoms, seek consultation with your doctor immediately as he will probably not want the Topamax continued. Once the Topamax is stopped, the symptoms of acute glaucoma will resolve. If allowed to continue for too long, however, permanent eye damage can occur.
- **Kidney stones:** During the research and development process, 32 of 2,086 patients developed kidney stones due to Topamax. Keeping your child well hydrated, by making sure he is getting plenty of fluids, will help him avoid this condition while taking Topamax.
- **Sudden unexplained death in epilepsy (SUDEP):** There were ten cases of sudden unexplained deaths in the 2,700 patients treated with Topamax for seizure disorder. The 2,700 were not being treated with Topamax for a psychiatric condition. The frequency of sudden death while taking Topamax was no different than is usually seen in seizure patients who are not taking Topamax.
- **Decreased sweating and high body temperature:** Children are at greater risk of developing this side effect than are adults. While taking Topamax, your child may develop a high temperature but feel relatively dry because his body is not sweating normally. This condition can require hospitalization to treat the high fever. Hot weather is often the cause of this side effect in children taking Topamax.

NEURONTIN

Neurontin was once a very popular medication in the treatment of mood disorder and for other impulse control problems. Research has now shown that Neurontin has no psychiatric benefit in treatment of such mood disorders as Bipolar Disorder or Major Depressive Disorder. Neurontin is still considered an effective seizure medication but it is not appropriate for use in mania control.

22

ANTIHYPERTENSIVES

REALISTIC EXPECTATIONS OF ANTIHYPERTENSIVE MEDICATIONS

Antihypertensive MEDICATIONS WERE originally developed to treat high blood pressure. However, psychiatrists have been using antihypertensive medications to treat psychiatric conditions in children for years. Antihypertensive medications are very effective at treating a number of different symptoms regardless of your child's diagnosis. Therefore, whatever his *diagnosis* may be, if your child has one of the following *symptoms*, antihypertensive medications may be helpful in bringing him relief.

- Hyperactivity
- Agitation
- Anger and irritability
- Violence and aggression
- Impulsivity
- Anxiety
- Tremors
- Motor tics

HOW ANTIHYPERTENSIVE MEDICATIONS
CAN AND CANNOT HELP YOUR CHILD

ANTIHYPERTENSIVE MEDICATIONS HAVE been used to treat anxiety, anger, and agitation for many years. These medications were standard treatment for anxiety until the newer serotonin antidepressants became more popular with doctors. Unfortunately, antidepressants can take six weeks to reduce anxiety. For more immediate relief of anxiety, doctors often prescribe benzodiazepines, which are very addicting when taken on a routine basis. An important feature of antihypertensive medications is that, unlike benzodiazepines, antihypertensives are not at all addicting. Antihypertensive medications provide doctors with an alternative to addicting benzodiazepines, when they need to treat anxiety with a fast-acting medication. Furthermore, children generally tolerate antihypertensive medications well. Conversely, kids do not always respond well to benzodiazepines for the treatment of anxiety. Benzodiazepines can cause *increased* agitation in children.

Antihypertensive medications work fairly rapidly to reduce hyperactivity, agitation, anxiety, and impulsivity. On the first day that your child starts taking antihypertensive medications, he may feel a little sedated. Within the next two days, that initial effect of sleepiness should have worn off and your child should start to see some benefit. Sometimes the dose will need to be adjusted several times to maximize the benefits. Medication adjustments need to made slowly to avoid causing too much sedation.

Antihypertensive medications can help your child, regardless of the diagnosis. Therefore, whether your child is agitated due to Bipolar Disorder, Asperger's Syndrome, AD/HD, or Oppositional Defiant Disorder (ODD), antihypertensive medications can reduce agitation. Antihypertensives can treat any of the target symptoms listed earlier in this chapter, regardless of the diagnosis. Even though antihypertensive medications do not have FDA approval for the treatment of any psychiatric diagnosis, it has become common practice to use them whenever they might be helpful.

It is important to keep in mind that just because antihypertensive medications can treat one symptom in a diagnosis, this does not mean that these medications can treat all the symptoms of that same diagnosis. Although antihypertensive medications are very calming and can reduce, to some degree, your child's anger and agitation, they cannot turn your child into a cooperative, agreeable child who takes responsibility for his own misdeeds. This partial progress can create an illusion of success and give the false impression that antihypertensive medications are able to provide a complete cure for a diagnosis such as ODD. In the case of ODD, successful treatment cannot be achieved by simply reducing your child's anger with sedating medication. Other psychotherapeutic interventions must be included for complete success. It is important to bear in mind that antihypertensive medications can be useful up to a point, but for many diagnoses they only play a small role.

THE RISKS OF MEDICATING YOUR CHILD WITH ANTIHYPERTENSIVE MEDICATIONS

FOLLOWING IS A list of the antihypertensive medications. They are organized by the type of drug. Two types of antihypertensives are included here: Beta Adrenergic Receptor Antagonists (also called Beta Blockers) and Alpha 2 Adrenergic Receptor Agonists (Alpha-Agonists). The most common and any of the dangerous side effects will be listed separately under each type of medication. The side effects of antihypertensive medications tend to be mild and temporary. Generally, most side effects resolve after a week of continual treatment.

BETA ADRENERGIC RECEPTOR ANTAGONISTS (BETA BLOCKERS)

Drug Name
- Inderal (propranalol)
- Tenormin (atenolol)
- Lopressor (metoprolol)

Common Side Effects of Beta Blockers
- Slow heart rate
- Low blood pressure
- Dizziness
- Fatigue or sleepiness

Rare but Not Dangerous Side Effects of Beta Blockers
- Nausea
- Diarrhea
- Constipation
- Insomnia
- Bad dreams
- Depression
- Shortness of breath

Rare but Potentially Serious Side Effects of Beta Blockers
- Withdrawal from Beta Blockers should always be managed very slowly. Abrupt discontinuation of Beta Blockers can cause a rebound of a child's blood pressure and induce a hypertensive crisis. Symptoms of a hypertensive crisis include: rapid rise in blood pressure, headache, agitation, and nervousness.
- Beta blockers should not be used in children with asthma, insulin-dependent diabetes, or hyperthyroidism. Beta Blockers aggravate these conditions.
- **Heart block:** If your child has a preexisting atrioventricular (A-V) conduction defect, he should probably not be treated with Beta Blockers. If your child does have an A-V conduction defect, and his doctor places him on a Beta Blocker, your child has the risk of developing a complete A-V heart block. This can be potentially fatal.

ALPHA 2 ADRENERGIC RECEPTOR AGONISTS (ALPHA-AGONISTS)

Drug Name
- Tenex (guaneficine)
- Catapres (clonidine)

Common Side Effects of Alpha-Agonists
- Sedation
- Fatigue or weakness
- Slow heart rate
- Low blood pressure
- Dizziness
- Dry mouth and dry eyes

Rare but Not Dangerous Side Effects of Alpha-Agonists
- Nausea
- Vomiting
- Constipation
- Insomnia
- Bad dreams
- Depression

Rare but Potentially Serious Side Effects of Alpha-Agonists
- Withdrawal from Alpha-Agonists should always be managed very

slowly. Abrupt discontinuation of Alpha-Agonists can cause a rebound of a child's blood pressure and induce a hypertensive crisis. Symptoms of a hypertensive crisis include: rapid rise in blood pressure, headache, agitation, and nervousness.

23

BENZODIAZEPINES

REALISTIC EXPECTATIONS OF BENZODIAZEPINES

BENZODIAZEPINES ARE VERY effective medications in the treatment of anxiety. They begin working within twenty minutes of ingestion. Just as you will find with any psychiatric medication, benzodiazepines target *symptoms* not a *diagnosis*. This means that regardless of your child's diagnosis, benzodiazepines would benefit the symptoms that this drug class is known to treat.

Benzodiazepines are very effective at reducing panic and anxiety. They can usually calm an extremely agitated or distraught adult within minutes. The following symptoms often respond to benzodiazepines, but this is not always true for children:

- Panic attacks
- Anxiety
- Fear of airplane flights and other phobic situations
- Social phobia
- Agitation
- Insomnia
- Managing alcohol withdrawal

How Benzodiazepines
Can and Cannot Help Your Child

BENZODIAZEPINES ARE VERY effective for treating anxiety in most adults. Unfortunately, this is not always true for children and teens. While some children do find relief from their anxiety on benzodiazepines, other children actually have the opposite reaction. Some anxious children find that benzodiazepines cause them increased anxiety and agitation.

Should your doctor decide to prescribe benzodiazepines to your child there is one very important feature of these medications that must be taken into consideration. Benzodiazepines have the potential of being addicting. Once your child is addicted, withdrawal from benzodiazepines causes tremendous anxiety. The increased anxiety during withdrawal can defeat the whole purpose of benzodiazepine treatment.

Benzodiazepines are best used on an intermittent or temporary basis. When your child takes benzodiazepines on a routine basis, he can develop a dependency. However, when taken on an "as needed" basis, the risk of addiction is very low. Instead of using benzodiazepines as the only treatment, your child's anxiety is best treated by combining a safe, nonaddicting medication, such as an antidepressant, with a benzodiazepine taken intermittently. Depending on the type of anxiety disorder, eventually, your child's anxiety could be successfully managed without antidepressants and with only the occasional use of a benzodiazepine.

If your child has insomnia, benzodiazepines could help him sleep. Of course, your child might have the opposite reaction, and benzodiazepines may cause him increased agitation, not sedation. Provided your child responds as adults do, he should fall asleep on benzodiazepines. Unfortunately, most people find that the sleep they get while taking benzodiazepines is unsatisfactory and they awaken "hung over." Benzodiazepines can inhibit stage four sleep, the most restful and restorative part of the sleep cycle. Without this deep portion of sleep, people feel tired the next day. There are better alternatives to benzodiazepines for treating insomnia.

Drug Name
- Xanax (alprazolam)
- Ativan (lorazepam)
- Klonapin (clonazepam)
- Restoril (temazepam)
- Halcion (triazolam)
- Librium (chlordiazepoxide)

- Dalmane (flurazepam)
- Serax (oxazepam)
- Valium (diazepam)

THE RISKS OF MEDICATING YOUR CHILD WITH BENZODIAZEPINES

THE POTENTIAL BENEFITS for your child of benzodiazepine treatment have to be weighed against the potential risks associated with them. Aside from the risk of addiction, benzodiazepines are generally safe medications.

Common Side Effects of Benzodiazepines
- Drowsiness
- Addiction develops with regular, routine use

Rare but Potentially Serious Side Effects of Benzodiazepines
The following less common or rare side effects are much more likely to occur when another sedative, such as alcohol, is taken along with the benzodiazepine.

- Dizziness
- Unsteadiness walking
- Slurred speech
- Confused or slow thinking
- Difficulty with memory
- Slowed breathing
- Amnesia
- Slowed reaction time

Special Issues Concerning Benzodiazepine
- Date rape is usually accomplished by secretly adding a benzodiazepine to a woman's alcoholic beverage. For example, if your daughter is drinking beer at a party and a boy slips benzodiazepine into her drink, she can be easily exploited. Furthermore, due to the amnesia benzodiazepines can cause, she may not remember being raped or who attacked her.
- An overdose of benzodiazepine alone is not particularly life threatening. On the other hand, an overdose of benzodiazepines combined with a significant amount of alcohol is easily lethal. In fact, it is a recipe for suicide.

- Of all the addicting drugs, there are only a few whose withdrawal can be dangerous. Once your child has developed an addiction to a drug and is consuming large quantities of the substance, abrupt discontinuation of that substance can create withdrawal symptoms that are not necessarily life threatening. The withdrawal from heroin, for example, is extremely painful for the addict, but it is not dangerous—in other words, the addict would not have to be medically managed through his withdrawal. On the other hand, withdrawal from an addiction to high doses of some of the benzodiazepines can be *very dangerous* and can even lead to death. If your child develops an addiction to one of these two benzodiazepines, Xanax or Ativan, you need to be concerned with how withdrawal is managed.

WHAT IS BUSPAR?

BUSPAR (BUSPIRONE) IS not a benzodiazepine and offers a nonaddicting alternative for the treatment of anxiety. However, BuSpar is not often used by doctors anymore to treat anxiety because it is not usually very effective. Its best quality is the low incidence of side effects. The *only* symptom BuSpar is designed to treat is anxiety.

Common Side Effects of BuSpar
- Headaches
- Nausea
- Dizziness

Rare Side Effects of BuSpar
- Insomnia

What Else
Can You Do
to Help
Your Child?

The Three Divisions of
Psychiatric Assessment and Treatment

FACTORS WITHIN YOUR child's life that can impact his mental health can be grouped into three areas: biological elements, psychological circumstances, and your child's social experiences. These components correlate to the three standard approaches to psychiatric treatment.

The following three chapters will describe the possible causes and cures of the conditions discussed in part 2, and are designed to help you generate ideas about strategies that could make a difference in your child's mental health care, whether the child is medicated or not. I urge you to share your ideas with your child's doctor and therapist who could translate your insights into successful treatment techniques tailored to suit your child's and your family's needs.

24

THE BIOLOGICAL ASPECTS OF MENTAL HEALTH

BIOLOGICAL CAUSES OF MENTAL ILLNESS

YOUR CHILD'S BIOLOGY is her physical body. The biological causes of mental illness include the chemical makeup with which your child was born, as well as those activities and experiences that have had or are having an impact upon her physical health. These are:

- **DNA:** The genetic makeup of your child's family members can predispose her to developing a psychiatric condition. In other words, if people related to your child by blood have a mental illness, the likelihood that your child will develop that same illness is greater than were this not the case.
- **Substance Abuse:** The abuse of alcohol and drugs by a parent during conception or pregnancy, or by the child herself, can cause a child to develop a psychiatric disorder.
- **Physical Exercise:** Having a very sedentary lifestyle can have a negative impact on your child's mental health. Being inactive in of itself will *not* cause a mental illness, but the lack of physical exercise can exacerbate an already existing illness.

- **Diet:** Not only can a steady diet of junk food make your child feel physically uncomfortable, but a bad diet—one that includes excessive amounts of processed sugars, artificial ingredients, and overprocessed elements stripped of their nutrients—can also contribute to the low energy and insomnia of such disorders as depression, or may produce agitation. I do *not* mean to imply that junk food causes mental illness. But a poor diet may create symptoms that mimic those of a disorder, or may "feed" symptoms already present in a psychiatric disorder.
- **Sleep:** Poor sleep can worsen the symptoms of an already existing mental illness. For example, by causing increased lethargy, increased irritability, and decreased concentration and focus, poor sleep makes a mood or anxiety disorder worse.
- **Medical Illnesses:** There are a number of physical illnesses that can cause what appears to be a mental illness. A physiological illness that causes a cluster of symptoms that looks like a mental illness is called a *medical mimic*. Some of the well-known medical mimics are: hyperthyroidism, kidney failure, mercury or lead poisoning, and allergies.

I know a brave mental-health crisis worker who stood up to a prison guard following the arrest of a man with kidney failure. The jailed man had been acting erratic, bizarre, and psychotic when the police picked him up. His strange behavior prompted a "psych consult." The crisis worker insisted on a medical evaluation, which the jailer initially refused. The crisis worker stood his ground and threatened to report the guard. A medical exam revealed later that day that the man's kidney transplant was failing. The kidney failure in turn had led to the development of psychosis. Once the man was treated for his physical illness, his mental health was completely restored.

I met and treated a boy at a hospital cancer unit who was unable to walk to school. He had been in therapy for the previous year. His therapist presumed the boy to be resisting school attendance for purely psychological reasons. As the boy's ability to walk grew weaker and weaker, his parents finally pursued a medical opinion. A cancerous tumor was found in the boy's lower spine that had affected his ability to walk. The tumor had been growing that entire year while the therapist had been treating the boy with talk therapy.

For such reasons as the examples above, it is important to keep in mind that medical mimics are always a possibility and can be very deceptive.

BIOLOGICAL APPROACHES TO MENTAL HEALTH

PSYCHIATRIC MEDICATIONS, WHICH directly affect the chemistry of the mind, are among the many biological methods that are available to address your child's mental health problems. However, there are a number of biological approaches other than psychiatric drugs. Listed below are other interventions that may help your child instead of, or in addition to, psychiatric medication. Remember, the more you include in any therapy regimen, the more benefit your child will derive from the treatment. Always discuss with your child's doctor and therapist what other interventions you are attempting.

- **Cessation of Substance Abuse:** Sobriety can hugely improve your child's mental health. The impact that alcohol and drugs can have on your child is devastating. Almost as remarkable is how much denial your child will have regarding that impact. I have been told by countless teenagers that, in spite of the fact all of their troubles began when they started smoking marijuana, the drug had had absolutely nothing to do with their problems. I have seen incredible changes in teens' mental health when they finally embraced sober living—honestly, completely, and over the long term. My clinical experience has taught me that addicted teens are master manipulators. Sadly, their parents are usually the most gullible to their children's tales of denial.

- **Physical Exercise:** New research by psychologist Andrea Dunn, PhD, has found that moderate exercise, if done at least two and half hours per week, can control depression just as well as can antidepressant medications. Although being inactive may not cause your child's mental illness, research shows exercise *may* successfully treat such mental illnesses as depression. However, we must be careful not to generalize these findings to assume exercise cures all cases of depression or other psychiatric disorders. Certainly, exercise alone would be completely inappropriate and ineffective for the treatment of schizophrenia, for example.

- **Diet:** A lot has been reported through the years on the impact of sugar or caffeine or colorful food dyes on children's behavior. No study has ever proven that any specific food product is the sole cause of a mental disorder. On the other hand, I think all nutritionists would agree that a healthy diet undoubtedly improves a child's physical health. What is good for the body is good for the brain; and what's bad, bad. When your child's diet is stripped of harmful substances and empty calories, and invigorated with nutrient-rich foods, he is likely to have more energy and concentrate better, which then improves his functioning in a classroom.

- **Sleep:** Getting good sleep every night can help your child feel more alert during the day, have more energy, and have increased concentration and focus. A regular bedtime even on weekends, the elimination of such distractions as electronic media or loud conversation while she falls asleep, less napping during the day, less caffeine intake, and more exercise—all contribute to better sleep and consequently better mental health. Research has shown that some depressed patients felt better after one night of partial sleep deprivation—but this does not mean that an interrupted sleep pattern, such as the typically poor sleep habits exhibited by some teenagers, is a healthy thing done on a regular basis.

- **Medical Illnesses:** Before you assume your child has a psychiatric disorder, the medical mimics must be investigated and eliminated. It is always a good idea to have your child receive a physical exam prior to being evaluated by a mental-health clinician. Sometimes a battery of blood tests will be required to rule out any of the medical mimics, such as allergies, hypothyroidism, or hypoglycemia. If any physical ailments are identified in your child, it makes sense to treat these first, before going on with other psychiatric treatments if they are even necessary at all.

- **Electroconvulsive therapy** (ECT) involves creating a controlled seizurelike episode, which is confined only to the brain as the body is completely relaxed by pretreatment with a paralyzing agent, such as the muscle relaxant succinylcholine. During the treatment the patient is anesthetized and intubated (that is, a tube is placed down the throat of the patient to help him breathe). Less than two seconds of electrical current is applied to the patient's head, delivered by electrodes taped above each temple with conducting jelly. The seizure, to be effective needs to last thirty seconds to one minute, and is monitored using an electroencephalogram, or EEG. The treatments are delivered to the patient three times per week for two to four weeks, sometimes longer. This treatment is reserved only for very resistant mood disorders and some psychotic disorders, when medications have failed. Although research does support ECT's use in children, it is not often used to treat children.

- **Light therapy** has been used successfully to treat depression in some patients, usually those with Seasonal Affective Disorder (SAD). It does not always work but has none of the potential risks associated with the side effects of many of the psychiatric medications. Light therapy involves spending a specified number of hours siting under a lamp with a bulb of the specific brightness of 10,000-lux, or in front of a light box that houses such bulbs. There is debate in the medical community about whether light therapy actually works.

25

THE PSYCHOLOGICAL ASPECTS OF MENTAL HEALTH

PSYCHOLOGICAL CAUSES OF MENTAL ILLNESS

THE PSYCHOLOGICAL CAUSES of mental illness are the emotional injuries experienced by your child that create misconceptions and confusion about himself and his relationships with others. These psychological wounds can result in mental illness. There are a multitude of ways that your child can be injured emotionally. I am not going to provide an exhaustive list of every different psychological hurt possible, but below you will find a sampling of the experiences that can lead to psychiatric problems.

- **Trauma and Abuse:** Children can be emotionally traumatized by being abused. Abuse can take many forms. Children can be physically abused or sexually exploited, which often does *not* include physical injury. Emotional and verbal abuse can be even more traumatic than physical harm. Any form of abuse can lead to mental illness in your child.

  Children can be traumatized indirectly by witnessing their caretaker being abused. Witnessing their mother being abused by a violent partner can be very unsettling for children. Likewise, a child can be traumatized by witnessing his mother abuse herself with drugs. Psychiatric disorders can develop in children simply as a reaction to witnessing abuse.

Natural disasters or auto accidents can be traumatic for children. Some children can be strongly impacted by simply learning of the loss or accidents of people with whom they closely identify. I treated a boy who developed severe anxiety when his aunt and uncle died in an auto accident. He lived in constant fear that his parents would meet the same fate.

- **Neglect and Abandonment:** Children are very vulnerable and needy. Neglect can be obvious and severe, such as not feeding or sheltering a child. Neglect can also be subtle. Children who do not get enough emotional stimulation from their caregivers, in the form of talking, playing and holding, suffer from neglect. Children can develop psychiatric problems if they do not receive the nurturing and attention that they require for healthy development.
- **Boundary Violations:** In mental health, we define healthy *boundaries* as the establishment of appropriate roles and relationships with the other people in our lives. The most important relationship to your child is his relationship with you, his parent. Therefore, the boundary you establish with your child is the most important one to form correctly and in a healthy way. Children need their parents to act like parents, *not* like buddies, pals, confidants, or best friends. Violating this fundamental boundary can lead to mental illness in a child. An example of a boundary violation is when a mother uses her child as a confidant to vent her frustrations about her miserable marriage.
- **Negative Indoctrination:** Teaching children to hate, or to develop strong prejudices, can lead to mental illness in children. When children are surrounded by violence and the glorification of crime, they can become emotionally impaired. This sort of indoctrination may prevent your child from having the capacity to feel compassion for others. This may lead to acts of indiscriminate violence during episodes of anger and frustration.

PSYCHOLOGICAL APPROACHES TO MENTAL ILLNESS

THE PSYCHOLOGICAL APPROACH to the treatment of mental illness targets your child's unhealthy thinking patterns and unrealistic beliefs. Misguided thinking can develop as a result of mental illness or can be the cause of your child's mental illness. Either way, psychotherapy is intended to correct your child's psychiatric problems using a psychological approach. A variety of therapies are described below. This is not a complete list of every type of therapy possible, rather a sampling of the most common offerings for children.

- **Individual Therapy:** Individual psychotherapy can take many forms. All forms of individual psychotherapy share a common setting: one patient with one therapist. This type of therapy can include a multitude of techniques: play therapy, supportive therapy, cognitive behavioral therapy (CBT), insight-oriented therapy, and psychoanalytical therapy. Individual therapy is delivered to your child directly. You may be asked by your child's therapist to join the two of them for part of the session, to update you on their progress. However, the majority of the session would be devoted to your child, one-on-one with his therapist.

- **Family Therapy:** This form of therapy involves your child and one or more members of his family. Many therapists like to start with you or your child alone for a session. Then slowly, the therapist will add more members of the family, to work with the therapist on resolving the conflicts you have with one another.

- **Parent Coaching:** This approach to correcting your child's mental health problems involves teaching you, the parent, skills to help your kid at home. Parent coaching teaches parents how to interact more effectively with a troubled child. Parent coaching is not intended to be psychotherapy for you as an individual. The aim here, essentially, is to deputize you as a therapeutic force within the home, where professionals are not available directly. This allows the work that is started with your child in the therapist's office to be continued at home by you. Parent coaching is really parenting training at a more sophisticated level. Parent coaching can help you build the kinds of parenting skills required by children with mental health issues.

- **Group Therapy:** Group therapy is a therapist-guided session that brings together two or more patients with similar issues. Patients with similar issues and common backgrounds would be appropriate in the same therapy group. In other words, a therapist would not include a teen girl who has been abused within a group of homeless schizophrenic men over forty years old. The idea behind group therapy is that, by working with others with similar problems, your child can feel less isolated in her mental illness and learn strategies for solving her own problems. You must be careful that the therapist leading the group has a strong enough presence and influence with the children that your child does not pick up more bad habits or ideas. Also, you want a therapist who can maintain healthy boundaries among the members of the group during and after the sessions.

- **12-Step Programs:** Twelve-step program meetings are comprised of people with a similar addiction, congregating to support one another in their sobriety and recovery. Two of the well-known 12-step programs for teenagers are Teen AA (Alcoholics Anonymous) and Teen NA (Narcotics Anonymous). For teenagers with addictions, the meetings require some adult supervision. These meetings are attended by young adult 12-step members who act as mentors and examples of healthy recovery for your teen.

  Teen AA and Teen NA usually invite parents to attend the meetings as well. Although your attendance is not usually required, you can gain an understanding of addicts and some insight into the process of recovery by attending these meetings. Your participation can also send the message to your child that you care about him and you take his recovery and 12-step program seriously.

  Not all the teens attending a 12-step meeting are on the road to a healthy recovery. Some teens attend reluctantly, as they are forced by their parents to go. These teenagers can exert a bad influence on your child. Your attendance is important to enable you to supervise your child's interaction with the other participants.

- **Mentors:** Mentors are people who provide a positive role model for your child. They can also give direct guidance and advice to your child. Usually, a mentor evolves in your child's life naturally. You might think a parent would be the most obvious candidate for a mentor, and you would be correct. Many times you, as a parent, can fulfill that role. Sometimes, however, your child will reject you as a mentor. This is when it is important to have a stand-in. Schoolteachers, coaches, grandparents, and clergy can provide this guidance for your child. If no one emerges naturally, you can ask for help from one of the potential candidates already mentioned here. Ask them to engage your child in a relationship over a common hobby or an ice-cream cone. Professional organizations such as Big Brothers or Big Sisters are specifically designed to provide just this sort of service to children. Always screen strangers carefully before inviting them into your child's life.

26

THE SOCIAL ASPECTS
OF MENTAL HEALTH

SOCIAL CAUSES OF MENTAL ILLNESS

ESSENTIALLY, THE SOCIAL causes of mental illness are the environmental factors that impact on your child negatively. Your child's social environment can have a significant effect on his mental health. Even though one child can endure a certain stressor does not mean that another child will be able to withstand that same stressor without developing mental health problems. Below is a sampling of the kinds of environmental stressors that can impact your child negatively. This is not a complete list of all social factors that cause or exacerbate mental illness in children.

- **Marital Conflict:** When there is conflict in your marriage, your child will feel uneasy. Whether the marital tension is overt or concealed, your child will be able to detect your unhappiness. Your child is a master at reading your emotional state. Of course, the worse the hostility, the greater the stress on your child. The greater the stress, the greater the potential for your child to develop emotional problems related to your difficult marriage.
- **Parenting Styles:** Parenting styles can have a monumental impact on your child's mental health. For example, a parenting style that is too

permissive can cause your child to become undisciplined and belligerent. If you respond to your belligerent child with hostility and accusations, implying that his behavior is intentionally wicked, this can cause other kinds of mental health problems for your child. There are so many variations on the theme of how your parenting style can affect your child, they cannot all be described here in this brief summary. More on parenting can be found in part 4 of this book.

- **School Environment:** Your child's experience at school can be affected by his teachers or his classmates. If the students at your child's school are bullies, that can cause one kind of problem. The school may be so overrun with drugs and violence that your child feels another sort of stress. Teachers working under horrible classroom conditions or who are not adequately trained can also cause problems for their students. I have treated children who were ridiculed by their teacher only once and the experience caused an escalating series of negative effects on the child's mental health.

- **Negative Friends:** If your child's friends are having behavioral problems, this can influence your child negatively. Your child's friends can encourage your child to try alcohol, commit petty theft, or defy your rules simply because these are the very things they are doing. Children are very invested in pleasing and keeping their friends. If your child is placed in a position of going along with behaviors he knows are wrong or else losing his friends, the choice is almost always to keep his friends.

SOCIAL APPROACHES TO MENTAL ILLNESS

THE SOCIAL APPROACHES to correcting mental illness center around changing your child's environment. The most important environment to your child's mental well-being is your home. The second most influential place is your child's school. His friends are obviously important, too, but most children make their friends at school. Following, you will find some examples of the sorts of social interventions you can make in your child's life to help improve his mental health.

- Peaceful home life: Marriage is a challenge under the best circumstances. When a couple starts having children, that challenge is magnified. The tranquillity in your home is something you cannot always control, because you represent only half of the marriage equation. If you are having problems in your marriage, seek marriage counseling together but attend therapy even if your spouse is not willing to come along. Although a happy marriage is the optimal situation, a divorce is sometimes better for your child's mental health. Your child's adjustment to divorce is not as damaging as the continued stress of an extremely hostile marriage.

- **Predictable and dependable routines:** Children are more comfortable with a life that is predictable and consistent. Not knowing where you are, who will be at the house when he gets home from school, and what to expect for dinner can be unsettling for children. Routines do not have to be held too rigidly. Routines just have to be in place for a child to feel secure. When your child can say, with some accuracy, where his parents are at any given moment, when his parents expect him home from school, and what the evening's schedule will be, he feels a little more secure. A child living in a chaotic household can feel anxious and insecure. A reliable and predictable routine gives a child a sense of security and makes it easier for him to prepare for the next day at school.

- **Effective parenting:** A healthy approach to parenting and child guidance can make significant improvements to your child's behavior problems. Of course, the sooner you start the greater your impact. Still, older children, even into the teenage years, can benefit from a healthier style of parenting. The virtues of appropriate parenting cannot be emphasized enough. For a more complete discussion on this topic, refer to chapter 27.

- **Positive school environment:** Your child spends a significant amount of his time in school. Work with school staff to change your child's negative experience at school. If your efforts reap no benefits and his experience in school has become toxic, then a change of schools should be considered. Sometimes your child's school troubles are academic failure; other times, social problems. Whether you place him in a private school, sell your house and move to a better school district, or school your child at home, your child's failures and misery at school must be addressed. If your child's school environment is a place where he views himself as successful and well liked, this experience can have a significantly positive impact on his mental health.

When your child has to change schools, you must make every effort to ease that transition. Investigating the school building when there are no students present, meeting with the teachers before school begins, and participating in summer activities where your child can meet his classmates prior to the start of school, are ways to help him adjust to a new school. Avoid moving your child in the middle of the school year if at all possible.

- **Extracurricular activities:** Hobbies, clubs, sports, and music are some of the many extracurricular activities that can aid your child's mental health. Self-esteem, which is so essential to mental health, is derived from only one experience, accomplishment. Sports, music, and hobbies can offer your child a way to feel that sense of accomplishment. Self-esteem does not come from therapy or parenting, although both can pave the way for self-esteem to develop. No, self-esteem comes from accomplishment.

  - Often, these activities can provide a healthier group of children from which your child can choose friends.
    Parents have been known to go too far with a good thing. Children can feel more stressed when there is too much going on in their lives. Encouraging one activity your child enjoys and pursues willingly is better for you both than insisting on a rigid schedule of several activities that are approached by the child with obvious reluctance.
  - For children who will not cooperate with choosing an activity, you may need to choose for him. Your child can also benefit from your participation. For example, you could enroll both you and your child in a martial arts class and then practice together at home. Once he is hooked, you may not need to attend.

- **Healthy friends:** Children, especially those over eight years old, will not choose friends based on your preferences. Kids want to pick their own friends. Criticizing your child's friends will not stop their friendship. Often, your complaints will only strengthen your child's resolve to stay in the friendship with someone you do not like. Parents can still exert some influence in this area. You can schedule a play date with another family who just happens to have a child your child's age. For older children, you can enroll your entire family in an activity that takes you all to an out-of-town event where same-age children will be present. Require that your child accompany your family on these outings.

Invite another family to come for a meal and request your child's assistance in entertaining the children from the visiting family. Anything you can do to expose your child to healthier peers will be beneficial. Unfortunately, asking him to stop a negative friendship almost never works.

27

YOUR ROLE IN RAISING MENTALLY HEALTHY KIDS

PARENTING IS ABSOLUTELY the most challenging, draining, and frustrating job on the planet. At the same time, there is no more important calling in this world. Done well, you will create a happy, well-adjusted, joyful human being, able to contribute to the world in a positive way. Done poorly, *you* will be helping to create a tormented, maladjusted youngster who is a constant irritant and burden to himself and to everyone around him. Moreover, his misery will continue throughout his adulthood.

In so much of life, a lot of trouble can be avoided if we address a job or problem early. Procrastination leads to more work, not an escape from work. That is certainly true of an undisciplined approach to parenting. The idea that if you just wait long enough, a child will eventually "grow out of" his negative behaviors has no basis in reality. The truth is that you will pay now or you will pay later, and you *always* pay *more* later. When you see your five-year-old having a kicking and screaming "meltdown" in a toy store, instead of telling yourself, "It's just the age, he'll grow out of it," you must realize that, without intervention, that behavior will not only continue indefinitely but escalate. Please try to imagine that same behavior in your sixteen-year-old son, one hundred pounds heavier, foul mouthed, and physically violent. No, the time to intervene with a child's behavior is *now*.

Discipline is not the enemy of enthusiasm or creativity. It is not the same as punishment. The misconception that firm discipline is harmful and alienates children from their parents is at the root of many of the childhood behavioral disorders I treat. Children do not learn to appreciate the value of self-discipline on their own; it must be taught to them and consistently reinforced. Self-discipline is absolutely necessary for a child to become happy, well adjusted, and responsible as an adult. In this chapter I challenge the belief that parents should be their child's "buddy," and I will provide the reasoning and methods to help you as a parent fulfill your vital role as your child's number one teacher and mentor.

Taking Advice

How may you gain the greatest benefit from this advice? It is essential that you be willing to unlearn some of your own behaviors and attitudes that may be contributing to your child's problems. Too often, as parents, we are determined to raise our children "our way," so much so that we fail to see that we are actually sabotaging our children's well-being. While you tell yourself you are taking a doctor's advice, you may in fact be modifying the expert's instructions so drastically to suit your own perceptions of what is right for your child, that your so-called newly acquired parenting techniques in no way resemble the clinician's original advice. You may not realize consciously that you are doing it, but it may be happening all the same unless you make a conscious effort to change.

This type of sabotage is clearly demonstrated in the example of a man who brought me his three-year-old son, Bobby, for a psychiatric evaluation. The man believed his son was "too hyperactive" and needed medication. The father was a very tall, heavyset man. Had he wanted to appear as the authority figure to Bobby, his formidable presence would have made that easy. When the two entered the clinic playroom for the evaluation, the father started to explain how he had done everything a father could possibly do to discipline the boy, and that nothing was working. He claimed to be using the methods in Thomas Phelan's book, *1-2-3 Magic*. The father insisted that the book's advice had been completely ineffective in correcting his child's behavior. I know the methods outlined in Phelan's book are excellent and very effective when applied properly. *1-2-3 Magic* requires that you give a child two warnings and, on the third reminder, a consequence is delivered, swiftly, calmly, and without apology.

During my evaluation, I watched this father follow his misbehaving youngster around my clinic's playroom, wagging his finger and repeating over and over to his son that he was "going to" give Bobby his first warning. Bobby set about the business of pulling all the toys onto the floor of the playroom in a fashion very typical of a three-year-old-boy. The father never reached warning number two (let alone the "magic" of three). Bobby's behavior never changed. This case is a perfect example of how, too often, good disciplinary advice is utilized incorrectly. This child's behavior continued unchanged *not* because the advice was faulty, but rather because the method was never properly implemented.

It is a leap of faith to trust a parenting expert and follow the person's advice. However, to benefit from an expert's advice, you must be willing to set aside your conviction that you already know what is best for your child. Obviously, your child would not be seeing a therapist or other behavioral specialist were that the case! This is not intended to insult or demean you as a parent, but to make you aware that your child needs to receive clear and constructive signals from you if she is to be her best.

As you read this chapter, examine each suggestion carefully *and* examine your ability to comply to the letter with that suggestion, as essential to your child's good mental health. Ask yourself if *you* might be acting like the man with the three-year-old boy, a man who understood on one level, and yet would not carry through on Phalen's advice because he thought it would be "mean" to actually hand out a consequence to such a small boy. *To benefit from parenting advice, a parent has to follow the advice given.*

What Is the Purpose of Childhood?

Many parents focus on the first eighteen years of their children's lives with little thought for childhood's ultimate purpose. These parents view childhood as a stage of life that exists in isolation from the rest of their child's life as an adult. Childhood is not seen, by such parents, as a time for children to work on developing self-discipline, responsibility, or social skills. To these parents, childhood should be a magical time of unending treats and fun. As a consequence, they rarely deny their children anything. Parents who constantly give in to their children's every want and desire will foster in their children willfulness, belligerence, and a complete lack of self-discipline. Without self-discipline, children emerge from childhood without the tools they require to have a fulfilling, gratifying, and happy adulthood.

The Goals of a Parent

Before setting out to accomplish anything, you must first establish exactly what it is you intend to achieve. In other words, you need to establish your goals.

This is particularly true in parenting. The goals of parenting have become diluted by various modern misconceptions about what constitutes a good childhood. There are good-hearted, well-meaning people who *themselves* are very well-adjusted, successful adults. Tragically, however, they simply lack the knowledge to guide *their child* into a successful adulthood of her own. Therefore, it must be understood that being a good person does not always equate to being a good parent; likewise, a bad parent is not necessarily a bad person. Let us start with some of the common but occasionally unhealthy goals that result in defiant and belligerent children.

WHAT CHILDHOOD IS *NOT*

CHILDHOOD IS *not* a nonstop trip to Disneyland. You are not your child's entertainment committee. Childhood is *not* about the size and the number of toys, treats, and outings that can possibly be showered upon your offspring in eighteen years. Our children's youth is *not* an opportunity for us to fulfill our own fantasies about a perfect family experience. Portrayals of family life in the movies and on television are unrealistic and a setup for disappointment for the parent who buys into this fantasy. Nor is childhood an opportunity for parents to compensate for their own poor experiences as kids. Lavishing your children with every extravagance you felt you were denied in your own childhood, or allowing them a permissiveness you always wanted but never received, will result in heartache and willfulness. Spoiling children leads to misery for the children and shame for the parents.

Forcing a reluctant child to participate in such activities as sports, acting, and beauty pageants, which the parent himself wishes he had the opportunity to enjoy as a child, is another bad idea. This is an obvious effort by the parents to relive their own incomplete childhood through their children, or to attempt to have a kind of superchild that fails to take into consideration the true capabilities of their son or daughter. We like to believe our children are brilliant and talented, and many are, but not necessarily in those areas in which we personally desire to excel. Parents need to recognize that children are not extensions by which to achieve glory for themselves, but individuals with their own set of abilities and interests. Immersion-teaching a child to play the violin may teach her to use the instrument correctly, perhaps even with technical brilliance, but unless she is truly gifted in that area it will not produce a talented violinist.

Finally, and possibly the most common mistake that good people make with their children, is trying to be popular with their child. Attempting to be your child's best friend will ultimately backfire on you. You will lose your child's respect and fail him as a parent. Children need parents to behave like adults. Being an effective parent and your child's best buddy at the same time is a complete contradiction. You are your child's guide, mentor, and teacher, and that means setting rules and limits, and making choices for your child that he is too young to make for himself. Parenting is an extremely difficult task, because it involves being responsible for not only oneself but for another person as well. This task is absolutely essential to your child's healthy development. If you are not willing to step up to the challenge and do this difficult job, unless you take control or completely turn over the reins of responsibility to another responsible adult who *can* do the job, your child is the one who will suffer.

What Is the Purpose of Parenting?

GUIDING A CHILD without first determining precisely where you are headed, will be confusing to the child and frustrating for the parent. Your purpose as a parent is inextricably linked to the purpose of your child's childhood:

> **It is absolutely imperative that parents understand that the one and most important goal of parenthood and primary purpose of childhood, is to prepare the child for adulthood.**

What Is the Purpose of Childhood?

THE PURPOSE OF childhood is to develop the skills needed for adulthood. To properly prepare your child for his adulthood, you must first determine exactly what constitutes a well-adjusted adult. Successful, well-adjusted, happy adults have all acquired the following traits: they are self-respecting, responsible, accountable, reliable, self-disciplined, and compassionate. Your mission as a parent is to equip your child with these character traits during childhood and adolescence, so that your son or daughter will be prepared for adulthood.

Your primary objective is to help your child develop self-respect. Teaching children to respect themselves starts by showing them respect, love, and compassion. As you start to equip your child with the qualities of a mature adult, you give your child more reasons to love herself. Loving and respecting herself is absolutely essential for your child to be able to love and respect others.

All parents want their children to have fun and enjoy their childhood. Kids should have fun. It is a necessary part of any healthy person's life. Yet, when a child's having a good or easy time becomes a parent's primary goal, the child can become completely unable to cope with adversity; instead he may become entitled, demanding, and unappreciative—which works in direct opposition to the goal of teaching a child how personal goals are achieved with patience and effort. You are not your child's fairy godmother, giving in to every whim and fancy, or solving problems for her that she needs to develop the strategies to solve herself. A child whose youth has been made easy for her, without challenges, will inevitably become a dissatisfied and frustrated individual. As an adult, she will find that happiness eludes her because she lacks the skills to manage her own life.

YOU ARE YOUR CHILD'S ROLE MODEL

WE'VE DISCUSSED YOUR goal, now for your *role*:

> Your role as a parent is to be a living example to your children
> of how to behave as an adult.

As I said, successful, well-adjusted, happy adults are reliable, honest, industrious, self-disciplined, and compassionate. These character traits are not easy qualities to acquire. Many of us may recognize these qualities as traits that we are still working to achieve for ourselves.

Children learn almost everything they believe and value in life *from watching what their parents do, not from listening to what their parents say.* What you present to your child as a role model has a very powerful impact upon him. What you preach, you must also live. You cannot teach your kids what you are unwilling to do, yourself. You cannot insist that your child be accountable, respectful, and responsible if you personally behave the opposite. For example, a parent who regularly emits criticisms, insults, and expletives as a basic conversational style is hardly the role model to produce a child polite and considerate toward others; the child will imitate his parent's method of communication as the correct way to behave. To help your children acquire positive skills, you must demonstrate that you value these traits and are working toward achieving them yourself.

I once assessed an undisciplined, ill-mannered, willful six-year-old boy. His mother explained that she had no organizational skills and no self-discipline, nor did she intend to work on acquiring these qualities. She did ask that I provide her son a medicine (she suggested Ritalin) that would give him these skills. I explained to this mother that there was no medication capable of bestowing these qualities on her child. When I told her that modifying the example she set for her son would be an essential part of his behavior-improvement program, she left my office, never to return. She refused to acknowledge that her child was out of control because *she* was out of control.

BE YOUR CHILD'S COACH

PARENTS SHOULD BE mentors, not pals. The role of a parent is a lot more like that of a coach with his team. An effective coach's goal is to prepare his team to meet the challenges on the field, so that the team can triumph and each member share in the satisfaction, self-respect, and self-esteem that comes from winning while exhibiting the best of good sportsmanship. The coach does not give much thought to how much fun his players are having while learning basic skills and team play, because having fun will not help prepare his young players for the challenges he knows they must face.

An effective parent must have a similar outlook. Your child needs you to guide and teach her. She relies on you to be strong, even while she resists you every step of the way. It is your job to keep your child focused upon both acquiring and maintaining positive behaviors; indulgent lapses that permit your child to exercise self-centeredness can upset the entire process. Unless you are prepared to face the unpleasant experience of bailing your child out of jail, being confronted by angry neighbors, or watching your child flunk out of high school, you will have to abandon the idea that you can always be popular with your child. Part of your role, like it or not, is cop, bad guy, disciplinarian, judge, and jury. In spite of all the grief that your child will certainly hand you if you refuse to allow her to break your rules, you must remain focused and steadfast. To be an effective parent, you must accept your role as a coach, one who sees the long-term, greater picture than your child may be incapable of fully understanding at this time.

BE PREPARED FOR HOSTILITY

AS YOU ENFORCE behavioral modifications, your child will not usually agree with your decisions, nor will he understand your motives. He may fight you on every little issue, and sometimes he will fight you just in retaliation for some other perceived slight. He may deliberately test the rules and limits you impose by behaving even worse than when your interventions began. Be prepared for this, and hold your ground. Your child will not appreciate that, by such measures, you are showing your love and concern for him by teaching him self-discipline and self-reliance. All he sees is that he is no longer getting away with things the way he used to, or that you are now responding differently than how he has grown accustomed to your reacting. Please don't feel guilty if you deny him the satisfaction of overturning your new regimen. Your child's lack of insight into the virtues of your mission, and your role as a strong parent, is due to his immaturity and lack of perspective. He will probably not come to understand or appreciate what it is you are trying to do for him until he is an adult himself. It is possible that he may not gain this insight until he has children of his own. The rewards of pride and satisfaction that you feel as a parent for a job well done, come many years later when your child is an adult.

You Can't Be Half a Parent

There are some parents who would prefer to put off some tasks in child rearing, to accomplish some of their own personal goals. This is doomed to create more work for you in the long run, and presents a number of risks for the child. The expression that "you are going to pay now or you will pay later, but you always pay more later" is especially applicable to parenting.

Putting off your parenting, nurturing, or disciplinarian duties creates much greater problem for your child and bigger challenges for you when your timing on parenting is out of step with the child's development. You could end up babying your child to the point that he is unable to take on age-appropriate responsibilities when the time arrives, because he has not mastered the necessary skills. Done correctly from the beginning, your child will be independent by the time he reaches adulthood. Done incorrectly, you might suffer as one of my patients did, whose son lived with her until he was forty years old. He had held only three jobs, and none for any longer than a week at a time, because the bosses were "too mean." His parents cooked his meals, did his laundry, and provided for his every financial need. He paid back their indulgence by spending their money on alcohol and drugs. This outcome was tragic for the son and heart wrenching for the parents, who ironically were very successful, self-disciplined adults themselves.

Parenting is already a horrendously difficult job that every parent struggles to do well, at times barely hanging on day to day. Even the most conscientious parents worry that they are doing a substandard job. This is why it is essential that the work of disciplining your child and preparing him for life start as early as possible.

Once you become a parent, your needs, your personal dreams, your hobbies and pursuits, your political agendas and career aspirations—all must take a backseat to your child's needs and your new role as a parent. If you hope to raise a healthy, well-balanced child, you must now see your first and foremost purpose on this earth as having become this child's parent. Your child needs you to value her as the single most important entity in your life. If that means putting some of your other interests or even a demanding career on hold until she graduates from high school, so be it.

You and Your Child Are in a 24/7 Partnership

DON'T TRY TO convince yourself that your self-serving endeavors do not interfere with your parenting tasks. Your child sees everything you do and "clocks" it all. Every time you say one thing but then do another, your child is watching you and learning what is acceptable behavior in the society he is being groomed to join. Your inconsistencies and hypocrisy are not missed by your child.

Children are so much more perceptive than you realize. They read you and know you better than you know yourself. If you put them first, they will see that. If you put your career, your politics, your hobbies, or your sports before them, they will know that, too. Children are not fooled by that clever diversion of yours by coaching their sports team as a cover for your own obsession with sports. This is not to say you should never coach your son's baseball team. Just make sure that your involvement is all about his growth and development as a team player and a good sport. This applies to acting, dancing, martial arts, and beauty pageants as well. Make sure you are not pushing him to do well so you can take a bow at the awards banquet.

On the flip side of this, a career that keeps you away from home for many hours beyond nine to five means that surrogates—including people you may not even know are having negative impact upon your child—are rearing your child for you. While it may be necessary to be a working parent, you need to be a *parent*, and not leave your child's development solely in the hands of other people to do *your job as a parent* for you. Parenting is not a skill that can be phoned in.

This may require you to make great sacrifices. You will not be able to see all the movies or attend all the clubs and adult parties you enjoyed before your children arrived. It is unhealthy and detrimental to take your young children to inappropriate social events. Your children are influenced by everything to which they are exposed. This includes adult situations and violence in movies, television, and video games, and inappropriate behavior among adults in your household. The convenience you may enjoy by dragging your baby to adult events will be far outweighed by the heartache you will experience later and the emotional problems your child will develop as a result of this exposure. Get a babysitter or skip the event.

Witnessing domestic violence or substance abuse or adult sexuality, even if it does not physically touch the child, hurts the child, who may be frightened or confused. Every child needs and deserves a healthy family life. Your child needs to feel her environment is safe and is not overwhelming for someone of her age. Create for your child a home that is child-centered without spoiling and indulging and free of inappropriate adult situations, and, in the long run, both you and your child will be much happier.

When the Parent Behaves like a Child

It is confusing and psychologically detrimental to your child if you, yourself, act like an adolescent. You need to behave like a responsible adult to be taken seriously by your child. As a parent you cannot wear a miniskirt, fishnet stockings, a tongue piercing, and tattoos in front of your child and still expect her to see you as an authority. Furthermore, once you have carried out every outrageous act of teenage rebellion in front of your child, what acts of defiance and rebellion will she have to resort to when it becomes her turn to be an insubordinate teen? Children will always up the ante. If you as a father have one ear piercing, your son will have to have multiple piercings; if you have a pierced tongue, your son will have to split his tongue. As a mom, if you wear a revealing, low-cut top, your daughter will have to wear a bra as a top, if you have one small discrete tattoo, your teen daughter may sneak off to get her entire back covered in tattoos. There is nothing wrong with tattoos, piercings, or revealing attire; that is just fine for any adult, even parents, as long as these cutting-edge, over-the-top fashions are not paraded around in front of your child. This has nothing whatsoever to do with morality—there is nothing in the world wrong with tattoos, piercings, and short skirts. This advice is intended to help you as a parent avoid unnecessary conflict and problems, more than enough will certainly come your way naturally as the parent of a teen. Whatever social statement you want to make will just have to take a backseat to being a responsible parent, if you want to raise well-adjusted children. If you still have issues with being an adult and acting your age, how can you honestly expect your child—who is a child—to behave better than you do? For your child's sake, you must become a rock of authority. This does not mean you need to fake a staid personality that is not your own. But it does mean that you need to make a sincere effort to act and look mature, to be thoughtful, considerate, and consistent in your behaviors.

Your Child's Reasoning Abilities

According to renowned child psychiatrist Jean Piaget, who devised a system identifying the cognitive levels of children as they mature, children are concrete thinkers up to the age of twelve and sometimes even older. Young children are not abstract thinkers until they reach twelve years old, which means they are completely unable to reason or understand complex or idiomatic explanations or arguments. The stages of cognitive development have nothing to do with the child's intelligence. The brightest child still has to pass through each and every developmental stage as with any milestone of development. This explains why trying to reason with even the most intelligent child under the age of twelve, can be ineffective and frustrating. Because he is unable to reason through an abstract concept, he may conclude something other than what you intended to communicate. For example, when you are trying to resolve a conflict between your children about who got the bigger piece of cake, it is best to simply state you are in charge, you made the choice, and that is how it goes, end of story. When you launch into a long dissertation on fairness, and the philosophy of the "grass is always greener," or you ask your six-year-old son to see this conflict from his sister's perspective had he gotten the bigger piece of cake, you will be talking completely over his head. Instead of helping your young, concrete-thinking son to understand and accept your decision, you will only add to his confusion and therefore his frustration. If you opt to give longwinded, abstract explanations to a concrete thinker, don't be surprised when he is not satisfied with your explanation and continues to badger you with the very same questions or, worse yet, he concludes that you have an elaborate plan to award him a second piece of cake or a bigger piece next time. Young children understand the concept that, the bigger you are— as adults always are to small children—the more authority you have. Let that work for you and for your child's benefit while they are still too young to be reasoned with and to grasp abstract concepts. When laying down the household rules with your child, the less explanation about the rationale behind the rules, the better. It is best to simply outline exactly what is expected and the consequences that will follow. Then, end the discussion there.

This principle applies as well when delivering unwelcome news to your young child such as handing out a punishment, ending a fun activity, or asking your child to complete a chore. When you launch into an explanation, your child tunes out the words and focuses on the fact that you are still engaged in the verbalizing part of the exchange. To a young child, this continued verbal engagement will be viewed as an opportunity to renegotiate the terms of your directives or the application of your rules. This is not about politeness, but clarity. If you hesitate to speak firmly to your child, couching phrases in apologies or hedging the issue by wording an order as a question, you suggest to your child that he has options. This is not the message you intended to give your child, yet this is how children perceive lengthy explanations.

Reasoning with a small child is a form of teasing a younger, less developed mind with implied promises you have no intention of fulfilling. The best approach when communicating with your young child is to state your instructions and expectations simply, without apology or rationalization, and making clear that the matter is nonnegotiable by refusing to allow your communications on the issue to become a prolonged conversation. Pleading and "why" questions from your child can be best answered by quietly restating that these are your rules, you are the parent, it is your prerogative and responsibility to make and enforce the rules. You can also tell your child that further arguing will bring unpleasant consequences for him. A parent who attempts to explain to a child the reasons why she finds it necessary to impose the rules of the house, or set limits that disappoint her child, will cause their child more frustration by asking him to operate intellectually beyond his capabilities.

Another way in which children can be set up for frustration unnecessarily is when a parent offers them choices that she doesn't plan to fulfill. For example, when you take your five-year-old son to the ice-cream store and ask him what he wants, get ready for tears if you have given too many open-ended choices to a child who is too young, too immature, and who lacks the self-discipline to limit himself. When he asks for the supersize banana split with five scoops of ice cream and three types of toppings, please remember it was you who uttered the words, "What do you want?"—and he told you, didn't he? Your lengthy explanations about how close it is to dinner, how his choice is more food than a five-year-old could eat, or how that much ice cream will probably give him a bellyache, will all fall on deaf ears. In your child's mind, you are going back on an implied promise. Not to render a child powerless, but you need to recognize which choices are within his scope, and only offer him a range of decisions for which a young child might reasonably be expected to provide input. In our ice-cream parlor example, why not simply limit the choices ahead of time by stating before you go into the store that he can have only one scoop of ice cream in any flavor he wants, not two scoops, not three, and no toppings. If you do not clarify both what he can have and what he cannot have, your child will already be thinking about exceptions to your rule that will likely invite an unnecessary and potentially angry conflict. Avoid this if you can, there will be plenty of battles that you have to fight that are unavoidable, why not do a little preparation, and avoid a few unnecessary battles. If you inadvertently make the mistake of offering up more than you intended, simply cut the discussion short by stating simply, calmly, and without explanation that you made a mistake in not stating clearly from the beginning what the parameters of his choices were and then state them plainly. That is enough.

28

PARENTING YOUR WILLFUL CHILD

WHAT ARE THE PRINCIPLES
OF DISCIPLINING YOUR CHILD?

AN EFFECTIVE PROGRAM, designed to change your child's willful behavior, starts with lots of patience coupled with the *three essential elements* of good discipline: rewards, consequences, and supervision. There are many different parenting programs that apply some measure of each of these elements; finding and learning a discipline system is usually not a problem for a concerned parent. The difficulty arises when it comes time to implement the program. You may find it a struggle to consistently deliver rewards when they have been earned or respond to poor behaviors by imposing reasonable consequences. Another way any parenting system can be sabotaged is when you do not supervise your child closely enough to track the behaviors that need to be rewarded or punished. Also, unless you are watching, you will not know if the consequences are completed. Finally, you may lose patience with your defiant child. The process of turning around your child's bad behavior is extremely slow. Children are notorious for pushing your buttons so that you lose perspective, become defensive, and lose your temper.

Let's walk through the three elements, to be clear that you understand what they entail.

Rewards

REWARDS ARE REALLY the key to engaging your child in any behavior-changing program. The prizes your child earns for good behavior have to be something she desires. If your child has just about everything she ever wanted, then why would she work to earn the rewards you are offering? If your boss paid you your full salary whether you came to the office or not, would you still go to work anyway? If your child has everything, she values nothing. For your parenting methods to work, the rewards have to be something desired and not already enjoyed on a regular basis. If your child has already been spoiled with every treat and toy imaginable, you will have to re-create a yearning and desire for treats, prizes, and rewards by slowing the gravy train back down to the basic essentials. How can you ever hope to motivate your child with the promise of a trip to McDonald's if you serve her a "happy meal" every day for her lunch? A couple of weeks lunching on peanut butter sandwiches, milk, and an apple, will not only re-create the desired motivation, but your child might actually eat healthier, too. You will need to decide what kinds of treats you are going to use as rewards for accomplishments and how you are going to track your child's progress toward their goal. Keep in mind that your time, attention, and verbal praise are the most reinforcing and motivating rewards you can give your children. When you use liberal doses of earned praise with your children, whenever possible, you will see your child's self-esteem expand and his motivation to please you growing as well.

Consequences

THE FIRST PRINCIPLE of handing out a consequence is: let the punishment fit the crime. For example, if your child arrives fifteen minutes late for her curfew, canceling her participation in the family's Christmas celebration would be overkill. A more fitting punishment would be to set her curfew fifteen minutes earlier the next time she goes out. A smaller punishment allows you to pile on additional or more severe consequences as needed. When you confiscate an item, it is helpful to return the item after a reasonably brief amount of time. You can always confiscate the item again later, if need be. However, if you take away everything too quickly, you will have nothing left to take.

Second, never assign a punishment you are not prepared to deliver. Do not tell your child he is grounded for the weekend and then allow him to spend the night at his friend's house Saturday night because you feel sorry for him. Pick another consequence or enforce the one you gave your child originally. Always follow through with the delivery of the consequence. A typical mistake many parents make is to confiscate a toy, then leave it in a place where the child can retrieve it later when the parent is not watching. Another example of the same kind of mistake is the parent who prohibits the child from watching TV as a punishment but then leaves the TV unattended. Your child is too immature, and the temptation is too great, for him to resist defying your restrictions to items that are readily accessible.

SUPERVISION

WHEN CHILDREN ARE supervised closely, they get into less trouble. Imagine how your driving would change if a police officer were sitting in the passenger's seat next to you while you were at the wheel. You would never get another traffic ticket again! Your child responds in essentially the same way when supervised. Supervising him closely gives him more opportunities to feel proud of his behavior. Remember, humans are creatures of habit. Therefore, the more your child practices good behavior, the more ingrained these behaviors become. Later, when he is *not* being supervised, he is more likely to behave appropriately simply because he has gotten into the habit.

YOU NEED TO HAVE PATIENCE

PATIENCE IS ESSENTIAL for raising kids. As much as you can, keep your cool. Try not to take personally the inconsiderate, selfish, and dishonest things your child may do. *Children are not born naturally compassionate and considerate; these are character traits that are taught to them by their parents.* Childhood is a period of time in life when a person is at her most self-centered. To your child, nothing in the world matters as much as her own wants and desires. The younger she is, the more she does not understand how unreasonable her demands may be. It takes years for a child to acquire the mental and emotional ability to truly empathize with another person's feelings, and to recognize when she is being hurtful. Remembering this may help you avoid taking things personally and help you maintain more patience with your child.

HOW TO SAY NO

TOO OFTEN PARENTS continue explaining the rationale for "no," by discussing the issue with their child much longer than is needed. You may feel driven to explain yourself to avoid the discomfort of feeling like the "bad guy." You may be under the misconception that your child is continuing to argue because he does not understand you and that a complete explanation will result in a fuller understanding by your child and an end to his incessant pleading. In truth, your child just wants to have his way and, regardless of how much time you spend rehashing the issue with your kid, he will almost never accept "no" for an answer, graciously. You may long to hear your child say, "Okay, Mom. I understand why I cannot have things my way. That's all right. I can accept this. No problem, Mom. Thanks for considering my request." This expectation is completely unrealistic.

The reality is that your child will do and say whatever it takes to get you to relent. The more you talk or apologize, the more ammunition you give your child to seize upon a loophole in your explanation. Children are very aware of how much we hate being the "bad guy." They are more aware of this quality about us than we are ourselves. They are not above manipulating us with guilt to get them what they want. Parents need to be strong enough to stomach all the manipulating, pleading and nagging from their children in order to make a "no" stick. Maintaining a flat "no" in the face of an adverse response by your child means you are being the good, effective parent your child needs you to be.

How to Deliver a Consequence

WHEN TELLING YOUR child he cannot have what he wants, it is best to adopt the attitude of the *benevolent bailiff*. What I mean by this is, be benevolent by showing earnest regret for the punishment that your child has brought upon himself. After all, he did create this problem by consciously disobeying you. So, like a dutiful bailiff, hold firm to the delivery of the consequences that your child has earned for himself by his refusal to comply with your rules. You can go ahead and provide general condolences to your child, but make no apologies. A helpful approach is to say out loud to your child, in the midst of delivering the bad news about a denied privilege or consequence, the following: "I cannot allow your anger, unhappiness, or disappointment about this situation to get in the way of my doing my duty as your parent. It is my responsibility to help you to become a person who you can respect. No self-respecting person would have done what you did. Hopefully, this consequence will act as a deterrent so that in the future you will be less likely to do this again. In time, you will come to realize that there will always be a consequence whenever you break my rules." Realize that this recitation is for your own benefit, not your child's. Generally, in such conversations with your children, they tune out most everything you say except what they want to hear.

Do not rescue your child from the restrictions he earns himself with his poor behavior. Most adults learn from their mistakes. Adults do not usually come to accept a truth about life simply because someone else said this is how it is; they need to experience the painful results of their actions to be able to move forward with new knowledge and wisdom. Your child is no different. The frustration that a punishment causes your child is precisely what drives the lesson home. Let your child experience anger and frustration; try not to rescue him from his uncomfortable emotions. The moment of greatest angst for your child is a window of opportunity to make an important association: if I act in the manner I just did, I will not be happy with the outcome. "No pain, no gain," is an expression that captures the truth about life and emotional growth as well as it does about exercise. When you deprive your child of his anger and frustration over enduring a consequence, you cheat him of the opportunity to learn and grow from his mistake.

WHEN TO START DISCIPLINING YOUR CHILD

WHEN IS THE BEST time to start teaching children that parents are in charge and that children cannot always have their way? The toddler period is the developmental stage when a child learns the rules in the game of life. This is a crucial period of time for your child to develop healthy social skills and avoid any reinforcement of defiant behaviors. When parents wait too long to teach their children the rules of social engagement, it becomes harder and harder for the child to learn these skills. Just like anyone at any age, children are creatures of habit: the longer they carry on with a behavior, good or bad, the harder it will be to change that pattern. Socially alienating maladaptive behaviors that become bad habits do not just resolve on their own; they have to be coerced out of children. Too often, parents succumb to the temptation to indulge their cute little toddler, only to be surprised and embarrassed when their child becomes willful. Indulging and spoiling can range from the blatant to the subtle. Either way, indulging your child leads to the same results: heartache and frustration for the parent and belligerence in the child. Therefore, begin teaching your child socially appropriate behaviors as early as six months old. When the very first sign of willful defiance rears its ugly head, immediately establish your role as parent—the person in charge.

HOW *NOT* TO PARENT YOUNG CHILDREN

WATCHING PARENTS manage toddlers in public places can demonstrate for you how children acquire poor social skills. For example, how often have you observed a well-meaning parent following a toddler while the child runs around a doctor's waiting room? He touches everything he can get his hands on, including all the occupants, their belongings, the magazines, lamps, and displays. This type of parent only attempts to stop the child after the tot has left his seat, grabbed a magazine, and thrown it to the floor. While the parent picks up the magazine to replace it, the toddler is already on to the next adventure. And so the forlorn parent hustles around the room, apologizing and trying to keep Junior's destruction to a minimum. All the while, the parent pleads with the child to "be good." Well-meaning parents permit this behavior because they believe in allowing the child "free expression." This kind of parent believes that the word "no" is a form of negativity that will hurt the little child's feelings and possibly stifle his creativity. Furthermore, if the parent were to demand the child stay in his seat like all the other people waiting in the lobby, the child would defiantly refuse. Ultimately, this sort of parent knows *not* confronting the toddler will avoid the vicious struggle that would ensue in such a confrontation.

SOCIAL EXPECTATIONS

LET US GO back now and review, step by step, why an absence of parental intervention is very detrimental to the child. When we are waiting in the office of a professional, such as a doctor, our society has laid down certain social norms to which we all adhere. We all know to sit still, wait our turn, not rearrange the physical features of the room, and not act overly familiar toward other clients. When a toddler experiences this social encounter for the first time and is allowed to behave as described above, he learns his unsociable behavior is acceptable. Little does the tot realize that his newly learned set of social rules will not apply when he gets older. Sometime between the ages of two years old and adulthood—probably sooner—this child will have to relearn the rules of social etiquette, because what society will tolerate from a two-year-old, it will not accept from an adult or older child.

It is vital that your child understand as early as possible that our society lives by general rules of behavior. Take a moment to think about how frustrating it is to learn a new game, skill, or job, when every time you return to the task, the rules have changed. Now imagine how much more frustrating this would be if your anger management skills were poorly developed. A child who has not acquired basic social skills in toddlerhood, later on will have a much harder time learning the social protocols expected of older childern, while at the same time he will have to unlearn his bad habits and relearn the rules he didn't process initially as a toddler. Tolerating, unchecked, in a young child what you find completely unacceptable in an older child, requires him to go through the frustration of being told he is wrong or bad for the very same behaviors that were once completely acceptable, or even "cute," only a few years earlier.

The key to the greatest success for your child, resulting in the least heartache and anger, is to start gently guiding and training her for adulthood as soon as she is ready to learn. In our example of the tot in the doctor's office, if your daughter is old enough to get out of her baby stroller, then she is old enough to learn how to sit properly in a waiting-room chair. Any other approach is a set up for future failure and frustration for you and your child.

Young children at this age are very fast learners and love to be praised for a job well done. Why not start teaching your child from his very first encounter with a social situation, what the accepted standard is? In a waiting room, adults and children alike are expected to stay in their own seat, reading or play-ing quietly. You must tell your child to stay seated and quiet when you first arrive, and continue to reinforce your directive throughout your visit. Yes, the first time or two may be tough, but think of all the frustration and tears you will spare her in the long run if she doesn't have to repeatedly relearn basic social etiquette. She will be happier and have a greater sense of mastery, self-confidence and self-respect when she feels more successful and appreciated by the world around her.

How to Teach Your Child Standards

PARENTS MAY APPROVE of their kids unconditionally, all the time. But children will encounter many others whose approval will not be so easy to acquire, such as teachers, coaches, siblings, and peers. These relationships are also important to your child's healthy emotional development. You cannot ignore your child's poorly developing social skills. Regardless of your unconditional love, if all your child's other relationships are frustrating and hostile, this could impact his self-esteem negatively. Believing your child is "too young to know better" delays the work he needs to do on his interpersonal skills. The sooner you start teaching your child social skills, the better he will get along with others and the happier he will be.

I know a young mother who entered a restaurant with her three small chil-dren, ages two, five, and six years. Because the children were properly social-ized to restaurants from the start of life, each knew what was expected of them in this setting. Thirty minutes later, a nearby diner came over to the table on his way out of the restaurant. He admitted to the young mother that when the family had first sat down, he was filled with dread about what he had expected would be a nice meal completely ruined by misbehaving children. Instead, the man went on to say, he was surprised and pleased by the excellent behavior of the three children. The children beamed with pride. This was an outcome where everyone won.

The argument that allowing children to tear about a restaurant or waiting room encourages a child's free expression and creativity has never been borne out as advantageous to a child's future creative powers. Usually, children who are indulged in their "free expression" develop maladaptive social behaviors that follow them to school and earn them the scorn of their teachers, and perhaps cause them to end up on Ritalin, with a presumed diagnosis of AD/HD.

AN EXAMPLE OF HOW TO ADDRESS WILLFUL BEHAVIOR IN A PUBLIC SETTING

WHEN VISITING A retail store, we as adults recognize the rules to which we must adhere. We recognize that our host, the retail-store owner, expects us not to run up and down his aisles, not to pull off the shelves things that we don't intend to buy, and not to strew merchandise on the floor or replace it in the wrong displays. Our host expects us not to disturb the other shoppers by screaming or clattering objects. Some parents allow their children to run up and down the aisles of a store as long as it is "not too fast or too loud." Children rarely resist the temptation to push the envelope to have more fun. Given this aspect of a child's nature, your expectations that your child will be able to determine when he is running too fast and yelling too loudly in the store, may be setting him up for failure. Do your child a favor: before you arrive in such a setting, tell him exactly what is expected of him during your visit to the store. Do not give your child the mixed message that it is acceptable to break the rules as long as he does not go too far. Your discussion should be worded not as a series of don'ts, but should include some positive behaviors you would like to see, such as to help you locate particular items on your shopping list or carry one of your potential purchases. Give him a chance to feel proud of himself. Expect the best of your child. He just might surprise you and bring out his best.

When your child asks you to buy something you do not want to buy, you simply need to say no. No further explanation is required. If your child continues to ask, plead, or nag, immediately lay out consequences for further nagging. If your child then takes the next step in his escalation and starts screaming, demanding, threatening, or kicking and thrashing on the floor, you must act decisively. When a child throws a tantrum, you must leave behind all the items you have gathered in your shopping cart and leave the store immediately.

If your child is small enough, pick him up off the floor and go directly to your car and drive home. If your child is too large to pick up and is refusing to accompany you out of the store, ask store security to help you lead the child from the premises. Once home, immediately apply a nonnegotiable consequence to this incident; for example, denying him any form of entertainment like TV for the remainder of the day; if he refuses to sit quietly at home, add another consequence in response to his continued disobedience. Finally, your child should not be allowed to accompany you to the store the next time you go. The most effective parenting interventions include quick, decisive consequences that logically fit the child's misbehavior. Skip the lectures and emotional displays of parental anger. Your child will not hear half of what you say in anger anyway. On the other hand, your actions will register with your child loud and clear. To address willful behavior most effectively, act swiftly, calmly, appropriately, and directly with little discussion.

REFUSAL TO COMPLETE A TASK

WHEN STANDARD ROUTINES and structure are worked into a child's schedule from the very beginning, many problems can be avoided. If, on the other hand, you have started late and your child has developed some willful behaviors, you will have to make an extra effort to gain the child's cooperation and compliance.

Let us say you are faced with the situation of asking your ten-year-old son to put down his video game and start his homework. If he asks for more time to complete his game (depending on the situation and the way he asks you) you might allow for ten more minutes of play time. Once you have decided that the time has come for the task to begin and your son refuses, you must spring into action. First, the toy must be confiscated and placed under lock and key. I suggest you place the confiscated item locked up in your car. Plan to move your child's possession to a remote location, such as your workplace or your friend's garage, if you intend to keep the item for a long period of time. If the offending item is large, such as a TV or a computer, then an essential piece can be taken, such as the power cord, keyboard, mouse, or joystick, to be locked up as described.

Then the child should be again asked to sit down to do his homework. Your assistance with the homework to get him started can work to prime the pump. When your son protests taking the toy away, you need to give him a time frame for which it is confiscated, such as four or twelve hours. Hours work better than days, as a day is too long and too vague a time frame. The beauty of this system is that, with each subsequent inappropriate action, you can add an hour or two, depending on the crime. For example, if your son swears at you when you take the toy out of his hands, you may add twelve hours. If he only grumbles and whines, you may add one hour, and so on. You can also add hours to the confiscation if your son does not start his homework as requested. Every ten minutes he waits to start working, you could add another hour of restriction. Again, the principle applies that the consequence should logically fit the misbehavior. If you have waited to start asserting yourself until your child is too old and too large to physically overpower, you will have to resort to gathering another adult family member (father, uncle, grandfather) to help you. Alternatively, you can confiscate items later from his room while he is out of the house.

29

PARENTING YOUR MENTALLY ILL CHILD

HOW PARENTING STAYS THE SAME

PARENTING A CHILD who has a psychiatric condition differs very little from parenting any other child. In fact, all the same parenting techniques outlined in chapters 27 and 28 that help well children, help children with psychiatric disorders, too. Your role as a parent does not change. The three pillars of good discipline still apply. You still need to follow through when you say no to your child. If anything, routines and structure are even *more* important for mentally ill children. Overall, most of your parenting approach must remain consistent regardless of what kind of illness your child may have.

Psychiatric hospital staffers know the value of structure and routine for mentally ill children, which is why the child psychiatric unit is run on a clearly defined schedule. The children are more comfortable and feel more reassured when they know what to expect throughout the day. Generally, discipline programs that help well children develop healthy behaviors, will help mentally ill children as much or more.

When parents do not discipline their mentally ill children, they get the worst of both worlds. For example, if you indulge your anxious child and do not apply any discipline, then you will have an anxious child who is also belligerent. Children with mental illness already have enough shame with which they struggle.

Do not add to their poor self-esteem by allowing them to become spoiled brats as well. Children can tell how others view and judge them. Though it may be unjust and unfair, the reality is: people are judgmental. Your child's peers will be the most critical of all. Children can be very cruel to each other. They may label or call your child names, including terms that don't even relate to your child's real problem, and may shun her. Your child needs to learn how to roll with such treatment and make friends in the face of such adversity. Help your child feel good about herself by helping her to build self-respect around the one area of her life over which she has some influence: her own behavior. Neither you nor your child can change the fact that she has a mental illness to battle. But, you can help her be proud of her accomplishments and her good behavior.

How Parenting Changes When a Child Is Mentally Ill

For the most part, the manner in which you parent your child with a psychiatric condition remains the same as it is with any other child. However, your approach to parenting will need to change in a couple of ways to accommodate your child's illness. One of the ways relates to how quickly you expect your child to learn new information and behaviors. Let me be clear that mental illness does not impede intelligence, per se. However, you will need to make allowances for your child when his symptoms interfere with his compliance with your parenting methods. If your child is also developmentally delayed or has mental retardation, even greater care will have to be made to make your instructions understandable, and closer supervision is required.

Allowing for Symptoms

You will have to make some allowances for your child's symptoms. That does not mean you must abandon your entire discipline program. For example, obsessive-compulsive children often have problems with rituals that require a great deal of time. Their rituals usually involve personal grooming and hygiene. This can create quite an issue when getting ready for school in the morning. You do not want to change your expectations of your OCD child because, just as with any other child, you still want him to learn to get ready on time for the school bus. Yet, expecting him to learn this skill and complete this task in the same amount of time as a child who has no mental illness, is unrealistic. If you make no adjustments for his OCD symptoms, but still expect him to meet your expectations in the same time frame as normal children, your mornings will probably not go well. Instead of success, you might find yourself becoming increasingly frustrated as he falls further and further behind schedule and melts into a puddle of tears and feelings of failure. Not only does this approach fail to meet your goals or teach your child to be get ready for school, this is really not how you want to send your child off in the morning.

To accommodate your child's symptoms without abandoning your good discipline technique, you must make modifications to how you arrive at your goal. You do not change the goal. In other words, you still expect your OCD child to be ready in time to meet the school bus in the morning. But, you can modify your child's routine to accommodate his OCD symptoms. Instead of waking up at the usual time, awaken him an hour earlier than any of the other children. Set a very firm schedule, with a set, simplified list of what absolutely must be accomplished before he leaves for school. Some of these steps may be achieved the night before, such as setting out clothing for the next day or making sure his schoolbag is packed and ready to go, by the door. Review the list with your child each morning. Develop intermediate goals throughout the morning with corresponding rewards—as in points toward a greater goal—for meeting each of these midway markers. Devise rewards to entice your child to follow your rules and morning routine, such as a treat after a week of getting to school on time every day. Provide your child regular verbal prompts and close supervision all along the way, and give him five-minute warnings before the deadlines of each of his intermediate steps. Give your child encouragement and verbal praise for meeting each of his intermediate goal; this will reinforce his positive accomplishments. Examine your environment for what may be unnecessarily distracting features that interfere with your child's progress; if another child is permitted to watch loud early-morning TV, obviously your OCD child might find it hard to concentrate on his list of tasks. Keep up as much as the routine as you can on weekends and during vacation periods, instead of allowing your child to indulge in unstructured behaviors on those mornings. Coach him through the cognitive behavioral techniques you were taught by his therapist to help him work through his symptoms as he advances through his morning routine.

As with all children, demonstrating your frustration with your OCD child's slow progress or failures with angry words and harsh criticism will not advance your cause or his learning. Try to remain calm, quiet, and patient but resolute at all times regardless of how frustrated you may feel. Your child will learn more when you maintain your composure. Children tend to blame their punishments on your anger, instead of appropriately on their own behavior, when you lose your temper while disciplining them. Initially, this approach may be very difficult and time intensive on your part, but in the long run your OCD child will feel great satisfaction when he is successful and you will feel relief as he overcomes his disability and learns to function more normally.

Should your child still miss the bus, because he was not cooperating with your regimen, definitely do not make excuses for him—let him feel some of the natural consequences for arriving late to school. If you decide to drive him to school late, do not sign a parental excuse for his tardy arrival, so that he can avoid the school imposed consequences. If the principal assigns your child an after-school detention, allow your child to serve the detention. Do not rescue him from the school's disciplinary actions, you would be forsaking all your effective parenting principles. Do not reduce your goals and expectations of your child, particularly if he has demonstrated that he is sometimes able to comply with the rules when he really tries. That kind of enabling creates more disability for your child, not less.

HELPING THE DEVELOPMENTALLY DELAYED CHILD

IF YOUR CHILD has mental retardation or one of the autistic spectrum disorders, you will need to make even greater accommodations to parent him. You will need to break down each goal into smaller parts and to provide much greater supervision. The task of parenting a child with one of the developmental disorders is so challenging that most parents are best advised to seek help and guidance from a professional. Most states and county government mental health departments have such staff available. If they cannot provide the help to you directly, they certainly will be able to refer you to an agency that can. When all else fails, there are private organizations, such as the Autism Society of America, that can refer you to resources in your area. Their contact information can be found in the resource section of this book. Parental support groups may also be useful for sharing tips other parents have received from clinicians, as well as what techniques they devised that work.

General principles still apply but will need significant modification, depending upon your child's disability. For example, you can expect both a well child and an autistic child to learn not to hit people. The difference is how you teach this lesson and your expectation for *how long* it will take to teach this lesson. This part of your approach would be quite different between your parenting of an autistic versus a normal child. You certainly do not want to adopt the philosophy that you should expect nothing from your autistic child because you feel sorry for her. Pity will not help your child reach her fullest potential. You will need to work much harder with your autistic or MR child to make minor achievements and be satisfied with seeing her accomplish much less than normal children usually do.

When it comes to behavioral modification programs, these kids need constant one-on-one supervision to learn new behaviors. Autistic children need tasks broken down into bite-size pieces, in a set series of steps. The prompts, reminders, rewards, and consequences have to be extremely consistent and almost rigidly uniform. Children with autism and MR need a great deal more supervision than do other children. When it comes to behavioral modification programs, these kids need constant one-on-one supervision to learn new behaviors. Just as with any other child, they do not respond well to anger. In fact, they can be particularly sensitive to loud voices and harsh reprimands, as they are already prone to being hypersensitive to environmental stimuli.

One of the primary features of autism is a rigid adherence to their routines. They are most comfortable when everything in their world is the same every day. This presents an obvious hurdle when your task is to change your autistic child's behavior. Because autistic children need a great deal more supervision, you cannot give a command and then walk away, expecting it will have been accomplished upon your return merely because you have offered an incentive for compliance. Furthermore, autistic children have a very difficult time with transitioning from one activity to the next. This means that your approach requires making many smaller intermediate steps on the way to your ultimate lesson. Therefore, if your final goal is to teach your autistic child not to hit, you will have to work hard at each minor step along the way. You may first need to teach him to be aware of where his hands are, with prompts such as, "Look where your hands are!" or "What are you touching now?" before you get to step two: keep your hands to yourself and ultimately step three: do not hit others.

Teaching autistic children requires very intense supervision, patience, hands-on redirection, and constant praise from you as your child works on each tiny intermediate step. This is an extremely painstaking process that many parents simply lack the endurance to manage. The parenting hardship explains why many autistic children are being raised in group homes with three shifts of round-the-clock nursing care.

Because parenting children with autism or mental retardation is such an involved endeavor, it cannot be adequately covered here. This discussion of specific parenting approaches for autistic and MR children is intended only to give you a flavor of what is involved in parenting children with severe mental disabilities such as Autism and MR.

Psychiatric Evaluation

Child's Name _____

Date of Birth _____

Age _____

Date Questions Completed _____

CURRENT PSYCHIATRIC HISTORY

Child's Current Symptoms? _____

_____

(defiance) _____

(aggression) _____

(anger) _____

(impulsive) _____

(mood) _____

(fears & phobia) _____

(obsessive rituals) _____

(energy) _____

(sleep) _____

(appetite) _____

(self-esteem) _____

(concentration) _____

(nightmares) _____

(hallucinations) _____

(delusions) _____

_____

_____

_____

History of Abuse or Trauma? _____

_____

   (physical, emotional, or sexual) _____

_____

_____

Talked about hurting himself or anyone else?_____

_____

   (suicide attempts or plans)_____

_____

Attempted to hurting himself or anyone else? _____

_____

_____

Psychiatric Medications:

   Current Psychiatric Medications?

   (name of med, dose, and schedule meds are taken)

_____

_____

_____

_____

   Past Psychiatric Medications?

   (name of med, dose, and schedule meds were taken)

_____

_____

_____

_____

PAST PSYCHIATRIC TREATMENT

Past Psychiatric Symptoms?_____

_____

_____

_____

Past Psychiatric Hospital Stay?_____

_____

Past Psychotherapy? _____

_____

Abuse of Drugs and Alcohol? _____

_____

_____

_____

_____

MEDICAL HISTORY?

(medical conditions)_____

(surgeries) _____

(head trauma) _____

(seizures) _____

(last physical exam) _____

(are immunizations up-to-date)_____

(recent hearing and sight exams)_____

_____

Nonpsychiatric Medications? _____

_____

_____

_____

_____

Allergies to Medications? _____

_____

DEVELOPMENTAL HISTORY?

(pregnancy) _____

(exposure to substances in utero)_____

(birth & delivery) _____

(age started walking, talking, & toilet trained) _____

(periods of developmental regression) _____

(bed-wetting) _____

_____

SCHOOL HISTORY?

(grade level in school) _____

(public, private, or home school) _____

(special education or gifted) _____

(academic performance) _____

(classroom behavior)_____

(number of schools attended)_____

(friendships with other students) _____

_____

_____

_____

SOCIAL HISTORY?

(family makeup: divorce, remarriage, brothers, sisters)_____

_____

_____

_____

_____

(marriage or relationship problems)_____

(do parents cooperate with each other on discipline)_____

(which parents work outside the home) _____

(home size, number of people he shares his room with) _____

(child's room environment: TV, DVD, X-Box, Play Station, stereo, phone, computer, etc.) _____

(noises and distractions in bedroom as he is going to sleep)_____

(who greets child after school or provides after-school child care)_____

_____

(study area at home & homework assistance)_____

_____

(hours each day he watches TV, plays video games, or is on computer for non-homework purposes)_____

_____

(use of Internet in secluded place in home or well monitored) _____

_____

(sports, hobbies, & clubs: any changes)_____

_____

(chores at home & work outside home) _____

(friendships: changes or losses) _____

(death, illness, or loss of important family members)_____

_____

(conduct problems or legal trouble)_____

_____

FAMILY HISTORY?

(people related by blood who have mental illness or addiction)_____

_____

_____

YOUR QUESTIONS FOR THE DOCTOR

_____

_____

_____

_____

_____

Disorders That Share the Symptoms of ADHD

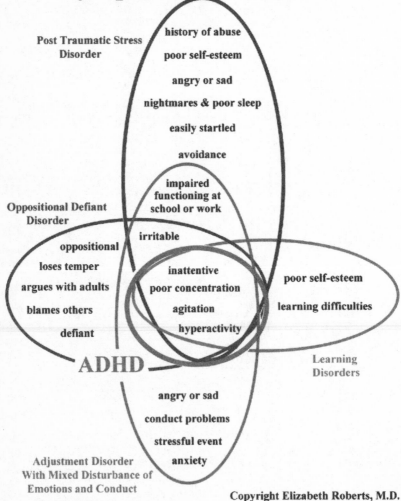

Post Traumatic Stress Disorder

history of abuse

poor self-esteem

angry or sad

nightmares & poor sleep

easily startled

avoidance

impaired functioning at school or work

Oppositional Defiant Disorder

irritable

oppositional

loses temper

argues with adults

blames others

defiant

inattentive

poor concentration

agitation

hyperactivity

poor self-esteem

learning difficulties

ADHD

Learning Disorders

angry or sad

conduct problems

stressful event

anxiety

Adjustment Disorder With Mixed Disturbance of Emotions and Conduct

Copyright Elizabeth Roberts, M.D.

Disorders That Share the Symptoms of ADHD

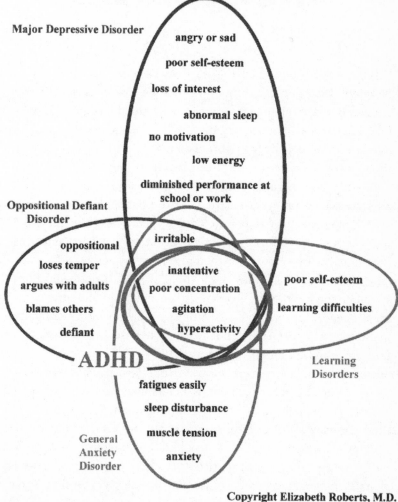

Major Depressive Disorder

angry or sad

poor self-esteem

loss of interest

abnormal sleep

no motivation

low energy

diminished performance at school or work

Oppositional Defiant Disorder

oppositional

loses temper

argues with adults

blames others

defiant

irritable

inattentive

poor concentration

agitation

hyperactivity

poor self-esteem

learning difficulties

ADHD

Learning Disorders

fatigues easily

sleep disturbance

muscle tension

anxiety

General Anxiety Disorder

Glossary

AD/HD: *See* Attention Deficit/Hyperactivity Disorder.

Adjustment Disorder: A psychiatric condition that consists of a group of symptoms that develops in response to an identifiable stressor. These symptoms can include depression, anxiety, and/or conduct disturbance in which the patient has violated the rights of others.

Alpha-Agonist: Term used as shorthand to refer to medications that are alpha 2 adrenergic receptor agonists, a type of high blood pressure medication, also referred to as an antihypertensive. The two alpha agonists most commonly used in psychiatry are Catapress (clonidine) and Tenex (guaneficine). These medications help address hyperactivity, agitation, anger, irritability, aggression, impulsivity, tremors, and motor tics. *See* chapter 22.

amphetamine: Amphetamines are a group of psychiatric medications that stimulate the brain, which improves concentration and attention. They are also referred to as stimulants. Amphetamines are most commonly used in psychiatry to treat AD/HD but do have other uses, such as weight reduction and to address fatigue. *See* chapter 19.

antidepressant: Antidepressants are a diverse group of psychiatric medications used to treat a number of symptoms including: depression, anxiety, panic, obsessions, compulsions, anger, and impulsiveness. *See* chapter 18.

antihypertensive: Antihypertensives are medications used to treat people with high blood pressure. There are a variety of different antihypertensives but there are two types in particular that psychiatrists use most often: alpha 2 adrenergic receptor agonists and beta-blockers. Antihypertensives are used to treat a number of symptoms including: hyperactivity, impulsivity, agitation, and anger outbursts. *See* chapter 22.

antipsychotic: Antipsychotics are psychiatric medications used to treat a number of symptoms including: hallucinations, psychotic delusions, paranoia, mania, agitation, and anger outbursts. *See* chapter 20.

Antisocial Personality Disorder: A personality disorder that is diagnosed in adults only and includes a number of character traits all of which involve criminal behavior and the violation of the rights of others.

anxiety: Anxiety is a psychiatric symptom or emotional experience of fear, nervousness, and worry.

Asperger's Disorder: A psychiatric condition considered to be a pervasive developmental delay, which develops from birth and includes the inability to be socially engaged or emotionally responsive to the needs and suffering of others. Asperger's is unique from the other pervasive developmental disorders in that the child retains the ability to use language fluently.

Attention Deficit/ Hyperactivity Disorder (AD/HD): A psychiatric condition which has to have been present (whether diagnosed or not) before the age of seven and includes symptoms of difficulty concentrating and restlessness. The dysfunction has to be severe enough that the child has difficulty functioning in at least two areas of their life such as school, sports, church, hobbies, clubs or home.

atypical: A term, which in psychiatry, is usually used to refer to the new antipsychotic medications such as Risperdal, Zyprexa, Seroquel, Geodon, and Abilify.

Autism: A term used to refer to Autistic Disorder, which is a psychiatric condition considered to be a pervasive developmental delay. Autism develops from birth and includes the inability to use language and to be socially engaged or emotionally responsive to the needs and suffering of others. *See* chapter 16.

benzodiazepine: Benzodiazepines are psychiatric medications used to treat anxiety, panic, insomnia, and seizures. Benzodiazepines are very addicting medications if used routinely over a period of time. *See* chapter 23.

Beta-Blocker: Term used as shorthand to refer to medications that are beta-adrenergic receptor agonists, a type of high blood pressure medication, also referred to as an antihypertensive. The beta-blockers most commonly used in psychiatry are Inderal (propranalol), Tenormin (atenolol), and Lopressor (metoprolol). These medications help address performance anxiety, agitation, anger, irritability, aggression, impulsivity, tremors, and motor tics. *See* chapter 22.

Bipolar Disorder: A psychiatric condition that includes episodes of mania and depression. *See* chapter 10.

Borderline Personality Disorder: A personality disorder that includes character traits of mood instability, erratic behavior, intensely dysfunctional relationships, and extreme anger. *See* chapter 11.

class (of drug): A category or type of medication. All the medications in a particular class will share a similar chemical makeup and/or mode of action and will cause a similar effect in the body. An example is the antipsychotic class of drugs, which all reduce hallucinations and delusions in a psychotic patient by blocking the same type of receptors in the brain.

Conduct Disorder: A personality disorder that is usually diagnosed in children and includes a number of character traits, all of which involve criminal behavior and the violation of the rights of others. *See* chapter 7.

Drug-Induced Disorder: A psychiatric condition which is the direct result of the use of drugs, whether prescribed or attained illicitly. *See* chapter 17.

Drug-Use Disorder: The term used to describe the condition of using, abusing, and being addicted to drugs. *See* chapter 17.

Dysthymic Disorder: A psychiatric condition of chronic depression that is not severe enough to qualify for Major Depressive Disorder but with which the child has suffered for over two years.

Generalized Anxiety Disorder: A psychiatric condition whose symptoms include fear, worry, insomnia, poor concentration, and restlessness. *See* chapter 12.

Intermittent Explosive Disorder: A psychiatric condition that includes anger outbursts during which people are assaulted or property destroyed, and the degree of anger expressed is much greater than the angering event would normally incite in people. *See* chapter 8.

Major Depressive Disorder: A psychiatric condition, which can include symptoms of sad mood, loss of joy, insomnia, poor concentration, restlessness, and hopelessness. *See* chapter 9.

MAO-Inhibitor: Monoamine oxidase inhibitors are antidepressants used to treat depression. They are particularly difficult to use, due to all the dietary restrictions and the drug-drug interactions. *See* chapter 18.

Mental Retardation (MR): A condition with which a child is born, characterized by below-average intelligence. Depending on the severity of the condition, children with MR to a varying degree do not function independently and require a great deal of assistance and supervision throughout their lives. *See* chapter 16.

mood stabilizer: A group of medications used to treat mania, depression, and psychosis. *See* chapter 21.

Multiple Personality Disorder: A personality disorder that is no longer considered a valid diagnosis. It was once very popular and included character traits of having several distinct personalities, each of which could operate independent of the other personalities. This diagnosis fell out of use, as it became increasingly more popular criminal defense to excuse and acquit murderers.

Obsessive Compulsive Disorder (OCD): A psychiatric condition that includes symptoms of intense adherence to rigid routines and anxiety about the consequences if these routines are not followed. *See* chapter 13.

Oppositional Defiant Disorder (ODD): A psychiatric condition that is usually only given to children, and which includes symptoms of belligerence, insubordination, hostility, and anger. *See* chapter 7.

Panic Disorder: A psychiatric condition that includes anxiety attacks that are intensely frightening but brief in duration. The child is constantly fearful of when the next attack may develop, which can drive the child indoors and curtail his interaction with the outside world. *See* chapter 12.

Personality Disorder: A psychiatric condition that reflects an enduring pattern of behaviors and symptoms that deviate significantly from cultural norms but are not considered a temporary mental state or illness from which a patient can recover and return to a normal baseline of behaviors. Personality disorders refer to the disordered character traits in a person that have been developed and established in childhood and tend to continue throughout the person's lifetime.

Pervasive Developmental Disorders (PDD): Refers to a group of developmental disorders, all of which share a common set of symptoms: the inability to be socially engaged or emotionally responsive to the needs and suffering of others. *See* chapter 16.

psychotropic: The types of prescription medications that are used to treat psychiatric conditions. The term can be used alone as a shorthand to refer to psychotropic medications. Examples of psychotropic medications are Prozac, Lithium, Ritalin, and Valium.

Post Traumatic Stress Disorder (PTSD): A psychiatric condition that develops in response to a traumatic event, such as a near-fatal car accident, rape, or a life-threatening natural disaster. The symptoms include feeling anxious, having nightmares, and reexperiencing the trauma repeatedly. *See* chapter 14.

Reactive Attachment Disorder: A psychiatric condition that develops in a young child in response to being neglected and abandoned during infancy.

The symptoms include having difficulty trusting and establishing healthy relationships with friends, family members, and loved ones.

Schizoaffective Disorder: A psychiatric condition that develops in young adult life and is generally considered a permanent condition for which medications can only ameliorate the symptoms while the patient is taking the drugs. Schizoaffective Disorder is not considered to be a condition from which one makes a full recovery and can return to a life free of the need for medications, but its prognosis is better than the fate of those with Schizophrenia. The symptoms of Schizoaffective Disorder can include depressed mood, mania, hallucinations both auditory and visual, delusions, and paranoia.

Schizophrenia: A psychiatric condition that develops in young adult life and is generally considered a permanent condition for which medications can only ameliorate the symptoms while the patient is taking the medication. Schizophrenia is not considered to be a condition from which one makes a full recovery and can return to a life free of the need for medications. The symptoms of Schizophrenia can include hallucinations both auditory and visual, delusions, and paranoia. *See* chapter 15.

Separation Anxiety: Separation Anxiety Disorder is a psychiatric condition that develops in children who are extremely frightened to be separated from their primary caregiver. The symptoms of Separation Anxiety Disorder can include nightmares, anxiety, nausea, and headaches when separation happens or is anticipated to happen in the near future.

Social Phobia: A psychiatric condition whose symptoms include fear, worry of humiliating oneself, nausea, and sweating when anticipating a social situation, such as meeting new people, giving a lecture or presentation, or performing on a stage or in sports. *See* chapter 12.

SSRI: Selective Serotonin Reuptake Inhibitors are a subtype of antidepressant class of psychiatric medications. Examples of SSRIs are Prozac, Paxil, Zoloft, Luvox, Celexa, and Lexapro. *See* chapter 18.

ENDNOTES

INTRODUCTION

1 Lawrence Diller, MD, *Running on Ritalin: A Physician Reflects* (New York: Bantam Books, 1998).

CHAPTER 5

1 "Psychotropic Practice Patterns for Youth: A 10-Year Perspective," *Archives of Pediatrics & Adolescent Medicine* 157 (January 2003): 17–25.

2 Janet Zimmerman, "Autism: The Struggle Within," *The Press Enterprise* (May 1, 2005).

3 Ibid.

CHAPTER 16

1 Megan Lane, "What Asperger's Syndrome Has Done for us," BBC News Online Magazine 12, no. 22, http://news.bbc.co.uk, accessed June 2, 2004.

CHAPTER 18

1 Dr. Julio Licinio, "Depression, Antidepressants and Suicidality: A Critical Appraisal," *Nature Reviews: Drug Discovery* 4 (February 1, 2005), 165–71.

2 www.cdc.gov.

REFERENCES

"About Autism." Center for Disease Control, Autism Information Center, www.cdc.gov.

Curtis, Lesley H., et. al. "Prevalence of Atypical Antispsychotic Drug Use among Commercially Insured Youths in the United States." *Archives of Pediatrics & Adolescent Medicine* 159 (April 2005): 362–66.

First, Michael B., H. Pincus, and A. Fanves, *Diagnostic and Statistical Manual of Mental Disorders, Fourth Edition, Text Revision* (DSM-IV-TR). Washington, D.C.: American Psychiatric Association, 2000.

Kaplan, H., B. Sadock, and J. Grebb, 1994. *Kaplan and Sadock's Synopsis of Psychiatry*. Baltimore, MD: Williams & Wilkins, 1994.

Helms, Marisa. "Shooting Fuels Debate over Safety of Prozac for Teens." Minnesota Public Radio News online magazine, http://news.minnesota.publicradio.org/features/2005/03/25, accessed March 25, 2005.

Lane, Megan. "What Asperger's Syndrome Has Done for Us." BBC News Online Magazine 12, no. 22, http://news.bbc.co.uk, accessed June 2, 2004.

Maag, Chris. "The Devil in Red Lake." *Time* 165, no. 14 (April 4, 2005).

Matthews, Anna. "FDA Revisits Issues of Antidepressants for Youth." *The Wall Street Journal Online*, http://online.wsj.com/public/us, accessed August 5, 2004.

Physicians' Desk Reference, 59th Edition. Montvale, NJ: Thomson PDR, 2005.

"Practice Parameters for the Assessment and Treatment of Children and Adolescents with Anxiety Disorders." *Journal of the American Academy of Child & Adolescent Psychiatry* 36(10S), Supplement 69S–84S (October 1997).

"Practice Parameters for the Assessment and Treatment of Children, Adolescents, and Adults with Attention Deficit/Hyperactivity Disorders." *Journal of the American Academy of Child & Adolescent Psychiatry* 36(10S) Supplement 85S–121S, October 1997.

"Practice Parameters for the Assessment and Treatment of Children, Adolescents and Adults with Autism and Other Pervasive Developmental Disorders." *Journal of the American Academy of Child & Adolescent Psychiatry* 38(12S) Supplement 32S–54S, December 1999.

"Practice Parameters for the Assessment and Treatment of Children and Adolescents with Bipolar Disorder." *Journal of the American Academy of Child & Adolescent Psychiatry* 36(10S) Supplement 157S–176S, October 1997.

"Practice Parameters for the Assessment and Treatment of Children and Adolescents with Conduct Disorder." *Journal of the American Academy of Child & Adolescent Psychiatry* 36(10S) Supplement 122S–139S, October 1997.

"Practice Parameters for the Assessment and Treatment of Children and Adolescents with

Depressive Disorders." *Journal of the American Academy of Child & Adolescent Psychiatry* 37(10S) Supplement 63S–83S, October 1998.

"Practice Parameters for the Assessment and Treatment of Children, Adolescents, and Adults with Mental Retardation and Comorbid Mental Disorders." *Journal of the American Academy of Child & Adolescent Psychiatry* 38(12S) Supplement 5S–31S, December 1999.

"Practice Parameters for the Assessment and Treatment of Children and Adolescents with Obsessive-Compulsive Disorder." *Journal of the American Academy of Child & Adolescent Psychiatry* 37(10S) Supplement 27S–45S, October 1998.

"Practice Parameters for the Assessment and Treatment of Children and Adolescents with Posttraumatic Stress Disorder." *Journal of the American Academy of Child & Adolescent Psychiatry* 37(10S) Supplement 4S–26S, October 1998.

"Practice Parameters for the Assessment and Treatment of Children and Adolescents with Schizophrenia." *Journal of the American Academy of Child & Adolescent Psychiatry* 36(10S) Supplement 177S–193S, October 1997.

"Practice Parameters for the Assessment and Treatment of Children and Adolescents with Substance Use Disorders." *Journal of the American Academy of Child & Adolescent Psychiatry* 36(10S) Supplement 140S–156S, October 1997.

Tucker, Miriam. "Recommended Exercise Also Curbs Depression." *Clinical Psychiatry News* 33, no. 5 (May 2005).

Zimmerman, Janet. "Autism: The Struggle Within." *The Press Enterprise*, May 1, 2005.

Zito, Julie M., et. al. "Psychotropic Practice Patterns for Youth: A 10-Year Perspective." *Archives of Pediatrics & Adolescent Medicine 157* (January 2003): 17–25.

RECOMMENDED READINGS AND RESOURCES

American Academy of Child and Adolescent Psychiatrists
Summaries available online for parents with questions about their children's behavioral problems.
www.aacap.org/publications/factsfam

American Foundation for Suicide Prevention
120 Wall Street, 22nd Floor
New York, NY 10005
phone 888-333-AFSP or 212-363-3500
fax 212-363-6237
www.afsp.org

Anxiety Disorders Association of America (ADAA)
11900 Parklawn Drive, Suite 100
Rockville, MD 20852
phone 301-231-9350
www.adaa.org

Autism Education Network
phone 408-558-9404
www.autismeducation.net

Autism Society of America
7910 Woodmont Avenue, Suite 300
Bethesda, Maryland 20814-3067
phone 800-328-8476
www.autism-society.org

ChADD: Children and Adults with Attention Deficit/Hyperactivity Disorder
Chapters are located throughout the country. They publish a magazine associated with membership: *Children with Attention Deficit Disorders*. They feature speakers at their meetings frequently. Their organization can be contacted at www.chadd.org, or contact Peg Nichols, Director of Communications and Media Relations at 301-306-7070 x102; Katrina Norfleet Brown, Senior Communications Specialist, at 301-306-7070 x117; or Bryan Goodman, Communications Associate, at 301-306-7070, x128.

Freedom from Fear
308 Seaview Avenue
Staten Island, NY 10305
phone 888-442-2022 or 718-351-1717
www.freedomfromfear.org

Hazelden Foundation Information and Education Services
Online bookstore dedicated exclusively to self-help books and books on recovery. Visit www.hazeldenbookplace.org or contact Kris Sanders, PO Box 176, Center City, MN 55012, phone 800-328-9000 x4064

NAMI: National Alliance for the Mentally Ill
Chapters are located throughout the country. They publish a magazine, *The Advocate,* and hold an annual convention. They are also an active advocacy group that lobbies Congress and organizes public rallies. Visit www.nami.org, or contact Bob Carolla, Director of Communications, Colonial Place Three, 2107 Wilson Boulevard, Suite 300, Arlington, VA 22201-3042, phone 703-524-7600, fax 703-516-7238, e-mail BobC@nami.org.

National Depressive and Manic-Depressive Association (National DMDA)
730 N. Franklin Street, Suite 501
Chicago, IL 60610-7204
phone 800-826-3632 or 312-642-0049
fax 312-642-7243
www.ndmda.org

National Mental Health Association (NMHA)
1021 Prince Street
Alexandria, VA 22314-2971
phone 703-684-7722
fax 703-684-5968
www.nmha.org

ACKNOWLEDGMENTS

I AM MOST thankful to my husband, Tom, for his advice, friendship, tolerance, and support with every step in the process of writing this book. From the inception of the project he has assisted with everything from the practical matters of locating an agent and publisher, to editing and crafting the manuscript, choosing the title, and providing his feedback on the content, his tireless efforts were invaluable. This book would not have been possible without his help.

I thank my three daughters; Jessica, Megan, and Jean, who helped me develop many of my parenting principles by allowing me to test my theories on them. They helped me to understand what works and what does not. I could not be prouder of their personal accomplishments and academic achievements.

Raising children has really helped me to appreciate my own parents more and to understand the sacrifices and efforts all parents make. I thank my mother, Barbara Wentworth Taylor, for teaching me the importance of perseverance, forgiveness, and dedication and showing me that it is never too late to start a new career path. I am thankful to my father, Stewart Roberts, for demonstrating, by his example, the value of education, duty, hard work, and self-discipline. My mother deserves extra thanks for her many excellent book title ideas which taken together with others were melded to create the final result.

I am very grateful to my agent, Linda Konner, who believed in this project and persevered until she found a publisher. I appreciated her warm support and encouragement of my writing, her faith in the book, and her efforts editing the original proposal. I thank her for placing the manuscript in the hands of my publisher at Marlowe & Company.

I thank my publisher, Matthew Lore, for his enthusiasm for this project and his confidence in me as a writer. I truly appreciate the opportunity he has given me to reach parents with this vital information, especially those who struggle every day, with weighty decisions about medicating their children. I am truly grateful to Matthew for everything he did to make this book a reality. I also thank my editor, Iris Bass.

A special thanks to my friend, psychiatry professor, and published author, Drew Ross, MD, for providing me with writing advice and many excellent suggestions for the book title which were used in conjunction with others.

I appreciate all of my child patients who willingly shared their stories with me and their parents who trusted me to care for their children. I am grateful to my professor, Alan Buffenstein, MD, who taught me that everything eventually becomes clear, in a complicated case, if one will simply spend enough time with the patient, listening.

INDEX

NOTE: *See* separate MEDICATIONS INDEX for a list of drugs by name.

I

J

K

U

T

V

W

INDEX OF MEDICATIONS

S

Serazone (nefazodone), 160
Seroquel (quetiapine), 55, 60, 63, 70, 77,
  85, 93, 123, 135, 173
Sinequan (doxepin), 55, 70, 77, 93, 97,
  101, 104, 117, 159–60
Strattera (atomoxetine), 54, 169–70

T

Tegretol (carbamazepine), 63, 70, 77,
  85, 93, 123, 129, 130, 135, 180, 183–85
Tenex (guanfacine), 55, 60, 70, 117
Tenormin (atenolol), 60, 70, 97, 101,
  130, 136
Thorazine (chlorpromazine), 60, 63, 70,
  77, 93, 123, 135, 173
Tofranil (imipramine), 55, 70, 77, 93, 97,
  101, 104, 117, 130, 135, 159–60
Topamax (topiramate), 60, 63, 70, 77,
  85, 93, 123, 129, 130, 135, 180, 187–88
Trileptal (oxcarbazepine), 60, 63, 70, 77,
  85, 93, 123, 129, 130, 135, 180, 185–86

V

Valium (diazepam), 97, 101, 130, 136

W

Wellbutrin XL (buproprion), 54, 70, 77,
  86, 93, 130, 135, 158

X

Xanax (alprazolam), 97, 101, 104, 130,
  136

Z

Zoloft (sertraline), 70, 77, 85, 93, 97,
  101, 104, 110, 117, 129, 135, 157
Zyprexa (olanzapine), 55, 60, 63, 70, 77,
  85, 93, 123, 135, 173